Ethics / Aesthetics:

Post-Modern Positions

PostModernPositions
A Monograph Series in Cultural Studies

Robert Merrill and Pat Wilkinson-Bus, series editors

1. Robert Merrill, ed. *Ethics / Aesthetics: Post-Modern Positions.*

2. Stephen-Paul Martin, *Open Form and the Feminine Imagination: The Politics of Reading in Twentieth-Century American Innovative Writing.* (Summer, 1988).

3. Keith C. Pheby, *Interventions: Displacing the Metaphysical Subject.* (Summer, 1988).

4. Douglas Kellner, ed. *Postmodernism / Jameson / Critique.* (Summer, 1988).

Maisonneuve Press
Publications of the Institute for Advanced Cultural Studies
P. O. Drawer 2980
Washington, DC 20013-2980

Ethics / Aesthetics:
Post-Modern Positions

by

Lyell Asher
Anthony Cascardi
Véronique M. Fóti
Geoffrey Harpham
D. Emily Hicks
Eugene W. Holland
Linda Hutcheon
Robert Merrill
Neal Oxenhandler
Richard Wasson
Rob Wilson

**Edited by
Robert Merrill**

PostModernPositions, Volume 1

 MAISONNEUVE PRESS

Publications of the Institute for Advanced Cultural Studies

Robert Merrill, ed. *Ethics / Aesthetics: Post-Modern Positions.*

Copyright © 1988 by Maisonneuve Press,
P. O. Drawer 2980, Washington, DC 20013-2980.

Maisonneuve Press is a division of the **Institute for Advanced Cultural Studies**, a non-profit collective of scholars concerned with the critical study of culture. Write to the Director for information about other Institute programs and activities of the Press.

Printed in the United States of America by BookCrafters, Chelsea, MI.

This book has been designed and manufactured for long life; the paper and binding meet the guidelines for durability as set forth by the Committee on Production Guidelines for Book Longevity of the Council on Library Resources.

Library of Congress Cataloging-in-Publication Data
Main entry under title:

Merrill, Robert, 1950-
    Ethics / aesthetics : post-modern positions.

    (PostModernPositions ; v. 1)
    Bibliography: p.
    1. Culture. 2. Aesthetics. 3. Postmodernism.
I. Asher, Lyell. II. Merrill, Robert, 1950-   . III. Series.
CB151.E74 1988   909.82'8   88-9257

ISBN 0-944624-00-6 (cloth binding)
ISBN 0-944624-01-4 (paper)

Contents

Acknowledgments

In the compilation of this volume of essays, I am indebted for the careful reading and valuable comments of Elisabeth Mantello, Annette Bus, Maria Hall, Patrick Wilkinson-Bus, and Dennis Crow. It is truly a privilege to work with such caring and dedicated people.

Forward—
Ethics / Aesthetics: A Post-Modern Position

Robert Merrill

"Aesthetics is the mother of ethics." Some form or another
of this equation between the beautiful and the good—most recently
advanced in this citation by the Russian-born poet, Joseph Brodsky,
in his 1987 Nobel Laureate lecture—has held the position of grand
referent, the *telos*, or explanatory termination for philosophical
discourse since Plato and from this position, of the possibility of
a unified good and beautiful, has seduced thought and action in
a most powerful way. I use the notion of seduction on purpose,
since under modernism the aesthetic as sublime, romantic,
pathetic, or beautiful has generally been alienated from the main
current of political and ethical consideration. J. S. Mill is typical
of the modern refusal of the seductiveness of beauty—conscious
but careful. Artists, too, such as Philip Sidney in the early period
of modernism or Romantics such as Percy Shelly later on held that
the aesthetic sense transcended the limitations of history and
everyday life to penetrate a realm not recognizeable in scientific
and empirical discourse. It remained for the aestheticism of the
nineteenth century and the formalism of the twentieth to refuse
ethics altogether and divorce totally the domains of ethics (i.e.
theories and practices of normative behavior) and aesthetics
(theories and practices of representation and the reception of

representations). R. S. Crane's often-noted remark that the subject of literature is "not the republic, but the republic of letters" (*Critics and Criticism* 376) indicates the possiblity of a thoroughly a-political aesthetic criticism and practice. If the discipline of art under modernism were to be ethically interested at all, its interest would flow from a privileged and autonomous position of taste, intuition, or pure beauty which is ontologically distinct from the sphere of ethics and politics. We are now, however, long past all that.

We are learning now to understand social situations, ourselves, and institutions as essentially "texts" which must be de-coded with the same basic strategies for reading, looking, and listening that one employs for works of art. Our perceptual categories give the only shape to whatever is called "real" that it can ever have, and thus response to the real is no different in nature from our response to art. As exclusive canons of master-works give way to include popular culture, spontaneous or even "found" artworks, conceptions of the aesthetic are returning once again to the level of the ethical. This recognition that no analytical vantage point outside of art and politics exists re-problematizes the old equation between ethics and aesthetics and is what makes discussions of art now so deeply political (in the sense of social constructions and economies of power) and discussions of the merely political (such as foreign policy, defense, and theories of the state) so fully artistic in the sense of the imaginary transformation of the world into representations of what might be.

In modernism, the zone of the beautiful and the good is the final resolution of the essential paradox in which mastery and liberation become one; that is, the individual through absolute mastery (of others and self) becomes absolutely free from the contingencies of individuality, this world, and others. This is the theme of Shelley's *Prometheus Unbound* just as much as it is of *The Federalist Papers* or Adam Smith's *Wealth of Nations*—the self-standing subject. It is thus that the discourse of ethics and aesthetics from a post-modern position cannot be separated from the discourse of power, excess, oppression, careerism, media exploitation, genocide, capitalism, migrations, schizophrenia— all of which constitute in this period of late modernism the technologies and practices for the aestheticization of the self, a project (the self or the state as art-work) which in both the dominant culture and alternative cultures is pursued through increasingly intense production of the signs which invoke the aesthetic and the ethical.

Craig Owens observes this tendency in the practice of recent artists: "what we witness . . . is a desperate, often hysterical attempt to recover some sense of mastery via the resurrection of heroic large-scale easel painting and monumental cast-bronze sculpture—mediums themselves identified with the cultural hegemony of Western Europe. Yet contemporary artists are able at best to simulate mastery, to manipulate its signs; since in the modern period mastery was invariably associated with human labor, aesthetic production has degenerated today into a massive deployment of the signs of artistic labor" ("Discourse of Others" 67). And it is no less true for corporate and governmental culture in the United States which displays an equally desperate quest for aestheticization of the self as modernist construct—white, male, Christian, industrialist—through monumentally styled office buildings, the Brooks Brothers suit (for male and female), designer food, business practices which amount only to the exercise of symbolic power, and, most of all, the Mercedes Benz which as the unification in design of the good (here, functional) and the beautiful and in production of industrial coordination and exploitation of human labor is pre-eminently the sign that one has finally achieved liberation and mastery, "made it to the top" (even if its stylistic lines thematize what can only be called a fascist aesthetics). Owens concludes, quite correctly as I believe, that such practices of simulation of mastery testify only to an increasing recognition of the loss of mastery—more precisely, to the failure of modern technologies of the self (both ideological and behavioral) to produce any sense of psychic wholeness or release from tensions, as explicitly promised in the modernist interpretation of the paradox of mastery / freedom.

What we get in contemporary life under the signs of ethics and aesthetics is what Arthur Kroker and David Cook have appropriately named "panic scenes," encompassing the "Panic God" of televangelism and the disappearing body under the "body McCarthyism" of AIDS and cocaine detection. These are sites which the technologies of modernism cannot transform and thus are sites which must either be erased as in the the panic dietary practices of anorexia and drug/alcohol addiction or covered-over as in the practices of body building and fashion dressing (see *Body Invaders: Panic Sex in America*). One, of course, takes over the praxis of anorexia or body building for precisely the same reason—aesthetically, the quest of the more beautiful body and ethically, to be a better person—and these two technologies encompass nicely the post-modern condition as the cultural logic of modernism that we find everywhere in the world: on one hand, the Christian renunciation and on the other, pagan indulgence; on one hand impoverished and homeless people and on the other the super-rich. Scarcity and abundance—nothing has changed, except for the intensity of the destructiveness of trying to employ an inadequate corpus of social, political, and aesthetic theory to resolve problems that the very theories themselves have brought about. The intensification of such dualities makes clear the criminal implication of the grand referent of the good and the beautiful in the horror of the culture of deprivation. In a world aimed so clearly at the solution of problems, why have we arrived at such a condition of fragmentation, polarity, and disintegration?

It is clear that the questions surrounding the technology of ethics and aesthetics need to be asked all over again, and it is the intention of the essays in this volume to do precisely that—though each in a vastly different manner and in total only a beginning. We cannot get beyond modernism until the lure of ethics and aesthetics as totalizing narratives or legitimations that mask contradictions and fissures is recognized (Anthony Cascardi) and re-grounded by learning, in Foucault's words "not to discover what we are but to refuse what we are" (Geoffrey Harpham). The essays that follow attempt to ask again the fundamental questions of ethics and aesthetics: Can there be poetry after Auschwitz? (Véronique Fóti) or paraphrasing William Carlos Williams, does the bomb put an end to all that (Rob Wilson)? Post-modernism (as Linda Hutcheon writes) raises a set of questions and problems that were not particularly problematic before when art was a category distinct from history or sociology. One of these important questions concerns the degree of autonomy from the political sphere that academic scholars exercise in determining such things as what literature receives scholarly acclaim—that is, what aesthetic experiences are promoted for consumption by students (Neal Oxenhandler). Taken together, these essays and this new way of thinking about our work as scholars, cultural theorists, and activists (if only in the ideological sphere) constitutes a general attempt to re-draw the boundaries of discourse and thus, to the extent that discursive and perceptual categories provide structure for the experienced-world, re-shape the realilty of what can be expected in life.

Fredric Jameson concludes his influential essay, "Post-modernism, or the Cultural Logic of Late Capitalism" by introducing a totalizing metaphor which, as I see it, should be adopted as an architectonics for the project of post-modern writing—in spite of post-structuralism and the diversity of methods and purposes and in spite of Jean-François Lyotard's unequivocal battle-cry of the post-modern: "Let us wage war on totality; let us be witness to the unpresentable; let us activate the differences and save the honor of the name" (*The Postmodern Condition* 82). Post-modernism must be destructive (deconstructive)—must take up philosophizing with a hammer and feeding the end of history (Baudrillard)—but it is well to remember Nietzsche's distinction between the anarchic and the nihilistic. The nihilistic begins in the discovery of the untenability of the highest values, "that the highest values devaluate themselves," but does not end in the absence of value itself—but rather in the process of revaluing all values ("European Nihilism," *The Will to Power*).

Post-modernism, as the essays in this collection illustrate, is the disorganized and often random program (oxymoron intended) to re-valuate by re-mapping or re-drawing the boundaries and "territorializations" of this late modern world we find ourselves in: "the alienated city [which] is above all a space in which people are unable to map (in their minds) either their own positions or the urban totality in which they find themselves" (Jameson 89). The totality which we should be waging war on is not any emerging post-modern one but rather the modernist one which as a constellation of theoretical discourses and master narratives legitimizes, centralizes, and exemplifies the privileged position of the white, male, Christian, industrialist. As long as all cognitive, aesthetic, or ethical maps are drawn to the scale of "I am the unified, self-controlled center of the universe . . . the rest of the world, which I define as Other, has meaning only in relation to me as man/father, possessor of the phallus," our cityscapes, mediascapes, landscapes, and mindscapes cannot help being, as Ann Jones puts it, "fundamentally oppressive, as phallogocentric" ("Writing the Body" 362). The modernist totality is oppressive and genocidal largely because of the *way* it structures discourse and human relations—not because it structures them to begin with. Modernist ethics and aesthetics have produced the culture of excess (both scarcity and abundance) not because they are related as theories and practices but because of the *way* they are related under the late-modernist political economy of the sign; deprivations are now necessary, not for material reasons, but for symbolic ones.

Post-modern writing as re-mapping and re-theorizing of fundamental human interests is a process of redistributing explanatory power (and thereby material power) through a shift to new dimensions, as Jameson basically sees it: "the compass introduces a new dimension into sea charts, a dimension that will utterly transform the problematic of the itinerary and allow us to pose the problem of a genuine cognitive mapping in a far more complex way. For the new instruments—compass, sextant and theodolite—do not merely correspond to new geographic and navigational problems . . . they also introduce a whole new coordinate" (90). The process of re-theorizing the objects and experiences of everyday life in the late modern world is precisely the process of transforming that world into one that will have to be recognized differently, ordered along different coordinates, and perhaps without any unified center at all, allowing us to take up again the pursuit of the good and the beautiful in practical and life-enhancing ways.

All of the essays in this volume undertake that project which Jameson calls "An aesthetic of cognitive mapping," a project which re-writes the rules by which subjects gain a sense of place in the global system. Let us hope simply that the work of this re-writing and the work of all others in field of post-modern theory will be unceasing in opening up the technologies of the self, or human ethics and aesthetics, to include where modernism excludes and to empower where modernism oppresses. If post-modernism is not a discourse and praxis of liberation, however differently demarcated and defined, then it has no need for the prefix "post—."

References:

Baudrillard, Jean. "The Year 2000 Has Already Happened." Trans. Nai-fei Ding and Kuan-Hsing Chen. *Body Invaders: Panic Sex in America.* Eds. Arthur and Marilouise Kroker. New York: St. Martin's Press, 1987. 35-44.

Crane, R. S., ed. *Critics and Criticism: Ancient and Modern.* Chicago: Chicago University Press, 1952.

Jameson, Fredric. "Postmodernism, or The Cultural Logic of Late Capitalism." *New Left Review* 146 (July-August 1984): 53-92.

Jones, Ann Rosalind. "Writing the Body: Toward an Understanding of l'Écriture féminine." *Feminist Criticism: Essays on Women, Literature, Theory.* Ed. Elaine Showalter. New York: Pantheon, 1985. 361-377.

Kroker, Arthur and David Cook. *The Postmodern Scene: Excremental Culture and Hyper-Aesthetics.* Montréal: New World Perspectives, 1987.

Kroker, Arthur and Marilouise, eds. *Body Invaders: Panic Sex in America.* New York: St. Martin's Press, 1987.

Lyotard, Jean-François. *The Postmodern Condition: A Report on Knowledge.* Trans. Geoff Bennington and Brian Massumi. Minneapolis: University of Minnesota Press, 1984.

Owens, Craig. "The Discourse of Others: Feminists and Postmodernism." *The Anti-Aesthetic.* Ed. Hal Foster. Port Townsend, WA: Bay Press, 1983. 57-82.

Nietzsche, Friedrich. *The Will to Power.* Trans. Walter Kaufmann and R. J. Hollingdale. New York: Random House, 1967.

A Postmodern Problematics

Linda Hutcheon,
University of Toronto

There is something about this postmodern beast with which we are obsessed today that remains baffling: why has postmodernism been both acclaimed and decried by both ends of the political spectrum? What is it about postmodernism that has caused it to be labelled both radically revolutionary and nostalgically neo-conservative? The simple and obvious answer is that everyone is talking about different cultural phenomena— which they all label as postmodern. Rather than add to the confusion, let me state right away that what I shall mean by that label is modelled on the first relatively uncontested use of it—in postmodern architecture. Transcoded into other art forms, the postmodern, in this sense, is parodic or ironic in its relation to the past—both formal and social, aesthetic and ideological. In fiction, the postmodern is what I would call "historiographic metafiction," self-reflexive yet historically grounded. And there are equivalent manifestations in painting, video, film, dance, and other literary forms, as well as in contemporary theory.

But confusion about corpus cannot be the only reason for the political ambivalences of postmodernism. There is also something about this art itself that is paradoxical or doubly-encoded on both the formal and ideological levels. On the one hand, fiction like Doctorow's *The Book of Daniel* or García Márquez's *Chronicle of a Death Foretold* overtly assert the arbitrariness and conventionality of the borders of genre. But they do so by self-reflexively insisting on those very borders. Historiographic metafiction is self-consciously fiction, even if its discourse overlaps with that of history or biography or theory. Those conventions are both installed and subverted, used and abused.

Paralleling this formal paradox of the postmodern is an ideological one, for this art is both critical of and yet complicitous with the cultural dominants of our time: liberal humanism and mass consumer culture. Thus, seeing—or privileging—only half of this contradiction would allow for those totally opposite interpretations and evaluations of postmodernism. This art both inscribes and contests prevailing norms, both aesthetic and ideological. In the light of this definition, there obviously is such a thing as postmodern theory: the now familiar and inherently self-contradictory theories such as those Foucaldian totalizing negations of totalization or essentializations of the inessentializable (power, for instance), or those Lyotardian master narratives whose paradoxical plot is our loss of faith in master narratives. In this light, what I would argue is that we should perhaps look to both theory *and* artistic practice to discern what the common denominators defining the postmodern might be.

As a look at any journal of theory these days shows, the debate over the meaning and, finally, value of postmodernism is very much a current one. Looking at postmodern art today in the light of the early terms of the debate—as articulated by Lyotard (*The Postmodern Condition*) and Habermas ("Modernity: An Incomplete Project")—I would see what I call the postmodern as straddling, or perhaps more accurately, sitting on the fence, between the two camps. One the one hand, it inscribes a metanarrative, with precise values and premises (à la Habermas) but it then proceeds to problematize both the product and the very process of inscription (à la Lyotard). Lately, though, the Lyotard/Habermas terms of reference have waned a little in popularity and the more fashionable frameworks of debate are either Marxist or what we might call neo-Nietzschean. The latter derives at once its rhetorical and theoretical base from the nihilistic theorists of excess and decay, the patron saints of continental apocalyptic thought: Nietzsche, Bataille, Baudrillard. But there is a very real sense in which the new terms of reference for the debate both fail to take into account their own position, the position from which the laments are launched. (Nor do they always grant the very real complexities of the phenomena they claim to be describing.) One of the lessons of the postmodern double encoding is that you cannot step outside of that which you contest, that you are always implicated in the values you *choose* to challenge.

And, while the bold assertion that the postmodern is "dehistoricized" has made for dramatic headlines for the new debaters, this is a claim which would seem to have little relation to the actual works of what I am calling postmodern art. Historiographic metafiction's self-reflexivity works in tight conjunction with its seeming opposite (historical grounding) in order to reveal both the limits and powers of literary and historical knowledge. To challenge history and its writing like this, however, is not to deny either; it is, instead, itself potentially a profoundly historical act.

Baudrillard's immensely influential article, "The Precession of Simulacra," makes the error of substituting for analysis of actual postmodern practice a generalized apocalyptic vision which collapses differences and rejects the possible creative and contestatory impulses within the postmodern. He has argued that mass media has neutralized reality for us, and it has done so in stages: first reflecting, then masking reality, and then masking the absence of reality, and finally, bearing no relation to reality at all. This is the simulacrum, the final destruction of meaning. What I would want to argue is that postmodern art works to contest the "simulacrization" process of mass culture—not by denying it or lamenting it—but by problematizing the entire notion of the representation of reality, and by therein suggesting the potential naivety of the view upon which Baudrillard's laments are based. It is not that truth and reference have ceased to exist, as Baudrillard so absolutely claims; it is that they have ceased to be unproblematic issues. But, we appear to have forgotten that, at least since Plato, they never really have been unproblematic, and so what postmodernism does is ask us to confront our amnesia.

We are not witnessing what Baudrillard sees as a degeneration into the hyperreal without origin or reality, but a questioning of what "real" can mean and of how we can know it. The function of the conjunction of the historiographic and the metafictive in much contemporary fiction, from that of John Fowles and E. L. Doctorow to that of Maxine Hong Kingston and John Berger, is to make the reader aware of the distinction between the brute *events* of the past real and the *facts* through which we give meaning to that past, by which we assume to know it. Baudrillard's simulacrum theory is too neat; it resolves tensions which I see as ongoing and unresolvable, and which perhaps should form the basis of any definition of postmodernism that pretends to be faithful to actual cultural practice.

Baudrillard himself is aware of some contradictions that cannot be resolved, however. He accepts that all culture, whatever its overt claims to the contrary, acts in accord with the political logic of the capitalist system. But postmodernism, I think, inverts the terms of that paradox. It does not pretend to operate outside that system, for it knows it cannot; it therefore overtly acknowledges its complicity, only covertly to work to subvert the system's values from within. It is what Michael Ryan has called an "enclave" or a pocket within the dominant that can contest it through a strategy of pluralized and diversified struggles (218). It is not apolitical, then, any more than it is ahistorical. It partakes of what Edward Saïd labels "critical consciousness" (241-242), for it is always aware of differences, resistances, reactions. The postmodern does not deny that all discourses (including my own—but also Baudrillard's) work to legitimize power; instead, it questions how and why, and does so by self-consciously, even didactically, investigating the politics of the production and reception of art. To challenge a dominant ideology, it recognizes, is itself another ideology. To claim that questioning is a value in itself is ideological; it is done in the name of its own power investment in institutional and intellectual exchanges within academic and critical discourse. And, of course, the very act of questioning is one of inscribing (and then contesting) that which is being queried. In other words, the very form of interrogation enacts the postmodern paradox of being both complicitious with and critical of the prevailing norms—which it has inscribed by its very questioning.

The paradoxes of postmodernism work to instruct us in theinadequacies of totalizing systems and of fixed institutionalized boundaries (epistemological and ontological). Historiographic metafiction's parody and self-reflexivity function both as markers of the literary and as challenges to its limitations. Its contradictory "contamination" of the self-consciously literary with the verifiably historical and referential challenges the borders we accept as existing between literature and the narrative discourses which surround it: history, biography, autobiography. This challenge to the limitations of the humanist privileging (and simultaneous marginalizing) of the literary has had repercussions that have overlapped with feminist and "minoritarian" contestings of the canon. Both theory and practice today work to show how, in Tony Bennett's terms, "literariness depends crucially not on the formal properties of a text in themselves but on the position which those properties establish for the text within matrices of the prevailing ideological field" (59).

Postmodern art is both self-reflexive and "worldly" (Saïd 35). Its deliberately unresolved paradoxes serve to underline, not to smooth over, the complex contradictions within our socially determined patterns of thinking and acting (Russell 190). And much literature today has also been aiming at analyzing the same thing, but my guess is that the theory is the better known to most of us. Novels like John Berger's *G.* overtly theorize (as they narrativize) almost all the notions to be found in post-structuralist and Marxist postmodern theory, but today I suspect we are more likely to read—and legitimate—the theory than the fiction. There obviously exists an intimate complicity between theory and practice, and I think that may explain why some of the most provocative studies of the postmodern are coming from artist-theorists: Paolo Portoghesi, Victor Burgin, Rosalind Krauss, David Antin.

What we find if we look at both theory and practice is a postmodern "problematics": a set of problems and basic issues that have been created by the various discourses of postmodernism, issues that were not particularly problematic before but certainly are now. For example, we now query those boundaries between the literary and the traditionally extra-literary, between fiction and non-fiction, and ultimately, between art and life. We can only interrogate these borders, though, because we still posit them. We think we know the difference. The paradoxes of postmodernism serve to call to our attention both our continuing postulation of that difference and also a newer epistemological doubt (*do* we know the difference? *can* we?). The focus of this doubt in postmodern art and theory is often on the historical. How can we know the past today? The questioning of historical knowledge is not new, but the powerful and unignorable conjunction of multiple challenges to any unproblematic concept of it in art and in theory today is one of the characteristics that I think define the postmodern.

A postmodern "problematics" would also take into account the many issues which result from these challenges to the modes of knowing and writing history, issues such as the textuality of the archive and the inveitable intertextuality of all writing. And it is not only literature that is involved in these challenges. What Renato Barilli has dubbed the art of the "Nuovi Nuovi" in Italian painting is reappraising the past of both local and international art and its relation to global informational mass culture. Similarly, postmodern architecture's parodic return to the history of architectural form is an ironic reworking of both the structural and ideological inheritance that was deliberately wiped out of architectural memory by High Modernism. Parody is the ironic mode of intertextuality which enables such critical—not nostalgic— revisitations of the past.

This self-reflexive, parodic interrogating of history has also brought about a questioning of the assumptions beneath both modernist aesthetic autonomy and unproblematic realistic reference (Solomon-Godeau 81). The entire notion of the referent in art has been problematized by the postmodern mingling of the historical and self-reflexive. This is most obvious, perhaps, in historiographic metafictions like *Ragtime*, where Sigmund Freud and Carl Jung can ride through the Cony Island Tunnel of Love together in a way they historically did not, but symbolically always had. What, then, is the referent of the language of this fiction—of any fiction, or, for that matter, of historiography? How can we come to know the real past? Postmodernism does not deny that it existed; it merely questions how we can know real past "events" today, except through their traces, their texts—the "facts" we construct and to which we grant meaning.

Postmodernism's challenges to our humanist notions of

history also involve challenges to its implied notion of subjectivity. In Victor Burgin's terms: "the 'individual' presupposed in humanism is an autonomous being, possessed of self-knowledge and an irreducible core of 'humanity', a 'human essence' in which we all partake, an essence which strives over history progressively to perfect and realize itself" (32). Any contestation of this basic belief—from Freud's to Foucault's—has been attacked as the "enemy of civilized aspirations." But feminist and Black theory and practice, to name only the most evident, have qualified the (male, white, Euro-centered) post-structuralist rejection of the cogito and of bourgeois subjectivity: they have argued that they cannot reject that which they do not have, that to which they have not been allowed access. Feminist theory and art, for instance, first inscribe female subjectivity before they contest it. And this is what makes much feminist and other de-centered (or "ex-centric") discourses have such a powerful impact on the postmodern by means of their inevitable and productive contradictions.

That all postmodern positions are, in a sense, ex-centric (paradoxically both inside and outside the dominant they contest) is no cause for despair or apocalyptic wailing. The postmodern view is that contradictions are inevitable and, indeed, the condition of social as well as cultural experience. To smooth them over would be bad faith, even if it would also be our normal reaction within a humanist context. The narrator of Salman Rushdie's novel, *Shame* puts it this way: "I myself manage to hold large numbers of wholly irreconcilable views simultaneously, without the least difficulty. I do not think others are less versatile" (242). Postmodernism refuses to eliminate (and indeed foregrounds) what Andreas Huyssen calls "the productive tension between the political and the aesthetic, between history and the text," (221) and it does so by historicizing and contextualizing the separation between those discourses, which within a humanist frame of reference, have been seen as almost mutually incompatible.

What postmodernism questions, though, is not just liberal humanism's assertion of the real but also the more fashionable neo-Nietzschean apocalyptic murder of the real. The various postmodern discourses do not "liquidate referentials" (in Baudrillard's terms) so much as force a rethinking of the entire notion of reference, a rethinking that makes problematic both the traditional realist transparency and the newer reduction of reference to simulacrum. It suggests that all we have *ever* had to work with is a system of signs, and that to call attention to this is not to deny the real, but to remember that we only *give meaning* to the real within those signifying systems. This is no radical new substitution of signs for the real. Postmodern art and theory merely foreground the fact that we can only know the real, especially the past real, through signs, and THAT is not the same as wholesale substitution. The postmodern still operates, in other words, in the realm of representation, not of simulation, even if it constantly questions the rules of that realm.

In writing of the avant-garde, Lyotard (*Le Postmoderne* 125) recently used the image of psychoanalysis: the attempt to understand the present by examining the past. The same image is suggestive for postmodernism's orientation toward the "presence of the past" (the title of the Venice Biennale that introduced postmodernism in architecture). It points to the postmodern rejection of either a positive utopian (Marxist) or negative apocalyptic (neo-Nietzschean) orientation toward the future (cf. Huyssen 169). Its aims are more limited, I think—to make us look to the past from the *acknowledged* distance of the present, a distance which inevitably conditions our ability to know the past. The ironies produced by that distancing are what prevent the postmodern from being nostalgic; there is no desire to return to the past as a time of simpler or more worthy values. These ironies also prevent any antiquarianism; there is no value to the past in and of itself. This is the conjunction of the present and the past that is intended to make us question—that is, analyze and try to understand—both how we make and make sense of our culture. Postmodernism may well be, as so many want to claim, the expression of a culture in crisis, but it is not in itself any revolutionary breakthrough. It is too contradictory, too wilfully compromised by that which it challenges.

Instead of looking to totalize, then, I think what we need to do is to interrogate the limits and powers of postmodernist discourse, by investigating the overlappings within a plurality of manifestations in both art and theory, overlappings that point to the consistently problematized issues that I think define postmodernism: issues like historical knowledge, subjectivity, narrativity, reference, textuality, discursive context. I would agree with Habermas that this art does not "emit any clear signals" but, then again, it does not try to. It tries to problematize and, thereby, to make us question. But it does not offer answers. It cannot, without betraying its own anti-totalizing ideology. Yet, both the detractors and promoters of postmodernism *have* found answers, and this is because the paradoxes of the postmodern do allow for answers—but only if you ignore the other half of the paradox. To Habermas' question: "But where are the works which might fill the negative slogan of 'postmodernism' with a positive content?" ("Neoconservative" 90), I would reply: everywhere—in today's fiction, in painting, in film, in photography, in dance, in architecture, in poetry, in drama. In this art's contradictions, as in those of contemporary theory, we may find no answers, but the questions that will make any answering process even possible are at least starting to be asked.

References:

Barilli, Renato. *Icons of Postmodernism: The Nuovi-Nuovi Artists.* Torino: Allemandi, 1986.

Baudrillard, Jean. "The Precession of Simulacra." *Art After Modernism: Rethinking Representation.* Ed. Brian Wallis. New York: New Museum of Contemporary Art; Boston: Godine, 1984. 253-81.

Bennett, Tony. *Formalism and Marxism.* London and New York: Methuen, 1979.

Bernstein, Richard J., ed. *Habermas and Modernity.* Cambridge: MIT Press, 1985.

Burgin, Victor. *The End of Art Theory: Criticism and Postmodernity.* Atlantic Highlands, NJ: Humanities Press International, 1986.

Foster, Hal, ed. *The Anti-Aesthetic: Essays on Postmodern Culture.* Port Townsend, WA: Bay Press, 1983.

Garvin, Harry R., ed. *Romanticism, Modernism, Postmodernism.* Lewisburg: Bucknell University Press; London: Associated University Press, 1980.

Habermas, Jürgen. "Modernity—An Incomplete Project." Trans. Seyla Ben-Habib. *The Anti-Aesthetic.* Ed. Hal Foster. Port Townsend, WA: Bay Press, 1983. 3-15.

_____. "Neoconservative Culture Criticism in the United States and West Germany: An Intellectual Movement in Two Political

Cultures." *Habermas and Modernity.* Ed. Richard J. Bernstein. Cambridge: MIT Press, 1985. 78-94.

Huyssen, Andreas. *After the Great Divide: Modernism, Mass Culture, Postmodernism.* Bloomington: Indiana University Press, 1986.

Lyotard, Jean-François. *The Postmodern Condition: A Report on Knowledge.* Trans. Geoff Bennington and Brian Massumi. Minneapolis: University of Minnesota Press, 1984.

_____. *Le Postmoderne expliqué aux enfants: Correspondance 1982-1985.* Paris: Editions Galilée, 1986.

Rushdie, Salman. *Shame.* London: Picador, 1983.

Russell, Charles. "The Context of the Concept." *Romanticism, Modernism, Postmodernism.* Ed. Harry R. Garvin. Lewisburg: Bucknell University Press; London: Associated University Press, 1980. 181-93.

Ryan, Michael. *Marxism and Deconstruction: A Critical Articulation.* Baltimore and London: The Johns Hopkins University Press, 1982.

Saïd, Edward W. *The World, the Text and the Critic.* Cambridge: Harvard University Press, 1983.

Solomon-Godeau, Abigail. "Photography After Art Photography." *Art After Modernism: Rethinking Representation.* Ed. Brian Wallis. New York: New Museum of Contemporary Art; Boston: Godine, 1984. 74-85.

Cultural Autonomy and *Nouveau Roman*

Neal Oxenhandler,
Dartmouth College

The relationship between writers and professors has always been adverserial. Socrates' scorn for professors of rhetoric is an archetype which continues to reappear until modern times. At the turn of the century, Alfred Jarry's Père Ubu, based on the despised Professor Heb, is exemplary; while Proust's malicious portrait of punmaster, Dr. Cottard, is derogatory in a different way. Professors who meddle in politics are sent to a special hell by the writer and ideologue Maurice Barrès, who found them an easy target. "One is always unfair when attacking professors," he wrote and, "I would rather be intelligent than an intellectual" (Brombart 25). Virginia Woolf's Professor Ramsey in *To the Lighthouse* is a monster of egotism, while James Joyce mercilessly portrayed his Jesuit teachers in *Portrait of the Artist.*

To all this the professors replied by ignoring living writers and refusing to allow their students to write doctoral dissertations on them. A writer only became interesting (and tolerable) once he was dead.

As we all know, the fifties and sixties saw a significant change in this centuries old quarrel. Academic critics began to be interested in living writers, not only admitting them as subjects of research, but even inviting them onto campus to read from their works. Reciprocally, the scorn that politicians had long held for professors began to abate. John F. Kennedy initiated the Washington-Cambridge shuttle, using Harvard intellectuals as an important resource. These new technocrats were, for the most part, social scientists; and it was not until the Reagan administration that humanist ideologues, most of whom had academic credentials, began to appear on the banks of the Potomac.

This article constitutes a reflection upon a special case of this relation between writers and professors, one that seems to represent a reversal of the long-standing hostility between them. I am talking about the rise to international eminence of the French *nouveau roman*. Why was this particular sub-genre of the novel, on the face of it so sharply counter to the American tradition of writing and reading, championed by the professors? How and why did they contribute to its invasion of the curriculum (both graduate and undergraduate) in the universities of Europe and, especially, the United States? Why, during the sixties, which was the period of resistance to Vietnam in the U.S. and to de Gaulle in France, did this apolitical form of fiction achieve dominancy among academic readers? Why were we so eager to promote a literature which pursued purely aesthetic goals, abandoning not merely the conventions of story and character but all forms of historical and social commitment? And finally, in this process of international transplantation, who gained and who lost?

Let us at the outset confront the view, expressed by Barthes and others, that the *nouveau roman* really *is* committed to a social and political program. At the very end of *Writing Degree Zero*, Barthes sees in modern writing the "anticipation of an absolutely homogenized condition of society . . ."(125) to be achieved through "the undoing of language, inseparable from the undoing (*déchirement*) of class" (126, my translation). As political statement, this is so broad as to appear perfectly safe; it is the statement of a *mandarin*, who has never worked in the blood and dust and boredom of the political arena. In fact, the only motives for social change in the *nouveau roman* are negative. So in a typical statement Jean Ricardou announces that he wants "to subvert these inverted and complicitous categories, such as those of work and pleasure" (Cérisy I, 242, my translation). In other words, Ricardou wants to repeat the act of the revolutionaries of 1789, who changed the calendar, thereby freeing energies bound by tradition and repetitive work. Again, we have a statement of such grandiosity that no consequences can flow from it.

In a chapter of a book in progress, Lynn Higgins argues that certain hermetic works of the 1960s must be read as encoded representation of a surrounding discourse; so, for example, Robbe-Grillett's *Marienbad* would really be "about" censorship in respect to the rape of Algeria (and a well-publicized case of the rape of an Algerian woman by French soldiers). Higgins writes: "Both *Muriel* and *Marienbad* speak around and through censorship of the film's historical context." This is a convincing argument, so far as it goes; its implicit point, with which I agree, is that there is no work which is completely autonomous, completely severed from its historical context: autonomy then would be a question of degree. By this criterion, the *nouveau roman* would still represent (along with the poetry of Scève in the 16th century and Mallarmé in the 19th) an extreme or limit-case of the phenomenon.

There are several ways of explaining the rise of cultural autonomy in the sixties. The Nobel laureate, Claude Simon, recently placed the responsibility for the rebirth of this tendency on the shoulders of Jean-Paul Sartre.[1]

According to Simon, Sartre's blindness to the failures of communism and his espousal of Maoism disgusted the young intellectuals and writers who looked to him for inspiration. In 1951, the year in which Sartre definitively accepted Stalinist Communism, he told an interviewer:

> For the time being, the Communist Party represents the proletariat for me. . . . It is impossible to take an anti-Communist position without being against the proletariat. (Lottman 282)

In 1970, he was attracted by "a moral conception of action and of human relations. That's what, in the beginning, the Maoists represented to me" (Cohen-Solal 617, my translation). Other, less judicious remarks were attributed to him during this period when he distributed pamphlets and participated in street debates which, he claimed, "perform in the street what should happen in the press" (Cohen-Solal 618-619).

While Sartre's reputation remained enormous until the time of his death, the decline in his political relevance was apparent in May 1968, when he found difficulty communicating with the students on their barricades and, after several public appearances, judiciously withdrew. But, as early as 1952, he had emerged scarred from the argument and break with Camus over the refusal of *Les Temps modernes* to acknowledge Russian slave-labor camps. Perhaps the most damning criticism of Sartre was that levelled against him by his old friend and co-founder of *Les Temps modernes*, Maurice Merleau-Ponty, who claimed that Sartre had become a *mandarin* (the classical 19th century term of contempt) who mistook his ability to conceptualize political issues for a form of political action:

> The action of revealing has its facilities and its torments which are those of contemplation. They are problems and solutions of mandarins. The myth of the mandarin reunites the fantasy of a total knowledge and pure action. By virtue of his knowledge, the mandarin is supposedly present everywhere a problem presents itself and capable of acting immediately, no matter where, without distance and by pure efficacy, as if what he did fell into an inert milieu and as if it were not, at the same time, only theater, manifestation, object of scandal or enthusiasm. (Kaelin 144)

Despite his many articles and polemics, Sartre stood above the fray, imposing a totalizing historicism on events. He believed that the media held the key to creating a climate of opinion favorable to revolution. Even when he allowed himself to be caught up in the wheels of communist publicity: "trapped, swallowed, solicited, unable to refuse an invitation or a request to publish" (Cohen-Solal 45), or when later he distributed Maoist pamphlets in the street side by side with youthful militants, even then Sartre was seen as (in the words of Michel Foucault) the "universal intellectual," rather than a man of combat or of action.

I find Simon's view a biased one; no one man can be held responsible for the depolitization of French intellectuals in the sixties. A better and more complex explanation was expressed by

Michel Foucault in an interview in *L'Arc*. Reflecting on what has been and now should be the historical position of the intellectual, Foucault said:

> All the exasperated theorizing about writing that we have witnessed in the sixties was undoubtedly a swansong: writers were struggling to maintain their political privilege; but whether or not there was really a 'theory' at issue, whether or not that theory required scientific credentials—founded on linguistics, semiology, psychoanalysis— whether or not that theory found accreditation through de Saussure or Chomsky, etc., the fact that it produced such mediocre literary works proves that the writer's practice was no longer the active matrix of social change. (23, my translation)

If the literature of the sixties (which includes the *nouveau roman*) was "mediocre," then how do we explain its success? Only half in jest, Roger Shattuck has suggested that it began with a "conspiracy" between Robbe-Grillet and Roland Barthes, each rising to prominence on the other's coat-tails (*The Innocent Eye* 207-208). As the principal artisan of applied structuralism, Barthes' role in the dissemination of the *nouveau roman* was crucial. The novels of Robbe-Grillet served as a pretext which allowed Barthes to promote his formalist views. Barthes attributed an "ineluctably nonrealistic status" to literature which made contact with the world of reference only through the "relay system" of language; in its colorless neutrality, Robbe-Grillet's fiction was an excellent example of such a relay.

Barthesian structuralism was (in the beginning) concerned entirely with the function, not the content of signs; it was interested only in their correlations and interactions. This functionalistic formalism, with its abandonment of all ontological claims, was the basis for Barthes' interest in Robbe-Grillet and his influential promotion of that writer.

But is is unlikely that a purely formalist fiction, with no ontological claims, could achieve worldwide prominence; and so there was a correction of Barthes' original position. In 1963, Barthes wrote the introduction to Bruce Morrissette's book on Robbe-Grillet. Here, Barthes dealt with the ontological question by cloning a second Robbe-Grillet. The first had been the *chosiste*, who refused transcendence in any form; the other was a *humaniste*, whose works link up with "models, archetype; with sources and echoes"; so Morrissette shows Robbe-Grillet's link with "an entire literary context." Barthes accepts Morrissette's effort to show a Robbe-Grillet who is "integrated, or better, reconciled with the traditional aims of the novel" (Barthes in Morrissette 11).

Any major literary success requires a "conspiracy" of the type Shattuck identifies, but in this instance he has omitted a number of the principal power-brokers. A central role was played by Robbe-Grillet's publisher, Jérôme Lindon, who believed in the *nouveau roman* and was willing to make sacrifices to help it survive:

> Against the *Dictionnaire des rues de Paris*, Jérôme Lindon exchanged the first fruits of the *nouveau roman*. . . . And the publisher indulged in a pleasure which he imagined a necessity, to build his list following the lead of his personal inclinations. (Hamon & Rotman 60, my translation)

That is surely admirable. We can also admire the energy with which Jean Ricardou undertook to turn the *nouveau roman* into the Cause of the decade. There were lengthy sessions at Cérisy; there were polemics and debates in the literary press; and there were the violent *éreintements* of the naive "pigeons" who fell into the traps set for them by the cabal of innovators. So Raymond Picard's *Nouvelle Critique ou nouvelle imposture?* was attacked from all sides and left in shreds.

There are certain questions that it is pointless to ask; but one wonders what would have become of Robbe-Grillet if Barthes had not put his prestige and his style in the novelist's service. It is true that Robbe-Grillet, who became an important editor for Lindon, promoted the work of other novelists who shared his aesthetic assumptions; and they, in turn, rewarded him with favorable reviews in the newspapers and journals to which they had entry.

But it was Barthes who brought the *nouveau roman* to a broader audience and, of crucial importance, to an **international** audience. Here, the work of Bruce Morrissette was used to great advantage. For, as suggested in the quotations above, Morrissette brought Robbe-Grillet back into the tradition and made him accessible to traditional exegesis. It is not surprising then that the

1977 Cérisy Colloquium on Robbe-Grillet was dedicated to Morrissette, who was unable to attend.

Though from the beginning the nouveau roman established itself via a complex network of connections in journalism and publishing, its flowering as a major literary event on the international scene came through a very different intermediary, one that had vast resources and access to a large captive audience—the American university. In the past ten years Les Editions de Minuit sold in the United States over 22,500 copies of *Le Voyeur*, which represents one half of the entire sales for this book since its publication in 1955. *La Jalousie*, which is Robbe-Grillet's other major success, sold more than twice as many copies world-wide as did *Le Voyeur* (i.e. 110,000) but approximately the same number in the United States—probably to the same colleges and universities where the earlier book had been taught. I am not clear on the reasons for the disparity in sales figures between the two novels[2]; it may be that *La Jalousie* had the wider sales because its content is less controversial and it has definite pedagogical advantages over the earlier book. In any event, the fact that one quarter of the book's sales were in this country confirms the fact that the American market has been a major factor in establishing the literary reputation of Robbe-Grillet.

On the face of it, the *nouveau roman* (along with much of postmodernism) should never have penetrated the native land of *Readers' Digest, Classic Comics*, and other forms of the easy "read." For the *nouveau roman* was based on an esthetic of difficulty; its masterpieces were indecisive, their themes hermetic and contradictory. Besides all this, and most serious of all, it did not give its undergraduate readers (who in earlier cohorts had flocked to Sartre and Camus) any clear message about the meaning of life. Its goals had nothing to do with those traditional goals of the novel—to move, to delight, to instruct.

It could be said, in fact, that the *nouveau roman*—though much more muted than the work of absurdists like Arrabal or moral radicals like Jean Genet—shared with the work of these writers the determination to assault and offend its readers. Here, in the politics of reading, we find something like a genuine political motive. While the great modernist writers (with the notable exception of Brecht) avoided overt political commitment, postmodernists were apolitical (Beckett) or anarchistic (Arrabal). Some masqueraded as nihilists or pocket revolutionaries, which did not prevent them from collecting their royalties. Others played the role of political gadflies and excelled in finding the open nerve (vestige of class or economic guilt) in their bourgeois audience, providing it with a few moments of cathartic discomfort, which did not prevent it from continuing to enjoy that *théâtre digestif* so vehemently attacked two decades earlier by Antonin Artaud. In the general attack on bourgeois values that began with Romanticism, the postmodernists were latecomers whose critique lacked context and hence the decisive social power of earlier writers such as Flaubert or Zola.

Another way to look at the social protest of the new novelists is to see it as providing what Barthes called in *Mythologies* an "innoculation." It caused a momentary discomfort, a brief spasm of guilt; this led not to action but to mental and emotional immunization against serious social concern and involvement.

Postmodernism has occasionally been effective in attacking bourgeois culture, not by arguing with it but by ridiculing it, as in the theater of Eugène Ionesco; or by making it seem, as in the works of Beckett, a vast and superannuated grotesquerie. Beckett's subtle undermining of traditional forms of cognition and of value-formation represents the most powerful attack on bourgeois society in all of postmodernism; yet (and this is the final paradox) Beckett is within that society and its beneficiary.

To what extent did the aesthetic program of the *nouveau roman* promote an ideological position?

The program of the *nouveau roman* was, at first, largely negative: to overthrow what Robbe-Grillet called "the tyranny of meaning." It wanted to liberate the reader from the metaphysical weight of the tradition by renewing language, freeing signifier from signified, voice from character, description from the obligation of bearing a narrative function. "Freedom," which has been the rallying cry in France since 1789, was seen as the ultimate goal of this new writing practice.

As the theory was elaborated, the novels ceased to be mere exercises in a decadent genre and became suspiciously positive and utilitarian. It was suggested that circular thinking without a precise object could provide a useful form of intellectual hygiene, a cleansing of the mind from the "referential illusion." But Jacques Derrida, who went further than anyone else in freeing signifier from signified and discrediting all forms of cognitive closure wrote, in *Of Grammatology*, in respect to Heidegger's slide into metaphysical thinking: "This would perhaps mean that one does not leave the epoch whose closure one can outline" (12). This statement by Derrida applies to the slippage that occurs in all attempts to achieve a purified *écriture;* it suggests that a writing practice, such as that of the *nouveau roman*, must be seen as an asymptote, tending toward a condition never wholly achieved.

In her introduction to an excellent book, *Three Decades of the French New Novel*, Lois Oppenheim undermines clichés associated with this broad range of writing styles inaccurately lumped under the single rubric of *nouveau roman*. Summarizing the essays she introduces, Oppenheim demonstrates that the text is not simply "a stratified composite of meanings isolated from any particular sensibility of their author and from any but a purely hypothetical mode of linguistic experience"; but rather, as Rybalka and others demonstrate, there is "a reinsertion of the author into the text and . . . of the text into the world" (7). Oppenheim's division of the evolution of the New Novel into three stages, all of which center in distinct ways on the question of reference, suggests that the New Novel does not, indeed, "leave the epoch whose closure it outlines."

One of the paradoxes of the reception of the *nouveau roman* in this country is the fact that it was promoted by a generation of young professors who had been in graduate school during the years of the Vietnam War. All of us, of course, are victims of whatever intellectual or artistic fad is current during our formative years; but in this instance, I believe that the frustration and emotional exhaustion produced by the War enhanced the appeal of this autonomous, self-contained form of art. This generation was ready to hear arguments against art as embodied meaning or as ontologized metaphor, notions identified with American new criticism. It was ready to believe that literature could by reduced to its language and that this language could be treated scientifically. Moreover the themes of the *nouveau roman* coincided with the 60s feelings about economic determinism and the randomness of history as well as views about the alienating quality of sex and the ubiquity of violence. The idea of a figure/ground reversal was appealing—modernism was seen to represent things (once revered but now dangerously passé) that postmodernism should be attacking.

The depreciation of experience which typifies the *nouveau roman* (in its way more radical than that of Proust) did not bother most critics of the sixties, though it did confuse their students. What captivated many in the *nouveau roman* was the delineation of a reading practice that had none of the messiness of life; instead, it had the neatness and clarity of a crossword puzzle. This practice appealed to the sixties generation as a clean well-lighted place where, with their students, they could explore the French language; or rather, they could explore a unique fictional *langage* captured like a butterfly within the meshes of the *langue*. They could find an appeasement of the mind in contemplating patterns and contours. There was a feeling of power in its very absence—the power **not** to respond to the confused solicitations of the broader society, the power to turn in tight intellectual circles till one could no longer tell the dancer from the dance.

Although the Vietnam protest was successful in achieving its primary goal, the cessation of the war, it did not succeed in developing a meaningful critique of the larger society: much of the reason for this lies in the fact that the late sixties and early seventies were a period of affluence, when the universities expanded enormously and everybody had good facilities and research grants. Young teachers entering the profession were awarded their part of the action. It would have been embarrassing to appear ungrateful; and besides, administrators toughened by years of protest and confrontation waited on the opposite side of the fence to mete out punishment.

There was no enduring Marxist tradition to energize a political opposition. In his introduction to *Postmodernism and Politics*, Jonathan Arac has given us a perceptive survey of the effort by postwar American intellectuals to retrieve an historically responsible position. He quotes a dispirited statement by Edward Saïd:

> . . . literary criticism is still 'only' literary criticism, Marxism only Marxism, and politics is mainly what the literary critic talks about longingly and hopelessly. (xxix)

Arac then quotes Fredric Jameson, in a statement that is somewhat blurred but more positive than Saïd's:

> We are, after all, fragmented beings, living in a host of separate reality-compartments simultaneously; *in each one of those* a certain kind of politics is possible, and if we have enough energy, it would be desirable to conduct all those forms of political activity simultaneously. So the 'metaphysical' question: what is politics . . . is worth-while only when it leads to enumeration of all the possible options, and not when it lures you into following the mirage of the single great strategic idea. (xxix)

"The single great strategic idea" recalls all those grandiose goals of the new novelists and their supporters. Nor is it only the autonomy of a disembodied fiction which is inculpated by Jameson's indictment. One thinks of that other form of theoretical gratuity called deconstruction. Still other structuralist and post-structuralist practices could by considered guilty of following this same mirage.

Those professors who championed the *nouveau roman* back in the 60s made a Faustian bargain. They abandoned their traditional role as critics of institutions and ideologies and shifted their investigations to the narrow arena of literary form. It was a failure of nerve, a seeming acquiescence (almost a century later) in the scorn heaped on them by Barrès as incompetents who had no business meddling in the really important issue of life, i.e. politics.

When you make a bargain with the devil, you get something in return. These academics acquired something that could be totally their own and upon which no alien claims could be made. The *nouveau roman* was the first literary form that could be read in the U.S. without a vast philosophical and historical baggage. Now for the first time, American academics need not feel inferior because they had not been born speaking French. For the first time, the congenitally inferior professor of French acquired real power. This was not the power to change the means and ends of production, nor power to change political structures, much less the defense community. Rather, he acquired the power to decree what should be read and how it should be read in a limited number of classrooms. Exegesis of the *nouveau roman* went on in the journals and at scholarly meetings. Despite the attempt to abolish interpretation, our strategy involved a surreptitious and hence contorted effort to extract levels of meaning from the *nouveau roman* which it was not meant to have. Some appropriated it as a vehicle for understanding French aesthetic life or what a colleague of mine at UCLA called by the high-sounding name of "French reality." Others claimed that it would cure our students of naive forms of reading, thereby making them into skeptical and informed citizens who would vote for the right candidates.

The appropriation of the *nouveau roman* frequently reached a level of passionate hyperbole. So one critic argued that Robbe-Grillet's *chosisme* (his obsessive focus on objects) could be understood in terms of Husserl's famous dictum "Back to the things themselves." This attempt to award the novelist up-to-date philosophical credentials was mistaken, but it is a measure of the seriousness with which the *nouveau roman* was taken in this country. The appropriation was mutual. Robbe-Grillet, who had no desire to be linked to phenomenology, attempted to explain his work in terms of T.S. Eliot's discredited notion of the "objective correlative."

One could also call the appropriation geographical: each of the *nouveaux romanciers* made his or her tour of American universities, culminating with a visit to California. I remember that Steve Nichols and I had the pleasure of showing Watts Towers to Nathalie Sarraute, who remained gracious despite a gale-force wind. A year earlier, I had taken Michel Butor for a tour of downtown L.A., including the now razed Clifton's Cafeteria with its replica of the Garden of Gethsemane. All of this showed up in his tribute to America, *Mobile*.

Meanwhile, French fiction continued to evolve; and while we were still explicating Robbe-Grillet, there appeared extraordinary novels based on an aesthetic opposed to the *nouveau roman*, novels signed with the names of J.M.G. Le Clézio and Michel Tournier.

The degree of aberration in our continuing fascination with the *nouveau roman* was commented upon by Françoise Verny, editor at Grasset, in a recent interview in the New York Times:

> There was a moment when the French lived under the
> dictatorship of the New Novel, but it seems to me that the

notions you had outside this country about its pre-eminence were a little out of date. For some time now, there has been a return to adventure, to immediacy, to a greater pluralism and independence. There are no schools these days, no currents, no dominant gathering places or literary reviews. We're in a period of individual ferment. (January 5, 1985)

During the past ten years, France has witnessed a broad sustained effort to redefine the role of the intellectual in respect to institutions and public life. A major document in this process was the special number of *L'Arc*, entitled "La Crise dans la tête," from which I have already quoted a remark by Foucault. Reading this document—and especially the interview with Foucault—one has the impression that, for better or for worse, the French intellectual is still a political creature, obsessed with defining his insertion in the body politic and finding his own specific levers of power.

I see no such effort of self-renewal and self-definition in the American community of letters; instead, we continue to witness a dismaying degree of careerism engaged in by our most celebrated professors. Accustomed to the rewards of the Great Society, these entrepreneurs, now in their fifties or early sixties, tour the lecture circuit, pulling down substantial fees and enjoying all the ballyhoo and prestige of film stars. The narrowness of their politics, as expressed in their lectures and books, seems to substantiate the view, proposed some years ago by Daniel Bell, that there is no real ideology behind American politics, only an enlightened pragmatism. More damaging is the view recently expressed by the conserative Irving Kristol, who uses against us the same argument that the French extreme right used against the theorists of the Revolution of 1789: We sacrifice realities (such as class structure and existing economic distribution) to abstractions such as the "common good." Kristol insists that this is sheer hypocrisy: intellectuals are motivated by self-interest, just as everybody else. On this point he is surely correct. How else explain the cynical game of musical chairs played by our intellectual stars? While the stakes are not as high, the competition in the academic NFL is hardly different from that search for the highest bidder engaged in by professional athletes.

To summarize and conclude: the *nouveau roman* marked a break with political involvement in the American academy from which (unlike the French, who never accorded the *nouveau roman* the adulation it won on this side of the Atlantic) we have never recovered. Moreover, our involvement with post-structuralism, deconstruction and semiotics has built upon this earlier fascination with "pure" forms of art and thought.

Today, as a new wave of intellectuals takes up positions in Washington—on the right this time rather than on the left [3]— we must look critically at the way we teach literature and the increasingly abstract character of our theoretical preoccupations. This preoccupation with theory and purified forms of thought points to a fundamental weakness in American intellectual life, a predisposition toward mandarinism and an unstated conviction of own inefficacy. Many of us, and especially those who are practicioners of literature, cannot escape the nagging suspicion that maybe, after all, we should follow the advice of the old proverb, recalled by Barrès: *A chacun son métier et les moutons seront bien gardés* (To each his own task and the sheep will be well cared-for, Brombert 25).

Or, can we reconcile both cultural and political imperatives? Can we find ways to change society by bringing our analytical and interpretive skills to bear on that referential world, so recently considered an illusion? I think that an authentic reading of texts involves their insertion in history and a determination of the meaning of the world. If this kind of reading practice is honest and complete, then it must eventually become an imperative for action.

Notes:

1. In a conversation with my colleague, Colette Gaudin. Simon is not kind to Sartre and writes (with feigned amazement) of Robbe-Grillet's descriptions of him as Sartre's spiritual heir: "Of course, I do not know the laws of genetics, but I must again confess that, despite careful self-examination, I discern nothing in myself which would allow me to claim this strange paternity. . ." (Oppenheim 75).

2. Figures provided by Les Editions de Minuit.

3. See "The Washington Intellectual," *The New Republic*, August 11 & 18, 1986.

References:

Arac, Jonathan. *Postmodernism and Politics*. Minneapolis: University of Minnesota Press, 1986.

Barthes, Roland. *Le Degré zéro de l'écriture*. Paris: Editions du Seuil, 1953.

Brombert, Victor. *The Intellectual Hero: Studies in the French Novel, 1880-1955*. Philadelphia: Lippencott, 1961.

Cohen-Solal, Annie. *Sartre, 1905-1980*. Paris: Gallimard, 1985.

Colloque de Cérisy: Robbe-Grillet. Vol. I *Roman/Cinéma*. Dir. Jean Ricardou. Paris: UGE, 1976.

Derrida, Jacques, *Of Grammatology*. Trans. Gayatri C. Spivak. Baltimore: The Johns Hopkins University Press, 1974, 1976.

Foucault, Michel. "Vérité et pouvoir." *L'Arc* 70 (1977): 16-26.

_____. "Distance, Aspect, Origine." *Théorie d'ensemble*. Paris: Editions du Seuil, 1968. 11-24.

Hamon, Hervé and Patrick Rotman. *Les Intellocrates*. Paris: Editions de Ramsay, 1981.

Kaelin, Eugene, F. *An Existentialist Aesthetic*. Madison: University of Wisconsin Press, 1966.

Lottman, Herbert R. *The Left Bank: Writers, Artists, and Politics from the Popular Front to the Cold War*. Boston: Houghton Mifflin, 1982.

Morrissette, Bruce. *Les Romans de Robbe-Grillet*. Préface de Roland Barthes. Paris: Les Editions de Minuit, 1963.

Oppenheim, Lois, ed. *Three Decades of the French New Novel*. Urbana: University of Illinois Press, 1986.

Shattuck, Roger. *The Innocent Eye*. New York: Farrar, Straus, Giroux, 1984.

History, Theory, (Post)Modernity

"There are no witnesses to changes of historical epoch."
—Blumenberg, *The Legitimacy of the Modern Age*, 469

"One can certainly wager that man would be erased, like a face drawn in sand at the edge of the sea."
—Foucault, *The Order of Things*, 387

Anthony J. Cascardi,
University of California, Berkeley

The following pages on history and theory are meant as a contribution to the larger debate concerning the relationship between modernity and postmodernism, as it has recently been focused in the writings of Jürgen Habermas, Jean-François Lyotard, Richard Rorty, and others.[1] While these discussions have been sharpened by the increasingly apparent contradictions of the "postmodern" age, it must at the outset be said that the "problem of modernity" is now nearly two centuries old, and dates at least from Hegel's critique of "modern philosophy" as the philosophy of subjective self-consciousness that found its culminating expression in Kant. Hegel's critique of subjectivity as the basis of modernity is combined, in the *Phenomenology* and elsewhere, with a series of insights into the religious, social, and economic transformations of history, which took decisive roles in the development of the modern world: the Reformation, which claimed a part in liberating consciousness from mystification; commodity capitalism, which confirmed the "desacralization" of nature accomplished elsewhere by rational means; and the French Revolution, which attempted to secure a realm of ethical freedom and thereby render concrete the notion of abstract right.

In Hegel's thought, modernity may properly be regarded as a realm of freedom, yet at the same time his judgment is that modernity failed to establish a legitimate social order, in part because it remained unable to reconcile its social and historical ambitions with the modes of rationality available to it. The dichotomy of history and theory is symptomatic of this failure, and it would not be too much to propose that the Hegelian dialectic was conceived in order to resolve the antinomic relationship of these terms. The French Revolution remained the decisive event of modernity for Hegel, but he ultimately viewed it as a threat to the ground of philosophy itself. Thus, as Habermas incisively observed, "in order not to sacrifice philosophy to the challenge posed by the revolution, Hegel elevated revolution to the primary principle of his philosophy" ("Hegel's Critique of the French Revolution" 121). In this respect—and notwithstanding the fact that thinkers from Nietzsche and Heidegger to Derrida have seen in Hegel the very culmination of the philosophy of subjectivity of the modern age[2]—Hegel attempts to distance himself from the modern paradigm in order to reconcile its antithetical terms.

We shall in conclusion see that Hegel's critique of modernity is possible only by virtue of a "double movement," in which the totality is divided into History and Reason, which are then recuperated into a self-surpassing Spiritual whole. This recuperative movement is necessary, for if philosophy is on the one hand identified with the activity of Reason, then it would seem incapable of acknowledging any world other than itself; and if philosophy recognizes the contingent and fragmented world of human nature and history, it would seem unable to take that world as an essential manifestation of Reason. As one Hegel scholar wrote of these conflicting goals, "from the outset and throughout, the Hegelian system seems faced with the choice between saving the claims of an absolute and therefore all-comprehensive philosophic thought, but at the price of loss of any actual world besides it, and saving the contingent world of human experience at the price of reducing philosophic thought itself to finiteness" (Fackenheim, *The Religious Dimension in Hegel's Thought* 76). To say that Hegel resolves this dilemma by recourse to "Spirit" is also to say that Hegel sacralizes human history, in effect subsuming the historical emergence of every new form of consciousness, including the self-assertion of modernist "reason," into a pattern which repeats the spiritual cycles of the Christian faith: as we shall also see, he thereby sacrifices the historical autonomy of the modern age.

To begin, however, I want to locate the antinomy of history and theory and the philosophical "founding" of modernity in the historical emergence of reason in the philosophy of Descartes; from there we may proceed to assess the postmodern and historicist critiques of reason in the work of Hans Blumenberg and Michel Foucault.[3] Descartes identified reason as the ordering of structures and quantities, and fashioned his philosophical method along these lines, yet he also claimed that his project was radically new and marked an unprecedented achievement of reason on the historical plane. Thus the Cartesian conception of reason may be taken as a defining characteristic of the modern age, but modernism is not reducible to it. Indeed, the "postmodern" challenge, brought sharply into focus in the work of critics such as Blumenberg and Foucault, has been to construct a vision of modernity which is not at the same time subordinate to the notion of a rationally centered whole. This is to say that any description of modernity must continue to make reference to culture as a totality, but therefore also to those elements within culture which Cartesian reason remained from the start unable to control (cf. Hegel: "what Enlightenment declares to be an error and a fiction is the very same thing as Enlightenment itself is," *Phenomenology of Spirit* 334, sec. 549).

Modernism so conceived is marked not only by the emergence of the "subject" and the mathematical ground which lends it support, but also by the consolidation of the powers of the absolutist state, by a redistribution of the authority of faith and science, by an increased mobility of the psyche, and by a reconception of the nature of the "literary" work of art. Together, these changes become visible in the period roughly contemporary with Descartes in the works of Cervantes, Hobbes, Pascal, and in various versions of the myth of Don Juan. And while each establishes a domain within a total cultural field that is at this moment in history constituted anew, the truth of modernist culture is revealed only in their differentiation from within. For while modernism may initially be described in speculative terms as a sociocultural whole, the meaning of its various elements can be grasped best as the relationship of mutually antithetical terms. The founding of epistemology as "first philosophy" by Descartes, for instance, depends on the containment of "literature" or "fiction" outside the realm of truth. Similarly, the Hobbesian conception of reason, which is closely linked to that of Descartes,[4] is unable to account for the founding of the modern state, which Hobbes regards as motivated by fear and dread. History and theory, in their part, remain sharply divided realms: as the example of the French Revolution would later bear out, historical events resist complete determination by the philosophy of subjectivity, just as Cartesian reason, which claimed unique applicability to motions in the sublunary world, remained unable to account for its own genesis on an historical plane.

Modernism in this and many other ways constitutes a "detotalized" whole, and is marked by what Max Weber described as the segmentation of culture into a series of separate value- or interest-spheres. Habermas sees in modernism the development of the "inner logic" of each of these spheres,[5] and regards it both substantively and historically as coextensive with the Enlightenment (viz., as that period in which reason came to manifest itself as the natural destiny of man). On these grounds he attempts a reconstruction of modernism from within its own "centered" point of view, and regards this as necessary for the preservation of its rational goals. By contrast, I take "modernism" as an already decentered cultural whole, which is to say as a totality no more than one facet of which may be held clearly in view at a time. The story that is told about the Cartesian conception of reason, including the history of corrections and historicist replies which it receives, may with equal legitimacy be narrated from the perspective of the mobile psyche of modernist desire; it may be told from the vantage point of the structures of terror and authority at work in the modern state; and it may be viewed in terms of the shifting and unequal balance of faith and science. Each provides a provisional center and is but a means for grasping the whole.

These preliminary facts are further confirmed when modernism is regarded as a trans-historical phenomenon and considered from a post-modern point of view. Habermas has consistently taken postmodernism at its face-value and sees it as the rejection of modernism; but I would argue that postmodernism deepens, rather than resolves, the contradictions of the modernist past. Indeed, the two most important postmodern critiques— those of history and of metaphysics—begin as responses to subjectivity and to that vision of history which subjectivity founds. Yet they conclude either in the loss of history as a potential value ground, or in historically indiscriminate critique of "Western metaphysics" as a whole. Moreover, these critiques are incompatible among themselves;[6] they are intelligible only against the background of a prior disjunction of reason and history, which in turn reveals their common inheritance from the modernist past.

Modernism thus conceived is not coextensive with the Enlightenment, as Habermas has claimed but rather is the field of a series of contradictions of which the dichotomy of history and theory is but one. This dichotomy is central to any effort to describe modernism, yet it remains unacknowledged by such thinkers as Hans Blumenberg and Michel Foucault. My critique of their work remains in important ways indebted to the Hegelian perspectives sketched above, yet it differs from Hegel in significant ways. For whereas Hegel conceived the problem of modernity as solvable only through the recovery by the philosophy of Spirit of the religious consciousness that modernity lost, I begin with the provisional acceptance of Blumenberg's assumption that the secular and historical character of modernity cannot be treated as the "loss of substance" of the sacred or ancient worlds. As a spokesman for modernity in a decidedly "postmodern" age, Blumenberg recognizes the contradictions of modernism and acknowledges their potentially damaging effects; his theses on the specific origins of modernity seem to me to need serious revision, yet his notions of the historical "reoccupation" of cultural positions offers a powerful alternative to the dominant trend in postmodern historiography, viz., the "archaeology" and "genealogy" of Michel Foucault.

Consider, then, the critique of modernity put forward by Foucault. In the opening chapters of *The Order of Things* and in the theoretical discussion surrounding that work, Foucault described the eclipse of the late Medieval and Renaissance world by what I have termed the modern age as exemplary of the phenomenon of historical discontinuity of which his "archaeological" method was designed to give account. If the historicist model of explanation took discontinuity as the sign of a temporal dislocation, which it was the historian's task to explain and remove, as the given of his analysis but also as that which was inassimilable by it ("the raw material of history, which presented itself in the form of dispersed events . . . which, through analysis, had to be rearranged, reduced, effaced"), archaeology was by contrast conceived as an enterprise in which all pre-existing forms of continuity could be held in suspense (*The Archaeology of Knowledge* 8). Insofar as the notion of continuity was presupposed by historicist explanation in its "classical" (i.e. nineteenth-century) form, the process of its interrogation by suspension or epoche may be regarded as the means by which history so-called transcends and finally cancels itself. Archaeology is post-history, and is followed by Foucault's version of "genealogy." This is not an account or logos of the genesis and transformation of historical paradigms, as Hegel had proposed to give, but something closer to Nietzsche's ideal of a history of absolute difference. As such, archaeology was forced to reject those images of the whole on which history so-called customarily relied. As Foucault wrote in "Nietzsche, Genealogy, History," "Nietzsche's criticism, beginning with the second of the *Untimely Meditations*, always questioned the form of history that reintroduces (and always assumes) a suprahistorical perspective: a history whose function is to compose the finally reduced diversity of time into a totality fully closed upon itself; a history that always encourages subjective recognitions and attributes a form of reconciliation to all the displacements of the past; a history whose perspective on all that precedes it implies the end of time, a completed development" ("Nietzsche, Genealogy, History" 153). Yet even within the limits of such concepts as "regularity," "order," "law," and "rule," which Foucault's archaeology genially accepted, there was an effort to internalize difference as the element which classical history necessarily had to elide: "[Archaeology] establishes that we are difference, that our reason is the difference of discourses, our history the difference of times, our selves the difference of masks. That difference, far from being the forgotten and recovered origin, is this dispersion that we are and make" (*Archaeology* 131).

The transition from "resemblance" or "similitude" to "representation" and "order" marking the rise to dominance of the modern age is exemplary of a variety of functions which, while contiguous in some chronological space, are from the vantage point of the new order of things seen as discontinuous with the past. As the concept of fixed essences comes under pressure, there is no longer a "nature" to secure the relationship of sign and signified. A system based on the comparison of structures and quantities comes to replace a hierarchy of intricate analogies and detailed correspondences; the network of similitudes, in principle infinite or bounded only by a transcendent plenitude, yields to an order of orders—a mathesis —in which it would be possible to give a complete analysis or enumeration of the whole. The theory and practice of mimesis shifts from imitation to representation, with a corresponding change in the focus of attention from human action (which, as an index of character, was considered to be imitation's proper object) to the concept of world, which as the object of representation was a creation of the seventeenth-century philosophy of mind. These changes correspond to the creation of philosophy as a science in the writings of Descartes, and to the differentiation of philosophical, historical, and aesthetic discourse. They are consolidated in the position of the subject, which Heidegger rightly saw as underlying the modern age (see "The Age of the World Picture").

The point of Foucault's analysis is that there is no rational process or movement which will account for the transformation of any one of these functions or moments into the next, or perhaps more accurately still, that it is only based on the presupposition of some underlying substance or ground (e.g. "history," "reason," "man") that such functions could be conceived as continuous among themselves. So seen, the purpose of *The Order of Things* is not simply to account for the phenomenon which historians of science have come to identify as a "paradigm shift," but to do so without reference to the notions of self-conception and purpose in terms of which discontinuities there have been understood. This is in part the reason why historical orders are seen by Foucault mysteriously to rise and then to suddenly disappear. I cite from the "Preface" to *The Order of Things*, which typifies this vision of abrupt and arbitrary historical change: "It is this (Classical) configuration that, from the nineteenth century onwards, *changes entirely*; the theory of representation *disappears* as the universal foundation of all possible orders; language as the spontaneous *tabula* . . . *is eclipsed* in its turn; a profound historicity *penetrates* into the heart of things" (*The Order of Things* xxiii). We see here evidence of that quality which Richard Rorty described as the peculiar "dryness" of Foucault's style, i.e., the systematic exclusion of any appeal to a self-interpreting community, or as Rorty puts it, the absence of any "we" ("Habermas and Lyotard on Postmodernity"). It may additionally be said that this "dryness" is symptomatic of an inability to theorize the relationship between knowledge and power, and suggests Foucault's deep-seated fear of power as well. Moreover, the dryness of Foucualt's style points toward the eventual disintegration of his "archaeological" stance, for it indicates, somewhat paradoxically, the *absence* of history as a ground on which to claim a stance (Foucault: "my discourse, far from determining the locus in which it speaks, is avoiding the ground on which it could find support," *Archaeology* 205). Phrased in slightly different terms, it could be said that the archaeologist's "dryness" results from the effort to speak difference itself, a project which when severed from the concept of a rational or social whole can only result in the dis-articulation of a stance.[7]

Following Nietzsche's remarks in *The Will to Power* (sec. 711)—"there is no 'totality;' . . . no evaluations of human existence, of human aims, can be made in regard to something that does not exist"—terms such as "discontinuity" and "difference" are often invoked in postmodern discourse in order to shatter the notion of a (rational, social, historical) whole. Yet the whole is not thereby altogether elided. Foucault substitutes for the whole the notion of the archive, which as a fully historicized positivity represents a lawlike formation demarcating all that can validly be said:

> To describe a group of statements not as the closed, plethoric totality of a meaning, but as an incomplete, fragmented figure; to describe a group of statements not with reference to the interiority of an intention, a thought, or a subject, but in

accordance with the dispersion of an exteriority; to describe
a group a statements, in order to rediscover not the moment
or the trace of their origin, but the specific forms of an
accumulation, is certainly not to uncover an interpretation,
to discover a foundation, or to free constituent acts; nor is it
to decide on a rationality, or to embrace a teleology. It is to
establish what I am quite willing to call a positivity.
(*Archaeology* 125)

The concept of mathesis, which Descartes invoked against
Aristotelian teleology at the beginning of the modern age, remains
powerfully operative in Foucault's appeal to regularity and rule,
and it remains likewise severed from the concepts of purpose and
end. In this light one may well understand Foucault's need to speak
of historical change as originating in a space which lies *outside*
that of existing thought ("Discontinuity—the fact that within the
space of a few years a culture sometimes ceases to think as it had
been thinking up till then and begins to think things in a new
way—probably begins with an *erosion from outside*, from the space
which is, for thought, *on the other side*," *The Order of Things* 50;
emphasis added). Yet it is unclear just how the notion of history
as a series of epistemes, insulated from one other, could provide
for such change; for the episteme is a finite totality, and must be
presumed to represent a given moment of history, fully present
to itself. *The Order of Things* begins with an allegorical account
of the incommensurability of epistemes through a reference to one
of Borges's tales, and it concludes with the indication of a possible
"future thought." "These [historical analyses] are not affirmations,"
Foucault writes; "they are at most questions to which it is not
possible to reply; they must be left in suspense, where they pose
themselves, only with the knowledge that the possibility of posing
them may well open the way to a future thought" (386). Yet
Foucault proves unable to formulate the language in which such
a thought might be expressed. Moreover, he rejects the possibility
that theory could comprehend, much less help project, the
transformation involved.[8]
 Only in a later interview does Foucault confront the question
of what it might mean to imagine a world which we might not
yet be able to inhabit: "I am well aware that I have never written
anything but fictions. I do not mean to say, however, that truth

is therefore absent. It seems to me that the possibility exists for fiction to function in truth, for a fictional discourse to induce effects of truth, and for bringing it about that a true discourse engenders or 'manufactures' something that does not as yet exist, that is, 'fictions' it. One 'fictions' history on the basis of a political reality that makes it true, one 'fictions' a politics not yet in existence on the basis of a historical truth" (*Power/Knowledge* 193). Yet in the majority of his work, the conception of history not simply as a succession of events but as a value-ground, i.e. as a drama of exemplary deeds and the repository of cultural models, is eclipsed by the positivist conception already noted, and history in this guise remains the master of theory. History controls language (discourse) and the projective powers of imagination as well. This mastery is evident in the inscrutable transformations of epochs, and also in the alliance of cognition and power implicit in the very terms "discourse" and "episteme." Yet the collapse of all forms of consciousness into manifestations of power implies the impossibility of a critique of history in view of any trans-historical goals, and explains why Habermas and other neo-Marxists have found it necessary to draw sharp boundaries between their work and Foucault's.[9] At the very least, it reveals the fact that Foucault embraces a stance towards history that is conditioned by conflicting demands. Foucault inherits from the modernist culture which he follows the will to revise all existing institutions and ideas; yet he seeks to reject modernist forms of discourse and the modes of consciousness they imply. These contradictory orientations are regarded as somehow overcome in the abandonment of the ideal that reason might provide the ground of an historical critique, and ultimately in the *dépassement* of the ground of history itself. History may thus be thought of as prior to theory, but it is for Foucault little more than a refuge for endangered subjective thought ("If the history of thought could remain the locus of uninterrupted continuities, if it could endlessly forge connexions that no analysis could undo without abstraction, if it could weave, around everything that men say and do, obscure syntheses that anticipate for him, prepare him, and lead him endlessly towards his future, it would provide a privileged shelter for the sovereignty of consciousness," *Archaeology* 12).

The relationship between history and theory in Foucault, which may be taken as indicative of their interrelationship in postmodernism more generally, is nonetheless intelligible as a transformation of the modernist project which superficially it rejects. As we shall see in relation to the work of Blumenberg, Foucault's alliance of knowledge and power gives expression, in postmodern guise, to one of the latent truths of the modern world. For although postmodernism openly declares a break with its modernist past, it would be more accurate to say that the reversal of history in its relationship to theory, which might conceivably serve for its transformative critique, is possible only because history and theory are themselves unreconciled in modernist thought. From its beginnings in the seventeenth century, modernism combines the project of a critique of all existing forms of consciousness and ideas with the notion that mathematics supplies the context-free "language of nature" and constitutes the natural language of thought. In the *Meditations*, the *Discourse on Method*, and the *Rules for the Direction of the Mind*, Descartes carried out a revisionary program calling for a critique of historical experience and the wisdom inherited from the past in favor of those truths which could be validated in solitude by the methods of the mathematical mind. Descartes clearly placed the claims of theory over against those of history, but rather than say that history was thus eliminated from modernism, it would be more accurate to say that Descartes construes history as open to the possibility of radical revision by speculative thought.

At the same time, the modernist project envisioned in the Cartesian texts was meant to provide the groundwork for a positive program of self-revision. To be sure, Descartes established the absolute certainty of mathematics as exemplary of rational activity and conceived his philosophical method as modeled on it ("I applied [the method] to certain other problems which I could put into something like mathematical form by detaching them from all the principles of the other sciences, which I did not find sufficiently secure," *Discourse* 125); but he never lost sight of the fact that the end of reason lies in praxis, or that the basis of action is human freedom, which knowledge is meant to secure. The work of reason in Descartes is directed towards what Habermas has called "emancipatory" interests, which operate through the transformation of nature, history, society, and the self. Yet the exercise of freedom with regard to history begins for Descartes with the prior abandonment of the encumbrances of the past: "regarding the opinions to which I had hitherto given credence, I thought that I could not do better than undertake to get rid of them, all at one go, in order to replace them afterwards with better ones, or with the same ones once I had squared them with the standards of reason" (*Discourse* 117). As Descartes sets himself the task of a rational historical critique, he invokes a division of history and reason ("science") of which reason is unable to give account: "even though we have read all the arguments of Plato and Aristotle, we shall never become philosophers if we are unable to make a sound judgment on matters which come up for discussion; in this case what we would seem to have learnt would not be science but history" (*Rules* 13).

The self-grounding nature of the reason which Descartes describes is conceived in terms of a mathematical substance which virtually insures that the moment of its own founding cannot be comprehended by it. The *cogito*, as "founding" act of thought, is thus not wholly ahistorical, but creates the impression within history of a radical discontinuity or gap. Hence the modernist desire to seek the absolute foundations of knowledge indicates a crisis in the relationship between reason and history that here manifests itself in the desire to begin entirely from oneself; the latter impulse, it might be added, is tantamount to the will to begin from nothing at all. As a result, the freedom which is expressed as what Hans Blumenberg would call modernist "self-assertion" becomes a manifestion of the phenomenon which Nietzsche would describe in terms of the "will to power" over the past. In this sense, it could be said that the subjective ground of Cartesian reason is not "foundational" at all, but groundless; it rests on foundations that can be secured only by the will.

In contrast to Foucault's postmodern critique of history, Blumenberg accepts the self description of modernity as that age in which reason manifested itself within history as man's natural vocation and definitively prevailed (see *The Legitimacy of the Modern Age*). Yet he also points to the paradoxical timelessness of Descartes' intention to make an absolute beginning in time, and to the antinomic vision of the shape of history which results therefrom:

> Reason's interpretation of itself as the faculty of an absolute
> beginning excludes the possibility that there could appear even
> so much as indications of a situation that calls for reason's
> application now, no sooner and no later. Reason, as the
> ultimate authority, has no need of a legitimation for setting
> itself in motion; but it also denies itself any reply to the
> question why it was ever out of operation and in need of a
> beginning. What God did before the Creation and why He
> decided on it—where reason was before Descartes and what
> make it prefer this medium and this point in time—these are
> questions that cannot be asked in the context of the system
> constituted by their basic concepts. (*Legitimacy* 145)

As Blumenberg goes on to say, modernism depends for its identity
on a sharply dualistic conception of its relationship to every former
age; that which precedes modernity is imagined as the province
of superstition, mythical thinking, or animistic beliefs. Yet any
"corrective" to the self-conception of modernity which would
propose to assimilate the prior history of reason to some unified
historical plan would only threaten the legitimacy of modernism
as an historical epoch. Attempts to bridge the gap between the
Middle Ages and the modern world by the invocation of an
unbroken continuum of rational activity, for instance, can be
understood as attempts to rationalize what was originally irrational
in modernism's understanding of itself; they threaten modernism's
epochal self-conception and jeopardize its claims to have brought
about a "final phase of self-possession and self-realization"
(*Legitimacy* 378).

Blumenberg's notion of historical method as the discovery of
"reoccupied positions" may fruitfully be juxtaposed to Foucault's
"archaeology" and its later, Nietzschean variant, "genealogy," on
a number of points. The invocation of cultural functions or
positions allows Blumenberg to conceive of meaning and purpose
in history without recourse to a thesis about the telos of history
as a whole. Moreover, Blumenberg conceives no substance (no
"reason" or "spirit") through which history is transformed; instead
he regards history as the repository of solutions to a series of
problems which we continue to confront. Accordingly, judgments

about the "legitimacy" of modernism must be based upon its ability to produce new and historically effective ideas. As for the category of "progress" and its crucial place in modern thought, it is worthwhile to recall that Blumenberg began his project as a response to the arguments of Karl Löwith, who in *Meaning and History* proposed that "progress" was modernity's re-appropriation of the eschatological pictures of history of the Jewish and Christian faith. It was hence a sign of the fundamental inauthenticity of the modern project, and of modernity's misinterpretation of the purpose of reason in the world. These facts about modernity were confirmed for Löwith in the Hegelian synthesis of reason and history, which relied on the recovery, by philosophy, of a religious substance that had been carried forward into modernity but remained nonetheless suppressed:

> Hegel himself did not feel the profound ambiguity in his great attempt to translate theology into philosophy and to realize the Kingdom of God in terms of the world's real history. He felt no difficulty in identifying the "idea of freedom," the realization of which is the ultimate meaning of history, with the "will of God"; for, as a "priest of the Absolute," "damned by God to be a philosopher," he knew this will and the plan of history. He did not know it as a prophet predicting future catastrophe but as a prophet in reverse, surveying and justifying the ways of the Spirit by its successes. (*Meaning in History* 58)

We shall, in conclusion, briefly return to Hegel's attempt to reconcile reason and history on spiritual grounds. But it must first be said that Blumenberg's critique of Löwith in his defense of the "legitimacy" of the modern age raises a series of questions about the origins and rationality of the category of the new as a defining feature of the modern world. We have seen for Foucault, the sources of the new remain unfathomable by reason. For Blumenberg, the legitimacy of the modern age is a function of its ability to articulate novel solutions to questions which may themselves be inherited from the past. For despite modernism's legitimate claims to historical autonomy, it can be seen that if modernity did not spring into existence from "outside" history, (which is also to say that if the philosophy of subjectivity, though "transcendentally" grounded, remains nonetheless an *historical* event), it must be traceable to pre-existing ideas. Blumenberg seeks to resolve this paradox of history and theory by combining the consciousness of an historical inheritance with an appeal to the powers of speculative thought. These methodological innovations remain valid despite the fact that Blumenberg's thesis regarding the specific origins of modernity in the second-overcoming of gnosticism is largely inconsistent with the proximity of such early modern writers as Descartes, Cervantes, Hobbes, and Pascal, to the already secularized culture of the high Renaissance. Moreover, Blumenberg seriously misinterprets the *querelle des anciens et des modernes* as an instance in which the moderns succeeded in freeing themselves from the "encumbrances" of the past. In both cases, Blumenberg ignores the prior attempts to reconcile history and reason on the grounds of a provisional and contingent totality, the *communitas*, in the civic humanism of the Renaissance. Indeed, as late as Montaigne, the past still constitutes a sphere of exemplary behavior and a scene of virtual action relevant to present purposes, rather than the store of potential errors as it had become for Descartes.

These arguments are not meant to suggest that what Descartes calls "reason," and what may more generally be referred to as a conjunction of modernist practices and beliefs, can only be understood in terms of the predecessor culture they negate. Examples drawn from pre-modern times offer no immediate alternatives to the problem of modernity if only because they deny modernist notions of reason their principal historical force, viz., that of something radically new, of the unprecedented achievement of reason on the historical plane. What Blumenberg proposes to explain through his thesis of reoccupied positions, however, is not just the novelty of modernity, but also its transformative effects on those questions which it inherits from the past. Thus the idea that "progress" lends meaning to the shape of history as a whole did not, in his view, become possible as a consequence of some prior theological eschatology; rather, originally modest notions of spiritual progress and salvation were extended to embrace the "philosophy of history" as a whole, at the same time presenting modernism with teleological questions which it had no framework to answer. Here again the contrast with Hegelian historiography is germane, for Hegel sought to resolve the contradictions of modernism by answering the question of the meaning of the totality of history. While Hegel may thus have succeeded in balancing the demands of history and theory, the origins and novelty of the modernist project nevertheless remain for him as mysterious as those objects which suddenly present themselves before consciousness as both necessary and yet wholly new ("it is just this necessity itself, or the *origination* of the new object, that presents itself to consciousness without its understanding how this happens, which proceeds for us, as it were, behind the back of consciousness," *Phenomenology* 56, sec. 87).

In contrast to the modernist gestures of Descartes, who spoke of razing the existing structures of knowledge to the ground in order to build from new foundations, Hegel proposed to stand on a ground which was not just foundational, or new, but which was totalizing, or absolute. The emergence of reason on an historical plane as the manifestation of that which was both necessary and new is thus concealed within a circle "that returns into itself, the circle that presupposes its beginning and reaches it only at the end" (*Phenomenology* 488, sec. 802). This is why Adorno's critique of Hegel, which was far more radical than Blumenberg's, had to reject both the dialectical totality and the modernist philosophy of origins which the dialectic was meant to correct: "The first and the absolutely new are complementary, and dialectical thought had to dispose of both of them. . . . Dialectics is the quest to see the new in the old instead of just the old in the new. As it mediates the new, so also it preserves the old as the mediated (*Against Epistemology* 38). In the dialectic, modernist "progress" becomes the movement through which reason is carried forward and also raised up; its medium and its validation are to be found in the long procession of historical cultures and individuals, in what Hegel calls "actual history." Hegel said that history is the court of the world's judgment, which suggests that it is both secular and rational. Yet Hegel's concept of history remained a sacred and sacrificial affair, one in which reason mimes a plan of spiritual death and redemption, sloughing off, but also recollecting, the prior stages of its existence as it moves ahead: "the two together," he wrote, "form alike the inwardizing [recollection] and the Calvary [sacrifice] of absolute Spirit" (*Phenomenology* 493, sec. 808).

Notes:

1. See Jürgen Habermas, *Der Philosophische Diskurs der Moderne*; Jean-François Lyotard, *The Postmodern Condition: A Report on Knowledge*; and the essays gathered in *Habermas and Modernity*.

2. This is a hotly contested point. See Heidegger, *Hegel's Concept of Experience*; Hans-Georg Gadamer, "Hegel and Heidegger," in *Hegel's Dialectic: Five Hermaneutical Studies*; Gilles Deluze, *Nietzsche and Philosophy*, especially pp. 147-194; and David Kolb, *The Critique of Pure Modernity: Hegel, Heidegger, and After*. Following Heidegger, Derrida reads Hegel as absolutizing, or infinitizing, the philosophy of subjectivity. For example: "On the one hand [Hegel] undoubtedly summed up the entire philosophy of the logos. He determined ontology as absolute logic; he assembled all the determinations of philosophy as presence; he assigned to presence the eschatology of parousia, of the self-proximity of infinite subjectivity" (*Of Grammatology* 24).

3. These aims are supported at a number of points by issues raised in a parallel study of mine, "Geneologies of Modernism."

4. Hobbes' relationship to Descartes has been the cause for some dispute, not least because of Hobbes' own written "Objections." Yet on such crucial questions as the mathematical nature of reason the two are in fundamental agreement.

5. See, for instance, Habermas, *Reason and the Rationalization of Society*, vol. 1 of *The Theory of Communicative Action*.

6. The dispute between Foucault and Derrida, including Derrida's response to Foucault's *Histoire de la folie* ("*Cogito* et histoire de la folie," published in *L'Ecriture et la différence*), is symptomatic in this regard.

7. This difficulty is shared by Derrida, whose work brings it into sharpest relief. He writes that "Difference is articulation" (*Of Grammatology* 66); yet, as Gillian Rose has pointed out, if this is so then it follows that "the *articulans* cannot itself be articulated, nor can it be articulate" (*Dialectic of Nihilism: Post-Structuralism and Law* 139). Implicit is the rejection of Hegel's claim to have achieved a complete (i.e. wholly articulate) discourse.

8. This is, to be sure, a difficult point. In work nearly contemporaneous with *The Order of Things*, Foucault seems to indicate that thought, as opposed to sight and speech, has the capacity to direct itself toward an "outside," i.e. to relations of power that have not yet been stratified. (See "La Pensée du dehors.") The gap between a thought which directs itself to the "outside," and visible or legible signs, nonetheless remains. Gilles Deluze provides some discussion of this point in *Foucault*, pp. 92-93.

9. See Habermas on Foucault in *Der philosophische Diskurs der Moderne*, and also Perry Anderson's critique of structuralism and post-structuralism, *In the Tracks of Historical Materialism*.

References:

Adorno, Theodor. *Against Epistemology*. Trans. Willis Domingo. Cambridge, MA: MIT Press, 1983.

Anderson, Perry. *In the Tracks of Historical Materialism*. London: Verso, 1983.

Blumenberg, Hans. *The Legitimacy of the Modern Age*. Trans. Robert M. Wallace. Cambridge, MA: MIT Press, 1983.

Cascardi, Anthony J. "Genealogies of Modernism." *Philosophy and Literature* 11 (1987).

Deleuze, Gilles. *Foucault*. Paris: Minuit, 1986.

_____. *Nietzsche and Philosophy*. Trans. Hugh Tomlinson. New York: Columbia University Press, 1983.

Derrida, Jacques. "*Cogito* and the History of Madness." *Writing and Difference*. Trans. Alan Bass. Chicago: University of Chicago Press, 1978. 31-63.

_____. *Of Grammatology*. Trans. Gayatri Spivak. Baltimore: Johns Hopkins University Press, 1976.

Descartes, René. *Discourse on Method*. *The Philosophical Writings of Descartes*. Vol. I. Trans. John Cottingham, Robert Stoothtoff, and Dugald Murdoch. Cambridge: Cambridge University Press, 1984.

_____. *Rules for the Direction of the Mind*. *The Philosophical Writings of Descartes*. Vol. I. Trans. John Cottingham, Robert Stoothtoff, and Dugald Murdoch. Cambridge: Cambridge University Press, 1984.

Fackenheim, Emil. *The Religious Dimension in Hegel's Thought*. 1967; Chicago: University of Chicago Press, 1982.

Foucault, Michel. *The Archeology of Knowledge*. Trans. A. M. Sheridan Smith. New York: Harper and Row, 1972.

_____. *Histoire de la folie à l'âge Classique*. Paris: Plon, 1961.

_____. "Nietzsche, Genealogy, History." *Language, Counter-Memory, Practice*. Trans. Donald F. Bouchard and Sherry Simon. Ithaca: Cornell University Press, 1977.

_____. *The Order of Things*. New York: Random House, 1970.

_____. "La Pensée du dehors." *Critique* 229 (juin, 1966): 523-546.

Gadamer, Hans-Georg. "Hegel and Heidegger." In *Hegel's Dialectic: Five Hermeneutical Studies*. Trans P. Christopher Smith. New Haven: Yale University Press, 1976.

Habermas, Jürgen. "Hegel's Critique of the French Revolution." In *Theory and Practice*. Trans. John Viertel. Boston: Beacon Press, 1974.

_____. *Der Philosophische Diskurs der Moderne*. Frankfurt am Main: Suhrkamp Verlag, 1985. Trans. Frederick Lawrence, *The Philosophical Discourse of Modernity*. Cambridge, MA: MIT Press, 1987.

_____. *The Theory of Communicative Action*. Vol. 1 of *Reason and the Rationalization of Society*. Trans. Thomas McCarthy. Boston: Beacon Press, 1981.

Hegel, Georg Wilhelm Friedrich. *Phenomenology of Spirit*. Trans. A. V. Miller. New York: Oxford University Press, 1977.

Heidegger, Martin. "The Age of the World Picture." *The Question Concerning Technology and Other Essays*. Trans. William Lovitt. New York: Harper and Row, 1977.

_____. *Hegel's Concept of Experience*. New York: Harper and Row, 1970.

Kolb, David. *The Critique of Pure Modernity: Hegel, Heidegger, and After*. Chicago: University of Chicago Press, 1986.

Löwith, Karl. *Meaning in History*. Chicago: University of Chicago Press, 1949.

Lyotard, Jean-François. *The Postmodern Condition: A Report on Knowledge*. Trans. Geoff Bennington and Brian Massumi. Minneapolis: University of Minnesota Press, 1984.

Nietzsche, Friedrich. *The Will to Power*. Trans. Walter Kaufmann and R. J. Hollingdale. New York: Vintage, 1967.

Rorty, Richard. "Habermas and Lyotard on Postmodernity." *Habermas and Modernity*. Ed. Richard J. Bernstein. Cambridge, MA: MIT Press, 1985. 161-175.

Rose, Gillian. *Dialectic of Nihilism: Post-Structuralism and Law*. Oxford: Basil Blackwell, 1984.

Deterritorialization and Border Writing

D. Emily Hicks,
San Diego State University

I. What is Border Writing?

Border writing is a mode of operation, not a definition. It is an attitude on the part of the writer towards more than one culture. Border writers give the reader the opportunity to practice multidimensional perception and nonsynchronous memory (Bloch 22-38). Border culture is a configuration of cultural practices in which the identity between cultural theory and praxis, that is, between any predetermined aesthetic and its implementation, has been replaced by a relationship of non-identity.

In Latin America and elsewhere, some border writing has been called "magic realism." I will argue that this term obscures important issues such as narrative non-linearity, the decentered subject, and the relationship of border writing to a multidimensional perspective. Rather than focusing on "magic realism," I want to analyze the border metaphor, and more specifically, its relationship to technology. I also want to consider the appropriateness of applying European post-modernist terminology to border writing by juxtaposing certain border texts with the category of "deterritorialization" of Gilles Deleuze and Felix Guattari. Finally, I will propose a model for analyzing the border text, a multi-dimensional model drawn from holography.

Some, but not all, contemporary Latin American literature is a literature of borders: cultural borders between Paris/Buenos Aires and Mexico City/New York; gender borders between women and men; and cultural borders between dollar-based and other-currency based societies. In border writing, the dominant cultures of Europe and the United States are presented in their inter-action with Latin American culture rather than as cultural models.

Latin American culture is not homogeneous. It is itself a culture that articulates borders between disparate traditions. The contemporary culture of Mexico, for example, emerges from a multi-layered semiotic matrix: the cultures of the Mixteca Indians, Spain, Lacandonian Indians, MacDonald's, ballet folklorico, punk rock. The heterogeneous cultures of Latin America exist in the spaces which emerge between a desire for memories of pre-Columbian cultures, a respect for the continuing traditions of indigenous cultures, and a problematic relationship with Spanish and other European cultures and the new-world culture of the United States.

In an article for *La Opinion*, I argued that border writing is the trace of the *coyote/shaman*, basing this view on Luisa Valenzeula who discusses the role of the writer as a *shaman* who writes in order to cure the reader. We can also see from Deleuze and Guattari's notion of the machine that the writer is a smuggler or *coyote*. If the border is a machine, then one of its elements is the smuggler who is bicultural, and to read is to cross over to another side where capital has not yet reduced the object to a commodity—to a place where psychic healing can occur.[1] North American critics of Latin American literature must realize that to continue to stress the "magical" or even certain post-modernist aspects of Latin American literature is to deny the larger, broader understanding of reality that informs these texts. Long before French criticism had been imported to North American literature departments, artists and writers in Latin America were already "appropriating" images and "decentering" the subject. We need only consider a few examples such as the Mexican artist Posada in the 19th Century, the Brazilian concrete poets in the 1960s, the writers of the "boom," and the artists of the *neo-gráfica* movement in Mexico.

To now recuperate a long tradition of experimentation with
the uncritical use of European post-structuralism is unnecessary.
Independent historical developments have led to "post-modernism"
in border writing. Harry Polkinhorn has written that "Chicano
writing at least in part short-circuited the power lines of
transmission of the European avant-garde and broader modernist
tendencies, which had much more of an impact on Latin American
practitioners (via Ultraismo to Huidobro, Estridentismo,
Noigandre's Concrete Poetry of the de Campos and Pagnatari,
Poem/Proceso, and later developments such as Espinosa's Post-
Arte group). By contrast with this richness of cultural
embeddedness, Chicano literature was born *ex nihilo*, as it were,
with connections less to a long tradition of oppositional art but
more to one of oppressed social experience" (Polkinhorn).

Franz Kafka, a Czech Jew who lived in Prague and wrote in
German is a well-known example of a writer of border literature.
Deleuze and Guattari call him a writer of "minor" literature. Border
writing emphasizes the differences in reference codes between two
or more cultures[2] and depicts, therefore, a kind of realism that
approaches the experience of border crossers, those who live in a
bilingual, bicultural, biconceptual reality. I am speaking of cultural,
not physical, borders: the sensibility which informs border
literature can exist among guest workers anywhere, including
European countries in which the country of origin does not share
a physical border with the host country.[3]

A term which has obscured border writing and which has
never been clearly defined is "magic realism." The term comes from
art history, where it has been used to describe Arnold Böcklin and
Giorgio de Chirico, both of whom have been associated with
surrealism. David Young and Keith Hollaman in *Magic Realist
Fiction* note that it may have been used first in relation to Latin
American literature in 1954 by Angel Flores. It was rejected by
Gregory Rabassa in 1973 because it "gave too much credence to
realism as a norm" (Young and Hollaman 1). "Magic realism" has,
however, continued in use by many critics, including Jean Franco,
often as a means of identification—has it outgrown its usefulness?
In the absence of a critical analysis of the historical and political
context of Latin American literature, the term "magic realism" can
serve to depoliticize the text. In *The Political Unconscious*, Fredric

Jameson writes, "Thus, in the first great period of bourgeois hegemony, the reinvention of romance finds its strategy in the substitution of new positivities (theology, psychology, the dramatic metaphor) for the older magic content . . . from Kafka to Cortázar" (134). Restated, these authors rely on more than one set of reference codes. The "dramatic metaphor," whether it be the "dialectical image" of Kafka, or the "magic realist" image of Julio Cortázar, nevertheless maintains certain elements of "the older magical content." What Mikhail Bakhtin in *Rabelais and His World* calls "the grotesque" has not been homogenized out of Kafka's and Cortázar's metaphors.

Unlike the term "magic realism," which maintains the binary opposition of magic / real, the term "border writing" does not obfuscate the deconstruction of this opposition that operates within certain border texts. Furthermore, the term "border writing" connotes a perspective that is not dominated by non-border regions. It hints at the subversive nature of this writing, a writing which disrupts the one-way flow of information in which the United States produces most of the mass media programming in the world and thereby controls the images of itself as well as that of other countries.

Border regions produce cultures which have certain common features. The Mexico-U.S. border provides a set of general categories: the *pollo* (the border crosser), the *mosco* (the helicopters of the United States Immigration and Naturalization Service), the *migra* (the United States immigration officer), the *coyote* (the person who brings the *pollo* across the border), the *turista* (the North American visitor to Mexico), and the *cholo* (the young inhabitant of the border region who is bicultural). The *coyote* and the *cholo* are the most bicultural because their lives depend on their ability to survive in the interstices of the two cultures.

In border writing, the reference code of the grotesque is very important. In the border region, the notion of the "grotesque" is linked to relations of power. The North American *turista* is fascinated and repulsed by "grotesque" culture: velvet paintings, ceramic sculptures of the Last Supper, and children selling chiclets. The Tijuanenses watch, amused and horrified, as surfers walk into the churches barefoot and drunk Marines stumble into shop displays on the street. The grotesque, suppressed in the nineteenth century European novel, is often confused by North American readers of Latin American literature with the "magical."

The inclusion of the grotesque is already an anti-centering strategy. Border writers are conscious of the gap or *differance* between the reader and the audience, and between the characters and the temporal setting (Derrida, *Writing and Difference*). Border narratives are decentered: there is no identity between the reader and individual character, but rather, an invitation to listen to a Voice of the Person which arises from an overlay of codes out of which characters and events emerge (Barthes). There is a displacement of time and space.

What makes border writing a world literature with a "universal" appeal is its emphasis upon the multiplicity of languages within any single language; by choosing a strategy of translation rather than representation, border writers ultimately undermine the distinction between original and alien culture. This notion of multiplicity of codes within a single language is taken from Bakhtin and informs Jacques Derrida's critique of Roman Jakobson's categories of translation. There is a resonance in Bloch's formulation of non-synchrony and the noncontemporaneous in, as Jacques Derrida phrases it, the "multiplicity of voices" (*The Ear of the Other*).

II. The Reader, the Border Text, and the Subject

The "magical" or grotesque content, in that it disrupts the rational, raises the question of linear narrative. How is the reader able to understand a non-linear narrative? Laura Mulvey, Teresa de Lauretis and Fredric Jameson have written on this issue. In "Visual Pleasure and Narrative Cinema," Mulvey argues that "sadism demands a story, depends on making something happen, forcing a change in another person, a battle of will and strength, victory/defeat, all occurring in a linear time with a beginning and an end." The structure of the relationship between the sadist and masochist resembles that of the relationship between narrative structure and the reader. Jameson imagines an alternative to bourgeois, linear narrative in the same way as "Mikhail Bakhtin's notion of the dialogic as a rupture of the one-dimensional text of bourgeois narrative as a carnivalesque dispersal of the hegemonic order of a dominant culture" (*Political Unconscious* 285). Border writers engage in a metacommentary about "story." Cortázar and Argentine writer Luisa Valenzuela in particular address their roles as narrators. They also demand that their readers address their roles as readers.

The reader of border writing will not always be able to perceive the "logic" of the text at first. The reader will not be able to hear a multiplicity of discourses within a single language—the four keys in a sequence of four chords, or the multiple sets of reference codes. For this reason, Cortázar had to invent the "lector complice"; similarly, much of post-modern art and culture is concerned with the active participation of the audience. A greater demand is made on the reader of border texts; in Derridean terms, the Ear of the Other must be heard.

The border crosser is both "self" and "other." The border crosser "subject" emerges from double strings of signifiers of two sets of reference codes, from both sides of the border. The border crosser is linked, in terms of identity, activity, legal status and human rights to the border machine, with its border patrol agents, secondary inspection, helicopters, shifts in policy and *maquiladoras*. According to Deleuze and Guattari, a machine may be defined as 1) a system of interruptions and breaks; 2) possessing its own set of codes; and 3) connected to other machines (*Anti-Oedipus* 36-41). The border machine, which produces the border subject, is subject to "flows" which depend on the labor needs of California growers; its codes are continually changing, as they are connected to and determined by the political and juridical machines of Washington and Mexico City.

Deleuze and Guattari have discussed the non-unified subject in relation to the writings of Kafka. They posit that the "statement" never refers back to a "subject" and that even the most individual "enunciation" is a particular case of "collective enunciation" (*Kafka* 84). In their discussion of K in *The Trial*, they argue that "Ultimately, it is less a question of K as a general function taken up by an individual than of K as a functioning of a polyvalent assemblage of which the solitary individual is only a part, the coming collectivity being another part, another piece of the machine—without our knowing yet what this assemblage will be: fascist? revolutionary? socialist? capitalist?" (85).

Another view of the decentered subject is suggested by Paul de Man in "Phenomenology and Materiality in Kant." De Man argues that Immanuel Kant's notion of the architectonic assumes, in rhetorical analytical terms, a consideration of the limbs of the body apart from any use. This leads him to a provocative conclusion: the dismemberment of the body corresponds to dismemberment of language "as meaning-tropes are replaced by the fragmentation" into words, syllables and letters (121-144). This dismemberment of language bears a similarity to Deleuze and Guattari's notion of deterritorialization. That is, the nineteenth century European notion of the subject is replaced in the work of the border writer by fragmentation into cultural, linguistic, and political deterritorialization.

III. Border Writing, the Object, and the Multi-Dimensional Perspective

In border writing, the subject is decentered and the object is not present or immediate but displaced. Michel Foucault has shown in his analysis of Velasquez' *Las Meninas* that painting was already freed from the task of representing objects in the Renaissance (*The Order of Things*). Border writers re-present the attitudes towards objects as they exist in more than one cultural context.

Maquiladoras advertise the opportunity to produce commodities in what Jean Baudrillard would call "hyperspace." Corporations are encouraged to manufacture in factories built on the border with their own "in-house" customs houses. Workers enter the plant from the Mexican side while management enters from the U.S. side. The "grotesque" elements of border life can be diminished by eliminating the need to "cross the border." What possible definition of the subject would the object produced in such an environment be a mirror of ?

The core of border writing is the border metaphor, which may be compared to Walter Benjamin's "dialectical image," where there is a joining of the subjective and the accidental to create objective meaning. In the border metaphor, we can no longer speak of a clearly defined "subjective" nor of objective meaning. Rather, in border writing, there is a refusal of the metonymic reduction in which a Western "subject" dominates an object. Instead of the "accidental," there is a broader view of the object in which it is presented within an historical—although not necessarily linear—past. This is the border "object" to which Gina Valdés refers in "Where You From": "my mouth still / tastes of naranjas / con chile / soy del sur / y del norte." The subject in this poem is dominated by the nostalgic memory for an object.

A model of analysis of border writing must be multi-dimensional. If we imagine the "real" to be a matrix of interaction between "subjects" and "objects" that can be partially translated, but which, in the final analysis, resists symbolization, then border reality might be conceived of as a framing of certain crucial inter-actions: nature and technology, humans and nature, popular culture and mass culture. The border metaphor summarizes these relationships by selecting two or more perspectives from which to "digitally sample" a portion of the matrix. Just as one part of a hologram can produce an entire image, the border metaphor is able to reproduce the whole culture to which it refers. Border metaphors are holographic in that they recreate the whole social order, but this is merely to say the "whole" in its fragmentation, as would Deleuze and Guattari (*Anti-Oedipus* 42).

IV. Border Writing, Technology, and the Holographic Model

The holographic "real" is less solid; it cannot be dominated as easily as the pre-holographic real. Border writing is rooted in a critique of technology. It is a "committed" art form in Theodor Adorno's sense of the term. Walter Benjamin's problematic angel of history is helplessly propelled toward the storm of plutonium; the industrialized world is on the edge of a storm worse than the storm that destroyed Macondo. Deterritorialized children grow up near chemical waste dump sites in Los Angeles. Where some in the industrialized world see "a chain of events," Benjamin's angel sees one single catastrophe, which now threatens to be nuclear holocaust. Where some see linearity, the angel sees a piling up of images. According to Kant, "the whole is articulated and not just piled on top of each other" (de Man 128). Physicist David Bohm describes the whole in terms of the implicate order (Martínez). Why can't the angel see that the whole is articulated? The angel of history would like to warn us, to make whole what has been smashed, to translate the disaster, but its wings are caught up in the storm. The "storm" is like that text that links the puppeteer to the puppet. The image of "making whole what has been smashed"—that is, of adopting a multi-dimensional perspective—recalls Benjamin's view of the task of the translator: "to piece together the fragments of a broken vessel." How are the translator and the angel of history alike?

Perception, like translation, is the piecing together of the fragments of a vessel. For Deleuze and Guattari the task of the translator is "to make use of the polylingualism of one's own language, to make a minor intensive use of it, to oppose the oppressed quality of this language to its oppressive quality, to find points of non-culture or underdevelopment, linguistic Third World zones by which a language can escape, an animal enters into things, an assemblage (*agencement*) comes into play" (*Kafka* 27).

According to Deleuze and Guattari, the three characteristics of "minor" literature are 1) the deterritorialization of language; 2) the connection of the individual to political immediacy, that is, everything is political; and 3) the collective assemblage of enunciation, that is, everything takes on a collective value (*Kafka* 17). In addition, they consider Kafka to be a border writer: "Not only is he at the turning point between two bureaucracies, the old and the new, but he is between the technical machine and the juridical statement. He has experienced their reunion in a single assemblage" (*Kafka* 82). As a border writer, he is a Czech Jew, a minority, but writes in a major language, German. Border writing, similarly, is deterritorialized, political, and collective.

In order to expand the definition of "minor literature" to include border writing, Deleuze and Guattari's categories can be rewritten to consider: 1) the displacement or "deterritorialization" of time and space through nonsynchronous memory and "reterritorialization" through nostalgia; 2) deterritorialization or nonsynchrony in relation to everyday life; 3) the decentered subject/active reader/assemblage/agent/border crosser/becoming animal; and 4) the political.

When one leaves her or his country or place of origin (deterritorialization), everyday life changes. The objects which continually reminded one of the past are gone. Now, the place of origin is a mental representation in memory. The process of reterritorialization begins. The hologram provides a model for conceptualizing the deterritorialized image. A hologram, unlike a window, a painting, or a photograph, is created by an interference pattern, just as the border text is created by the interference, interaction, or border between two cultures. "Border" literacy, or the ability to read border literature, is a kind of border crossing as well as a democratic thought process; it avoids a single perspective, such as a stereotypic, middle class, Western cultural bias. It takes a critical view of authority and supports the imaginative.

A holographic image is created when light from a laser beam is split into two beams and reflected off an object. The interaction between the two resulting patterns of light is called an "interference pattern." It can be recorded on a holographic plate. A border writer records this pattern in the border text, most clearly visible in the border metaphor. The holographic plate can be re-illuminated by a laser positioned at the same angle as one of the two beams, the object beam. This will produce a holographic image of the original object. The border metaphor reconstructs the relationship to the object rather than the object itself: as a metaphor, it does not merely represent an object but rather produces an interaction between the connotative matrices of an object in more than one culture.

Border writing offers a new form of knowledge: information about and understanding of the present to the past in terms of the possibilities of the future. It refuses the metonymic reduction of reality to the instrumental logic of Western thought. As Valenzuela puts it, the word is sick: in order to heal it, the writer must free it from the teleological and bring it across the border into the architectonic. This historic journey will reterritorialize it. The global body needs to be healed. Border writing holds out the possibility, through its combination of perception and memory, of subverting the rationality of collective suicide, of calming the storm of progress blowing from Paradise—the ability to withstand the pull of the future destruction to which one's face is turned.

Notes:

1. Hicks, "La Palabra enferma, una charla con Luisa Valenzuela," (*La Opinión*, 22 June 1986: 6). Valenzuela states, "De alguna manera la palabra está enferma y los escritores tratamos de devolverle toda su salud, para que el lector entienda lo que se le está diciendo en ese discurso político tan lleno de mentiras . . . para que el lector aprenda a reconocer la mentira."
2. See the discussions of the five codes in Roland Barthes, *S/Z*, trans. Richard Miller (New York: Hill and Wang, 1974).
3. See George Lipsitz, "Cruising Around the Historic Bloc," *Cultural Critique*, 5 (Winter 1986-87): 157-178.

References:

Adorno, Theodor. "Commitment." *The Essential Frankfurt Reader*. Eds. Andrew Arato and Eike Gebhardt. New York: Urizen, 1978. 300-318.

Bakhtin, Mikhail. *Rabelais and His World*. Trans. Helene Iswolsky. Cambridge, MA: MIT Press, 1968.

Barthes, Roland. *S/Z*. Trans. Richard Miller. New York: Hill and Wang, 1974.

Benjamin, Walter. "The Task of the Translator." *Illuminations*. Ed. Hannah Arendt. Trans. Harry Zohn. New York: Schocken, 1973. 69-82.

Bloch, Ernst. "Nonsynchronism and the Obligation to its Dialectics." *New German Critique* 11 (Spring, 1977): 22-38.

Cortázar, Julio. *Rayuela*. Buenos Aires: Sudamericana, 1963.

Deleuze, Gilles and Félix Guattari. *Anti-Oedipus: Capitalism and Schizophrenia*. Trans. Robert Hurley, et al. New York: Viking, 1977.

_____. *Kafka*. Trans. Terry Cochran. Minneapolis: University of Minnesota Press, 1986.

Derrida, Jacques. "Differance." *Writing and Difference*. Trans. Alan Bass. Chicago: University of Chicago Press, 1978.

_____. *The Ear of the Other*. New York: Schocken Books, 1984.

Foucault, Michel. *The Order of Things*. New York: Random House, 1970.

Hicks, Emily. "La palabra enferma, una charla con Luisa Valenzuela." *La Opinión* 22 June 22, 1986: 6.

Jameson, Fredric. *The Political Unconscious: Narrative as Socially Symbolic Act.* Ithaca, NY: Cornell University Press, 1981.

—————. "On Magic Realism and Film." *Critical Inquiry* 12 (January 1986): 301-325.

de Lauretis, Teresa. *Alice Doesn't: Feminism, Semiotics, Cinema.* Bloomington: Indiana University Press, 1984.

Lipsitz, George. "Cruising Around the Historic Bloc." *Cultural Critique* 5 (Winter 1986-87): 157-178.

de Man, Paul. "Phenomenology and Materiality in Kant." *Hermeneutics.* Eds. Gary Shapiro and Alan Sica. Amherst: University of Massachusetts Press, 1984.

Martínez, J. Nelly. "From a Mimetic to a Holographic Paradigm in Fiction." Unpublished manuscript.

Mulvey, Laura. "Visual Pleasure and Narrative Cinema" *Screen* 16 (Autumn 1975): 6-18.

Polkinhorn, Harry. "Chain Link: Towards a Theory of Border Writing." Unpublished manuscript.

Valdés, Gina. "Where You From." *The Broken Line / La Línea Quebrada* 1.1 (May 1986). n. pag.

Young, David and Keith Hollaman, eds. *Magic Realist Fiction.* New York: Longman, 1984.

The Ideology of Lack in Lackanianism

L'Oedipe ... ne saurait tenir indéfiniment l'affiche
dans des formes de societé où se perd de plus en
plus le sens de tragédie.

—J. Lacan

Eugene W. Holland,
Ohio State University

The aim of this essay is to expose the value-system underlying
what I call "Lackanianism." Inevitably (and as was the case with
Derrida), "Lacan" has been transformed in translation for and
assimilation by an American audience composed primarily of
academic literary critics rather than practicing psychoanalysts or
French intellectuals. The extent to which translators and disciples
of Lacan are faithful to him is not my concern—hence the
designation "Lackanians" (with a "k") to refer to such figures as
Kaja Silverman (Silverman, 1983), Ellie Ragland-Sullivan (Ragland-
Sullivan, 1986), Juliet Flower MacCannell (MacCannell, 1986), et
al.: it is *their* ideology I want to challenge here. In doing so, I draw
on a notion of excess suggested by the work of Georges Bataille
(Bataille, 1967 and 1985) and on the theory of schizoanalysis
developed by Deleuze and Guattari in *The Anti-Oedipus* (1977).

The basic thrust of schizoanalysis is to radicalize and
historicize psychoanalysis (Holland, 1987). For my present purpose,
the key feature of this critique is its insistence on the Freudian

• *59*

notion of *nachträglichkeit* ("deferred action"; Lacan's *après coup*). At an important turning-point in the development of the theory of psychoanalysis, Freud had rejected his original hypothesis, that real childhood traumas necessarily "cause" later psychological disturbances, in favor of a more "dialectical" view (Holland, 1985). On this view, later disturbances endow initially meaningless childhood memory traces with traumatic significance only *after the fact—"après coup."* From this important insight, Deleuze and Guattari draw a radical conclusion: that it is not "family romance" nor the Oedipal triangle that constitute the prime determinants of psychic life, but rather social relations *at large.* In one specific case, as we shall see below, it is true that certain social relations produce family romance itself as their privileged vehicle of representation in the psyche. But the anthropological and historical data marshalled by schizoanalysis shows that this case represents a determinate historical exception, not a universal rule. And from their analysis of contemporary social relations, Deleuze and Guattari conclude that, for the most part, the Oedipus complex is a thing of the past: it is only used now by regressive institutions (among them conventional psychoanalysis) to counter the anti-oedipal tendencies of society at large and re-impose feelings of inadequacy, the better to shore up out-moded forms of social control.

Schizoanalysis thus attacks the fundamental Lackanian notion of "lack" head-on by arguing that, rather than being intrinsic to the structure of subjectivity, lack is imposed on or injected into subjectivity by strictly social (and hence historically variable) forces. Lackanians usually represent the structure of the psyche according to the diagram below (the so-called "L-schema," Lacan, 1966: 66 and 1971: 63; Wilden, 1968: 107), where "S" represents the (unconsciously determined) subject of speech, "a" the (part-) objects to which the subject relates in the world, "a'" the ("alienated") image of self or ego founded on the mirror stage, and "A" the Other whose discourse structures the subject's unconscious:

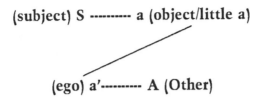

The diagonal line represents the Imaginary relation, while the relation of subject to Other (not graphed here) is constituted in the Symbolic Order governed by castration and the Law. Schizoanalysis challenges this representation by cutting it in half, as it were, accepting the top half of the schema while denying the bottom half universal validity. By refusing the Imaginary/Symbolic dyad central to (most) Lackanianism (Deleuze & Guattari 79-83), schizoanalysis opens the question of subjectivity to far-ranging social and historical analysis.

Bataille's anthropological perspective, meanwhile, suggests a different approach. Few purely mechanical exercises would go as far in illuminating the ideological bias of Lackanianism as simply substituting the term "excess" for "lack" wherever the latter appears in Lackanian discourse; the concrete content of the doctrine would remain nearly the same, but its evaluative tenor would be diametrically reversed. It may not be possible to re-write all of Lackanianism in this way, but one example should indicate the direction such a critique would take; we will then be in a position to assess the importance of Bataille's notion of excess to Deleuze and Guattari's critique of Oedipal and Lackanian psychoanalysis.

The notion of lack appears again and again in the Lackanian understanding of psychic structure and development; surely not the least important occasion is the famous mirror-stage, where the relatively un-coordinated child perceives its apparently coordinated image in a mirror (or perceives such coordination in an (older) other). Lackanians often cite passages describing the mirror-stage as a "jubilant assumption of his [sic] specular image by the child at the infans stage, still sunk in his motor incapacity and nursling dependence" (Silverman 157) or as a "drama whose internal dynamic shifts from insufficiency to anticipation" (Jameson 358). And what they focus on exclusively is the incapacity and insufficiency: on lack, on what the infant is bodily lacking yet perceives in the mirror. No attention whatsoever is paid to anticipation and jubilation. But if we decide to emphasize anticipation instead (recalling the significance of the notion of nachträglichkeit), there is no lack, only excess. What the infant perceives in the mirror at this point is perceived due to the fact that the development of certain cognitive faculties exceeds that of motor skills. Such a disparity may indeed forever engage the subject in a "line of fiction" (to cite another oft-quoted phrase), but this in turn need mean no more than that the realm of possibilities can or does always exceed the realm of reality.

The disparity between cognitive and motor abilities in the infant has important consequences bearing on the distinction and relations between "primal" and "secondary" repression (between refoulement and répression in current French psychoanalytic terminology [Laplanche and Pontalis, 1973], or psychic and social repression in schizoanalytic terms). To the extent that the infant's biological drives cannot induce motor response immediately to secure gratification on its own behalf, they become desire and invest memory traces of previous gratifications instead; here again, "cognitive" ability supplements (exceeds and makes up for) motor inability. To be sure, the transformation of drive into desire is indeterminate; excess energy in the psyche is mobile, connects with images that are only associated—by the mechanisms of condensation and displacement—with previous satisfactions of the drive. Hence the radical contingency of desire, and the corollary impossibility of referring from the associated images back to the nature of the drive itself with any certainty. But this is no great loss, not the root of some grievous "insufficiency of being" (Ragland-Sullivan 272); it means simply that the human being is free from strict instinctual determination. The famous "metonymy of desire" entails not tragic alienation, but mediation of drives in a psychic apparatus characterized, again, by excess.

The spillover of psychic energy (unable, for the time being, to induce motor response) into the investment of images of gratification is crucial, according to schizoanalysis, for it is here that "secondary" repression— *répression*; real, social repression— will be grafted onto the effects of primal repression, in the space opened by the indeterminacy of desire relative to biological drive; here that social forces will intervene to distort desire by replacing (schizophrenic) contingent images with fixed representations of gratification that specify the socially-sanctioned aims and taboos of desire. It is here, then, that the excess characteristic of the human psyche can be transformed into lack and loss (as when the mere infantile *inability* to gratify drives becomes a ["mature"] willingness to delay intentionally their gratification or even a [neurotic] *refusal* to gratify them altogether)—*can* be but does not *have to* be so transformed. Schizoanalysis insists that the extent to which psychic excess will be transformed by social repression into loss depends entirely on the nature of the demands that a given social formation makes on the individual. These demands have varied historically according to social formation; Deleuze and Guattari present a typology of them in one chapter of *The Anti-Oedipus* (Ch. 3), and claim that one historically unprecedented feature of the capitalist social formation is its tendency to reduce the social demands made on the individual subject (although this tendency is severely counteracted at the same time by another tendency of capitalism to resuscitate and re-impose historically older forms of demand).

This double-inscription of the psyche through primal and secondary repression lies at the heart of schizoanalysis, and in fact corresponds to the bisection of the Lackanian L-schema I alluded to above, distinguishing the top and bottom halves. The top half —comprising the «subject--little a» relation—represents the excessive, "schizophrenic" subject in direct contact with the Real; the bottom half represents the structure of social repression bearing on the desiring subject *under capitalism*. Only under capitalism, Deleuze and Guattari insist (119-120 and *passim*), is the nuclear family selected out of all social institutions to graft its specific representation of desire—the "Oedipus complex"—onto primal repression; only under capitalism is desire apparently restricted to the triangle Mommy-Daddy-me, which gives rise to the Symbolic/Imaginary matrix so dear to Lackanianism.

Indeed, the basic error of all psychoanalysis has been to mistake this particular representation—grounded in the social structure of capitalist society and its "nuclear" family—for desire itself (Deleuze & Guattari 114-120, 313 and *passim*). This mistake is no doubt due in large part to the very nature of the "talking cure," whose *referent* (the unconscious) is accessible only through interpretation of the discourses of the analysand, as the *signified* of the discourse of the analyst—one of the defining features of language being the confusion it can foster between signified and referent: the possibility of being mistaken and of lying. In order to recover a sense of the reality of desire from the deformations imposed by contemporary society, Deleuze and Gauttari compare the capitalist social formation with two others (the "savage" and the "barbaric") considered as ideal types of non-power and power society respectively. They examine each according to the nature of its "double-inscription" of desire, that is, according to the type of social ("secondary") repression it imposes on "primal" repression. I now put the terms "primal" and "secondary" in scare quotes because schizoanalysis reverses the priority assigned to them by conventional psychoanalysis. In this socio-historical perspective, the libidinal structure and dynamic of the mode of social production (social repression, *répression*) conditions the forms psychic repression will take in the individual (while both are made possible by "primal" repression [*refoulement*] in the infant).

Each mode of production has a specific focal point for the investment of human energy; the nature of this "socius" (in schizoanalytic terms) determines how a social formation inscribes libidinal energy and subjects it to social production. From the socius and its system of double-inscription stem the schizoanalysts' other analytic categories, principal among which for my purpose here is the notion of "anti-production." Derived from Bataille's notion of *dépense*, anti-production comprises any expenditure of goods that contributes neither to further production nor to the reproduction of life itself. As Bataille insists, no society is really organized around needs; needs are an after-effect of social organization which is itself always centered on the expenditure (*dépense*) of surplus. (Only an individual-centered psychology or anthropology places needs before desire, which is why schizoanalysis reverses the priority of "primary" and "secondary" repression, instead referring to them as "psychic" and "social" repression respectively.)

So it is socially-instigated anti-production that introduces lack into psychic life, rather than the other way around. "Desire does not lack anything," according to schizoanalysis; "the objective being of desire is the Real in and of itself. . . . Desire is not bolstered by needs, but rather the contrary; needs are derived from desire: they are counter-products within the real that desire produces" (Deleuze & Guattari 27). The point of studying different modes of social-libidinal production is to examine how each ideal type counter-produces needs and lack in its subjects, and finally to understand how the capitalist mode of production uses the nuclear family (and then psychoanalysis) to produce and impose the Oedipus.

The system of anti-production in primitive societies arises out of the temporary accumulation of specific goods—objects the tribe deems to be of special value or significance. Schizoanalysis calls this "coded surplus-value" because social codes reflect collective agreement as to what is of social value and therefore worth accumulating. Extensive accumulation, however, is not permitted. Ritual orgies of waste and expenditure (such as *potlatch*) prevent accumulation as each clan earns prestige by either destroying or dispersing its goods when its turn comes. Anti-production at this "savage" stage is thus sporadic and reciprocal, and functions to prevent power from accruing to any one family or clan.

Anti-production serves precisely the opposite function in despotic formations, which represent power society par excellence. Instead of a patchwork of debts and responsibilities following the lines of lineage and alliance, all now flow directly to the despot himself, transforming the sporadic and reciprocal relations of primitive anti-production into an infinite and uni-directional debt.

This tribute is not payable in various locally-coded "currencies," either: objects of special significance to this or that particular group mean nothing to the despot. Rather *one* single representative of value— gold—becomes the privileged signifier of universal value, and this "over-coded" surplus—reflecting not collective agreement but an *imposed standard* of value—flows continually toward the coffers of the despot. As sole agent of anti-production, the despot is the object of universal envy, so his position of power is characterized by schizoanalysis as paranoid.

The capitalist mode of production, unlike the others which code and over-code, *de-codes*. By means of money and the market system, capitalism substitutes a quantitative calculus for the qualitative codes that organized social life in previous formations. Social production is no longer organized locally, nor by and for the sake of a transcendent instance of anti-production such as the despot, but by the market and for the sake of immanent, self-renewing production. The new socius is capital itself, and the basic dynamic of capitalist society is the production of surplus for its own sake. For capitalist surplus is a surplus of *flows*, not of codes or over-codes: surplus-value arises from the differential between the flow of money invested in factors of production—labor, materials, technology—and the flow of money returning at the end of the production/consumption cycle. It matters not at all *what* (qualitatively) is produced, only *that* production occurs and surplus-value is realized.

And what the realization of surplus-value requires, given the inherent tendency of capitalism to over-produce on a continually larger and larger scale, is a vast system of anti-production installed at the heart of production itself to keep its wheels turning. Such was the intended effect, for example, of Keynesian economics and the New Deal, though it was really achieved only by the Second World War; and such is the ongoing function of "advertising, civil government, militarism, imperialism," and perhaps most sinister of all, the nuclear arms race. "This apparatus of anti-production is characteristic of the entire capitalist system, (whose) supreme goal is to introduce lack where there is always too much" (Deleuze & Guattari 235). Anti-production today culminates not in the transcendent glory of, say, the Palace at Versailles, but in the morbid greed of the military-industrial complex and the patent insanity of the nuclear-arms race: such is the social determination of lack under advanced capitalism (Deleuze & Guattari 262, 335-337).

The capitalist socius differs radically from its predecessors in that it is inscribed digitally: it registers only abstract quantities: forces and means of production and consumption. It thus lets loose de-coded flows of experience—fosters schizophrenia, according to schizoanalysis—and leaves the social repression of people to other, subordinate institutions, primarily the nuclear family. Because the family is excluded under capitalism from any socially productive functions except human reproduction, it is in a perfect position to carry out the double-inscription of the psyche by imposing on it the repressing representations of desire characteristic of the capitalist social formation.

And capitalism's characteristic representation of desire is the Oedipus. The power-relation of despotism—gradually effaced in the realm of the public by capitalism's digital inscription of the socius—reappears at the heart of the nuclear family. The father now occupies the paranoid position as the head of the household. As family despot, he has exclusive rights to the mother, his wife; their sons, his subjects, are thus supposed to envy him his possession of the mother (Deleuze & Guattari 216-217). But desire itself is indeterminate ("schizophrenic"), not oedipal: "the Oedipus," Deleuze and Guattari insist, "begins in the mind of the father" (Deleuze & Guattari 178). "Oedipus is first the idea of an adult paranoiac, before it is the childhood feeling of a neurotic" (Deleuze & Guattari 274). And this is not even its real origin; his paranoia only takes shape on the basis of the investments the father makes in the historically-constituted social domain: "The father is first in relation to the child, but only because what is first is the social investment in relation to the family investment, the investment of the social field in which the father, the child, and the family are immersed" (Deleuze & Guattari 273-276; see also 104, 178-179, 364-365).

What's more, whenever the family unit itself fails to impose this oedipal representation on desire—and this is increasingly the case as the degradation of work and the impact of private media and state education tend to diminish the authority of the father—

psychoanalysis steps in to finish off the job of domesticating desire (Deleuze & Guattari 307). For if need be, the psychoanalyst himself will shoulder the mantle of the despot—by way of the famous "transference"—to ensure that no desire escapes from oedipal triangulation. Oedipal psychoanalysis thus appears as an archaic despotism installed in the privatized family to oppress desire so early and so effectively that repression itself comes to be desired.

Lackanianism's projection of the family oedipus onto the whole of society via the Symbolic/Imaginary dichotomy does not change the profoundly reactionary nature of the oedipal enterprise; it only extends and generalizes its parameters. Granted, one *can* project the structure of the family triangle onto the whole of contemporary social relations; it might go something like this: the unmediated ("Imaginary") fusion with mother nature that is labor and the enjoyment of the fruits of labor is proscribed by the ("Symbolic") castrating mediation of capital and the Law of extraction of surplus-value (Deleuze & Guattari 264). But little is gained thereby, and the ultimate effect of such a projection is to *naturalize* some of the worst features of contemporary society, to lose sight of their social origins and historical contingency. The problem with Lackanianism, to conclude this analysis, is its tendency to substitute angst for acts: it retains Law, the Name-of-the-Father, Castration— the whole panoply of notions functioning to eternalize and to justify Lack in terms of the tragedy of human nature, when in fact the real determinants of lack are socio-historical—and therefore subject to change.

"The Oedipus cannot play forever in a society that is losing the sense of tragedy" (Lacan, 1971: 174, my translation): *that* loss may be the best news about Lackanianism one could imagine.

References:

Bataille, Georges. *La part maudite.* 1949; Paris: Minuit, 1967.
————. "The Notion of Expenditure." *Visions of Excess: Selected Writings, 1927-1939.* Ed. Allan Stoekl. Minneapolis: University of Minnesota Press, 1985. 116-129.
Deleuze, Gilles and Felix Guattari. *The Anti-Oedipus: Capitalism and Schizophrenia.* Trans. Mark Seem, et al. 1972; New York: Viking, 1977.

Holland, Eugene W. "The Suppression of Politics in the Establishment of Psychoanalysis." *Salmagundi* 66 (Winter-Spring 1985): 155-170.

_____. "'Introduction to the Non-Fascist Life': Deleuze and Guattari's 'Revolutionary' Semiotics.'" *Esprit Createur* 27.2 (Summer 1987): 19-29.

Jameson, Fredric. "Imaginary and Symbolic in Lacan: Marxism, Psychoanalytic Criticism, and the Problem of the Subject." *Yale French Studies* 55/56 (1977): 338-395.

Lacan, Jacques. *Ecrits I.* Paris: Editions du Seuil, 1966.

_____. *Ecrits II.* Paris: Editions du Seuil, 1971.

Laplanche, J. and J. B. Pontalis. *The Language of Psychoanalysis.* Trans. D. Michelson-Smith. 1967; New York: Norton, 1973.

MacCannell, Juliet Flower. *Figuring Lacan: Criticism and the Cultural Unconscious.* Lincoln: University of Nebraska Press, 1986.

Silverman, Kaja. *The Subject of Semiotics.* Oxford: Oxford University Press, 1983.

Wilden, Anthony. *The Language of the Self.* Baltimore: Johns Hopkins University Press, 1968.

Foucault and the "Ethics" of Power

Geoffrey Galt Harpham,
Tulane University

Much of the contemporary renewal of interest in ethics among philosophers and literary theorists can be traced to the later work of Michel Foucault, especially to the *History of Sexuality* series. In these volumes, Foucault finally turns directly to a subject that had occupied the margins of his attention in much of his earlier work, and, according to some of his critics, articulates a new conception of ethics in the process. This new conception is not based on any notion of the best life, nor on any notion of man's essence, nor on any principle of a fundamental obligation to obey the moral law. It is, rather, "an ethic of who we are said to be" (Rajchman, "Ethics after Foucault" 166), of how we are constituted as the subjects of our own experience by practices that are relative, contingent and local, rather than universal or eternal. It raises, as Aristotle and Kant do not, the question of how we make and describe our ideals, and therefore the question of who we might become. Accordingly, John Rajchman has argued that Foucault seeks to replace traditional ethical notions of obligation or human essence with the notions of choice and becoming. The "fundamental category" of Foucauldian ethics, Rajchman writes, is "the category of freedom" (165).

I do not want to contest this assertion as much as I want to complicate it, and to implicate the idea of freedom in the web of restraints that condition and empower it. At the same time, I want to suggest that the new or modern ethic proposed by Foucault depends on and reinforces, if not a traditional ethics, then at least the ascesis and discipline on which any conception of ethics must be founded.

The last place to look for asceticism might seem to be in the domain of sexuality. But the emphasis in Foucault's work on sexuality is not pleasure in itself but rather the regulatory and disciplinary functions served by the discourses that articulate and organize the network of experiences known by the collective title of sexuality. In fact, in the first volume of this series, *La Volonté de savoir*, the idea of pleasure in itself exists in uneasy suspension with another idea of pleasure as an effect of power. The Christian institution of confession, for example, produced in the confessor a sense of mastery and detachment, but also "a physical effect of blissful suffering from feeling in one's body the pangs of temptation and the love that resists it" (23). Defining the conditions and categories of pleasure, the discourses of sexuality actually produced it, effecting *"perpetual spirals of power and pleasure"* (45). The power-saturated discourses that monitored and regulated sexuality may have been instituted because of their social usefulness, but they were suffered because they felt good.

One of the most interesting aspects of Foucault's treatment of this ambivalence is his own ambivalence towards it. Take for example his analysis of the 1867 incident in which a simple-minded farm hand "obtained a few caresses from a little girl, just as he had done before and seen done by the village urchins round about him" (31). Instantly discourses flocked to the site to define the "degenerescence" of the farm hand (fortuitously named Jouy) through techniques of scientific, legal, medical and psychological investigation. Foucault appears outraged by this "regulated and polymorphous incitement to discourse," which multiplied forms of perversion even as it purported to define and "constitute a sexuality that is economically useful and politically conservative" (34, 37). But he is particularly scandalized by what might be called discursive perversion through which, by a kind of contagious magic, the discourse of sexuality produces "a sensualization of power and a gain of pleasure" that rewards the overseeing control and reinvigorates the process of investigation: "Pleasure spread to the power that harried it; power anchored the pleasure it uncovered" (44-45). By comparison with the innocent fondlings of Jouy and his fellow village pederasts, the discourses radiated at them represent an unprincipled abandon, an uncivil refusal to respect boundaries, a violation of privacy that was "in actual fact, and directly, perverse"(47). Perversion is thus a consequence not of degeneration in the racial stock but of "the encroachment of a type of power on bodies and their pleasures" (48).

In other words, perversion is discredited as an analytic category in the case of Jouy himself and then introduced in the case of the Jouy-discourses. Foucault is no less certain of the definition of perversion than any of his Victorian analysts, but his target is discourse rather than body-pleasures. While Foucault understands in a fundamentally new way the relation between sexuality and discourse, and has gone a very long way toward the defetishization of sexuality, he is still capable of considering perverted the pleasure that attends the exercise of power, the sexuality of discourse, or, to put a finer point on it, the "sexuality of history."

Why does Foucault retain the category of perversion? One clue may be provided by the section in which he opposes the Western "*scientia sexualis*" which sustains the will to knowledge and truth primarily through confession, to the "*ars erotica*" of certain non-Western societies. Such societies draw truth "from pleasure itself, understood as a practice and accumulated as experience" (57), while the Western confessing cultures systematically violate the sanctity of silent practice. Perversely, this violation procures a new and intense form of pleasure. In other words, the will to controlling knowledge can be considered only a special case, or, as Foucault concedes in a telling passage, "an extraordinarily subtle form of *ars erotica*" the "Western, sublimated version of that seemingly lost tradition" (71). Western techniques of control do not deny pleasure; they appropriate and complicate it, so that, within Western discourse, one could argue, pleasure is pre-perverted.

Nevertheless, it seems strange that Foucault should think in terms he so persuasively condemns. Foucault appears at this point confused by his own critique, which argues for the possibility at least of an unconstrained pleasure vulnerable to domination and perversion by a malignant power-knowledge mechanism. But he was already in possession of the idea that would eventually lead him out of this confusion. The "event," as Foucault says in his essay on "Nietzsche, Geneology, History," is "not a decision, a treaty, a reign, or a battle, but the reversal of a relationship of forces, the usurpation of power, the appropriation of a vocabulary turned against those who had once used it . . . the entry of a masked 'other'" (154). In this respect power as described in volume one is a true event, "tolerable only on a condition that it mask a substantial part of itself" (86). What power masks is, however, not only its "mechanisms," as Foucault says, nor its indifference to Law, its capricious imposition of brute force; power masks its pleasure, the source of its perversion. Moreover, the proposition may be reversed. At least within Western cultures, pleasure itself always masks an "other"—power—in order to please. Even in the case of the hapless Jouy, the little girl is forced to submit to subjugation, dominance, appropriation, exploitation.

These functions are heightened in de Sade, in whose work sex is subjected to an unrestricted exercise of power that "knows no other law but its own." As Foucault reads him, de Sade writes of a sexuality utterly subordinated to "a unique and naked sovereignty: an unlimited right of all-powerful monstrosity" (149). In the Sadean event, the pleasure of sex can be altogether obliterated by its triumphant "other." Jouy's pure pleasure and de Sade's pure power indicate how impure—how "eventful"—pleasure and power really are. We can now be more specific than Foucault about what is masked, and can even assert that what the "other" masks is precisely its intimacy with that which is being "entered"; indeed, the "other" is itself masked *as* an other.

Foucault's text itself sustains a more or less continual "monstrosity" through what might be called "dialogic moments" in which "other" voices are heard in resistance to the dominant voice. In "What Is an Author?" Foucault had applauded the way in which Marx and Freud, as "founders of discursive practices," had "cleared a space for the introduction of elements other than their own" (132), creating and validating differences rather than seeking to eliminate them. If that is the criterion, Foucault himself belongs in that august company. Balancing the negations and exclusions that generally characterize his rhetoric, Foucault frequently opens up his text to objections, questions, attacks, counter-arguments, repeatedly accusing "himself" of being duplicitous, obstinate, confused, stubborn, heedless. These "dialogic moments" take the form alternatively of confession, with an "other" voice serving as the conscience; and of a display of conceptual might, with the "other" voices captured and paraded through the streets. In some instances the charges are never answered but are simply left to fester, more like cancer than a cyst; other such confessional moments conclude with gestures of containment or neutralization, and still others with weak replies, abrupt changes of the subject, contemptuous dismissal, or even acceptance of the charges.

This peculiar strategy is found throughout Foucault, most conspicuously in the "Conclusion" to *The Archeology of Knowledge*, which is cast as a dialogue; but it has special force in *La Volonté de savoir* since the subject of much of the text is confessional practices as forms of domination and control. From one point of view this entire text is a machine for the incorporation of alien elements, the entry of masked "others." This machine works to dominate and control both those alien elements and the "self"; and, we may speculate, to purchase pleasure, which issues from a sort of inter-vocal friction, and from the quivering destabilization of the argument.

What I am suggesting is that the same formula Foucault applies to the relation between discourse and pleasure operates in his own text. This formula seems latent and unarticulate until, midway through volume one, Foucault abruptly introduces the concept of resistance, which emerges, as Baudrillard says, as "a divine surprise on page 126" (51; in the English translation of Foucault, the surprise occurs on page 95). "Where there is power," Foucault says, "there is resistance, and yet, or rather consequently, this resistance is never in a position of exteriority in relation to power" (95). Resistance springs from the necessity of accounting for the "unexpressed" element in power, as a designation for the pleasure of power and the power of pleasure. Not quite a simple reaction to power, nor yet an inevitable mirroring, nor even something one might consciously will, resistances are "the odd term in relations of power; they are inscribed in the latter as an irreducible opposite" (96). A reproachful Edward Saïd calls resistance "the ceaseless but regularly defeated" antagonist of triumphant power ("Michel Foucault" 5). But it is both more and less than that. The odd man in, resistance mediates between the "inside" and "outside" of power, providing the pleasurable friction, the painful opposition that characterizes the relations between pleasure and the power-knowledge complex.

Resisted power is doubled, mirrored, self-contradicted, self-confirmed—as multiple, relational, and unstable in its being as it is in its functioning. And yet only resistance can make power coherent. Without resistance power is omnipotent and infinitely efficient; without resistance power has no possible connection to pleasure because no contact with its other; without resistance power has no "other" and no need to conceal a part of itself; without resistance power is formless, theoretical, an impossible singularity on a denuded, radically simplified landscape—indeed, on no landscape at all. Without resistance, in short, power is inconceivable.

Many of Foucault's politically oriented critics are dismayed by the double effect of this concept: while resistance to the powers that seek to constitute us appears as a principle of ethical and political response, Foucault's analysis implicates resistance in power, and thus suggests that resistance is no more principled than its "other." Resistance is neither an addition to nor an aspect of power; it is the site and condition of power. We cannot think of power without resistance any more than we can think of an electrical impulse without the circuit that provides its resistance. In this sense, all power is electrical. Even to speak of "power" and "resistance" as though they were independent terms may be a case of what Nietzsche calls language "doubling the deed," but we cannot correct language's error by resolving the two terms into one. Power-resistance condition(s) thought to seeing that one and two are not necessarily the only choices we have. There is, in addition, a figure of relation that is neither single nor double but both.

Foucault's political "position" is rendered both analytically incisive and pragmatically "soft" by the fact that resistance to instituted power is necessary not so much on ideological or ethical grounds, but on a far more fundamental basis. Resistance can be desired, planned and undertaken, but it does not originate with the conscious will of the intending subject, for the power-situation testifies to its presence from the first. There are powerful ethical and political reasons for wanting to think in terms of an act of resistance freely undertaken by the unconditioned subject. But there are prices—even ethical and political prices—to be paid for such a conception as well. Not only is the free act perpetually vulnerable to subversion and perversion by the power it seeks to overturn and appropriate; it is also the site of various forms of self-congratulation and self-delusion. Resistance as I am developing the notion intervenes between us and our self-esteem both by denying the ethical superiority of resistant acts or commitments and even by suggesting that these acts or commitments are not the creation, the product, of the intending will. People and groups can modify and direct power as a counter to resistance; but they can neither invent nor fully control either power or resistance. Nor can they eliminate the politically irresponsible or ethically unserious phenomenon of pleasure. If power produces knowledge, it also, through its resistances, produces pleasure. Thus there are three key terms, not two: power-knowledge-pleasure: each the "unspoken" or "masked" resistance to the other two.

At the end, Foucault suggests that the "rallying point for the counterattack against the deployment of sexuality ought not to be sex-desire, but bodies and pleasures" (157). In this crucial but problematic formulation of a nonsexual economy of pleasure (why should bodies and pleasures be any more historically or conceptually substantial than sex?), Foucault attempts to escape from and oppose the domination of the power-knowledge network. But his own text suggests that no such escape is possible. Indeed, when volume two appeared (*L'Usage des plaisirs*, translated as *The Use of Pleasure*), eight years after the first, Foucault had surrendered this rather primitive optimism in favor of a new species of pleasure that would issue not from bodies but from, for example, writing. While the "introduction of the individual into the realm of documentation" is described in *Discipline and Punish* (1975) as a coercive instrument of normalization, it is rehabilitated at the beginning of *The Use of Pleasure*, in which writing is presented as a "kind of curiosity" that "enables one to get free of oneself," almost to achieve an exhilarating weightlessness. The philosophical essay, Foucault notes, may serve as a kind of confession, "an *askesis*, an exercise of oneself in the activity of thought" ("*un exercice de soi dans la pensée*," 8, 9). It is tempting to think that the hinge for this sonnet-like turn in Foucault's thinking away from bodily pleasure occurred with the passage in *La Volonté de savoir* in which resistance was for the first time situated within power. At that point, it became possible to think of discourse as both an instrument of and an opposition to power. By the same token, writing can be seen as a way of centering the self and decentering it, a way of liberation and mastery, of reduction and enrichment. At the moment Foucault discovers resistance, he becomes capable of seeing the power of writing over the subject and the power that writing grants to the subject as phases of the same complex phenomenon.

After the first volume of the sexuality series, Foucault suspended the project for several years before writing *Les Aveux de la chair* (the confessions of the flesh). Largely a study of the relation of writing to the technique of the self in early Christian culture, this fourth volume in the series—second in order of composition—indicates a suddenly heightened interest in the methods and preoccupations of institutional asceticism. He finds even in the fanaticism of the early Christians a more expansive economy than he had supposed when he wrote in the first volume that asceticism was marked by a "renunciation of pleasure or a disqualification of the flesh" (123); he now recognizes that each such renunciation or disqualification is attended by pleasure in another key.

On the other hand, as the project sinks deeper into the past, pleasure as a thing in itself seems to recede, to become implicated in "use," especially in the production of a form, "a precisely measured conduct that was plainly visible to all and deserving to be long remembered" (*Use of Pleasure* 91). The turn taken in the middle of the first volume, then, continues through the end of the volume, and carries through the next three volumes as an exploration and increasing appreciation of ascetic strategies of temperance, exercise, and regulation in defining a "style" of selfhood. This appreciation consists not so much of an insistence on freedom as a critique of the interrelatedness of knowledge, power and pleasure. It is not so much an ethics as an ascetics. A strategy of resistance as well as the essence of philosophy and writing, asceticism conceptualizes the power-knowledge-pleasure complex and enables Foucault to move decisively "beyond perversion," beyond the thought that pleasure is the perversion of power and power the perversion of pleasure.

This move was not unanticipated. With the later volumes of the sexuality series, in fact, the ascetic orientation of Foucault's earlier work comes suddenly into focus. Both the early "archeology," with its emphasis on the humbling of the subject beneath the anonymity of discourse, and the subsequent "genealogy," with its insistence on the embodied subject as the martyr of history, specify types of ascesis, versions of sainthood.

Not all of Foucault's critics are capable of following him beyond perversion. Leo Bersani accuses him of allowing himself to be "seduced by a structure of domination" in the second and third volumes of the sexuality series ("Pedagogy and Pederasty" 18). Subscribing to "an exceptionally parsimonious economy of the self designed to center the self and to subjugate the other," Foucault has, according to Bersani, perversely aligned his own writing with "the Greek ethic of sexual asceticism" in order to conceal a deeper perversion, "to paganize and thereby to render somewhat less problematic a perhaps ambivalent interest in Christian self-mortification" (19), an interest that appears to be "a new kind of surrender" to "the fundamental assumptions of Western humanistic culture." "Nothing is more ominous," Bersani writes, "than the unanimous reverence with which Volumes 2 and 3 have been received in France, or the hagiographical industry already at work on—really against—Foucault's life and writing" (20). To counter the perverse perversity of an imminent beatification, Bersani recalls the joyous perversity of the earlier Foucault, whose language was "anything but an ascesis," and who would never have attempted "to detach language from the excitement of its performance . . . to elude the exuberant despair of being had, of being penetrated and possessed, by a language at once inescapably intimate and inescapably alien" (21). According to Bersani, Foucault's late work took an historicist turn for the worse, substituting objectivity for "succulence," self-denial for a "thrill" which had been in happier times "crucial" ("The Subject of Power" 5, 6). But Bersani has not understood the ways in which factors of mastery, power, and impersonality in Foucault's work were bound up—in resistance—with the exuberance, excess, delectation and "indolence" about which he had been so excited. Misunderstanding this, he has also misunderstood how the forms of denial documented by Foucault in his last work can provide their own species of exhilaration. Like Foucault himself before the advent of the "divine surprise," he is still resisting resistance.

Foucault's influence on American thought has been great, though complicated. In terms of literary criticism, the "Foucauldian" project is occupied chiefly with tracing the lines of social force inscribed in, and generated by, the text. This project has provided a salutary diversion of attention away from the more narrowly textual interests of deconstruction. But in the power-resistance dynamic, Foucault opens up an equally promising prospect for literary theory, a new conception of the task, the discipline, the epistemology of criticism. To see criticism in resistance with the text is to understand how the critic necessarily and appropriately determines and disturbs the text by which he or she is in turn determined and disturbed. This is neither an abject submission to the "law of the text," as advocated in recent work by J. Hillis Miller and other neo-formalists, nor a lordly creation of the text, as in the more extravagant styles of a reader-response criticism; rather, it would be a pleasurable, power-generating, knowledge-producing engagement—an entanglement, a submission, a production, an erotics all at once, with a priori privilege granted to none. It is, incidentally, under such a conception that I would place this essay.

The task "of our days," Foucault said in a late essay, "is not to discover what we are but to refuse what we are" ("The Subject and Power" 216). A task for all days, and yet a hopeless assignment; for on what Nietzsche calls this "distinctively ascetic planet," this refusal *is* what we are.

References:

Baudrillard, Jean. "Forgetting Foucault." *Humanities in Society* 3.1 (1980): 87-111. (Originally published as *Oublier Foucault*, 1977).
Bersani, Leo. "Pedagogy and Pederasty." *Raritan* 5.1 (1985): 14-21.
_____. "The Subject of Power." *Diacritics* 7.3 (1977): 2-21.

Foucault, Michel. *History of Sexuality: An Introduction.* Trans. Robert Hurley. *History of Sexuality,* vol.1. New York: Vintage Books, 1980. (Originally published as *La Volonté de Savoir,* 1976).

_____. *The Use of Pleasure.* Trans Robert Hurley. *History of Sexuality,* vol 2. New York: Pantheon, 1985. (Originally published as *L'Usage des plaisirs,* 1984).

_____. *Les Aveux de la chair* (The Confessions of the Flesh). *History of Sexuality,* vol. 4. Paris: Gallimard, 1985.

_____. "Nietzsche, Geneology, History." *Language, Counter-Memory, Practice: Selected Essays and Interviews.* Ed and trans. Colin Gordon. New York: Pantheon Books, 1980. 139-164.

_____. "The Subject and Power." Trans. Leslie Sawyer. *Michel Foucault: Beyond Structuralism and Hermeneutics,* 2nd edition. Eds. Hubert L. Dreyfus and Paul Rabinow. Chicago: University of Chicago Press, 1983. 208-226.

_____. "What Is an Author?" *Textual Strategies: Perspectives in Post-Structuralist Criticism.* Ed. Josué V. Harari. Ithaca: Cornell University Press, 1979. 141-160.

Rajchman, John. "Ethics After Foucault." *Social Text* 13/14 (Winter/Spring, 1986): 165-183.

Saïd, Edward. "Michael Foucault, 1927-1984." *Raritan* 4.2 (1984): 1-11. (Foucault was actually born in 1926).

The Contrary Politics of Postmodernism:
Woody Allen's *Zelig* and Italo Calvino's *Marcovaldo*

Richard Wasson,
Rutgers University

In a well known scene in Woody Allen's film, the fabled Zelig stands with the historical Herbert Hoover surveying a celebratory crowd. The camera glides about the scene, calling attention to itself. At first it appears that the wit of the scene depends on Zelig's imitation of the gestures of authority, on the contrast between the man of real power and the little man who can only imitate him. But the antics of the camera make clear that both president and imitator participate in the sign production of the medium; both are aping the *gestes*, the motions, the facial expressions, the stances that conventionally signify power and authority. Put another way, authority rests in the conventions and codes established by the media, not in an individual or an office.

In Italo Calvino's story, "The City All to Himself," Marcovaldo, a warehouse employee who moves cartons about all day, is on vacation. Too poor to leave the city, he wanders its deserted streets in splendid isolation. Born a peasant, he imagines the "paint and tar and glass and stucco" of his gritty north Italian industrial city turned into "bark and scales and clots" (98). But into this fabulous isolation comes the crew "of the TV report *August Follies*." Discovering Marcovaldo, they interview him; but rather than listen to his imaginative and utopian vision, they incorporate it into their system of signs: "At every three syllables he uttered, the young man moved in, twisting the microphone towards himself, 'Ah, so you mean to say that . . .' and he would go on talking for ten minutes" (99).

Marcovaldo's discourse about his utopian city is not only nullified by the medium's production of signs, but the vacationing Marcovaldo is hired as a grip, reduced again to his unseen labor. The crew sets up scaffolds and lights, a famous movie star arrives and is filmed "diving into the main fountain of the city" (100). The wit reveals the medium denying Marcovaldo's imagination, discourse and deeds; the city he envisions and the city in which he labors are replaced with a third and wholly artificial city imaged in the frolicking movie star. A fabricated world of the rich and the famous is produced for the camera at the expense of both the working city and the city Marcovaldo imagines.

These two scenes, one from Allen's film, the other from Calvino's tales, embody the contrarieties of the stylistic politics of postmodernism which sees itself as challenging, as resisting, as transgressing and/or dismantling established systems of sign production. Social realism defined the realm of material production as the arena in which contending class forces battled over ownership, distribution of goods and wealth. In social realist theory, the task of the artist is to represent that struggle and its implications. Most frequently, as in films like *Salt of the Earth* or post-revolutionary South American films, social realists see themselves as bringing people and events usually excluded from the conventional representations into new texts. Implicit in social realism is the notion that the writer or film maker is allied with one side of the forces represented in the text, though that relationship may not take an overt place in the text.

Postmodernism, whether following the lead of the Frankfurt School or more recent theorists like Jean Baudrillard, displaces the central social struggle from the arena of material production to the arena of sign production, to the realm of culture. Within that realm the struggle is between those who accept and reproduce the dominant cultural code and those who resist such "fetishism of the signifyer." For postmodernism, social realism, regardless of particular political content, too often participates in the conventional codes of representation and is therefore conservative. For example, realist conventions hold that reality could be adequately represented through carefully controlled and neutral forms of writing and filming. The "radical" claim of postmodernist political aesthetics is that no such neutrality exists; rather the so-called realist forms conceal within themselves essentially bourgeois notions of reality, representation, conflict, character, and society. Most obviously, realism contains a fixed ratio between author, text, reader and reality that posits the author as some sort of all knowing observer, the text as a window on the world and the reader as passive consumer. For postmodernism these are all elements of a more or less hidden code which determines meaning. Postmodernism insists on revealing that code, that machine which shapes the writing and reading. For postmodernism, writer and reader face a sign producing system or machine and it is the operation of the machine that is crucial. The exposure of boundaries and closures of the code pre-occupies postmodernism which sees both writer and reader facing a sign system, not reality.[1]

Two of the means by which postmodernism supposedly achieves these ends are fabulation and collage, both of which are employed in these works. Fabulation, as Robert Scholes defined it some years ago, grows out of a sense that the techniques of realism cannot capture reality and that new "fictional skills" were needed. Fabulation deployed new techniques which produced "peace and joy" in the audience by inculcating a "delight in design." Turning away from "direct representation of the surface of reality," fabulation "returns toward actual human life by the way of ethically controlled fantasy" (3). A second postmodernist impulse is found in the collagic, which critics and writers as diverse as Barthelme, Benjamin, Adorno have seen as a means not of imitating reality, but of intervening in it. As Peter Bürger comments:

> The insertion of reality fragments into the work of art fundamentally transforms the work. The artist not only renounces the shaping of the whole, but gives the painting a different status, since parts no longer have the relationship to reality characteristic of the organic work of art. They are no longer pointing to reality, they *are* reality. (78)

For Greg Ulmer such collages are created not to represent the world but to "intervene" in it: "not to reflect, but to change reality" (86).

From this perspective, the collage of Zelig and Hoover removes the boundary between fable and documentary; both are shown to be dependent on the machinery of sign production—in this case, upon a code which designates the *gestes*, the stances, the movements, and the facial expressions which signify authority. The comedy of the scene rests not on the situation of the man with no authority imitating an authoritative person who embodies it, but rather on the premise that both are poseurs acting in conformity with a code that bestows authority on its user. In fact Zelig's fabulous emulative *tic* rests less with his ability to imitate "real" others than on his mimicry of the signs the popular media deploy to designate gangsters, swinging Black jazz musicians, sad-eyed Indians, or jargon-spewing psychiatrists. Reality, the film's wit points out, is merely the enactment of the dominant code deployed to represent it.

Within its witty exploration of this production, the film is careful to call attention to the media, in particular the film as the ultimate determiner of significance. For example, Zelig's psychiatrist, Dr. Fletcher, decides to advance her professional reputation by filming her sessions with Zelig. The film shows its audience the careful placement of camera, lights, microphone, and the muffling of the camera sounds by the cinematographer's coat while the voiceover explains the techniques of filming. The consequence is not the capturing of reality, but its transformation into theater. Zelig spots the devices, waves to the camera and grins as he discovers his new significance. He imitates a psychiatrist, forcing Fletcher to play patient in order to catch him out. A mode designed to simply capture "raw" reality transforms it into a theater of sign production.

Having established the media as the key producer of signification, the film goes on to establish it as an arena of struggle. In one scene, a mellifluously voiced radio announcer asks Dr. Fletcher's mother a series of questions designed to produce answers that delineate the American myth of *poor-but-morally-disciplined* parents sacrificing much so that their children might be successful. Instead, Mrs. Fletcher, each of her unusual gestures designating her sign-resistant eccentricity, recites the narrative of a well-off family composed of her own idiosyncratic self, her alcoholic and alienated husband and two difficult daughters, the most unruly and least approved of which is Dr. Fletcher. Both her *gestes* and her words resist and even transgress the code embodied in the announcer's media style and questions.

While this segment of the film wittily contests the media's reproduction of the American myth, its more ambitious challenge is less successful. By posing Zelig's protean and fluid self against the image of the directed Charles Lindbergh, the film challenges the central character type in the American success story. In one scene, the disciplined and taciturn pilot leans against *The Spirit of St. Louis* while the narrative voiceover explains the national need for heroes that the aviator fulfilled. Disciplined, pleasure postponing, directed toward a goal that distinguishes his individuality from all others, Lindbergh is the sign of the bourgeois hero of the American myth of success. Zelig, on the other hand, represents the protean self that refuses to fix itself and from moment to moment and takes on the image of some "other." Of course, in a society dominated by the ideology of self represented by Lindbergh, Zelig is defined as the "sick" outsider in need of "cure." Wittily enough, the film shows us a supposedly "cured" Zelig lecturing school children about the relation of the values of hard work and honesty to success. For Zelig however, conformity to such values brings him only calumny, law suits and contempt. So disagreeably does society treat him that he flees to Nazi Germany. When Fletcher finds him, they steal a Luftwaffe plane, and Zelig imitates a pilot. He flies upside down from Germany to the United States, thus surpassing the heroic Lindbergh on two counts. Now restored to public favor, he is welcomed back and given the key to New York City. Before a cheering crowd, he delivers a zingy one-liner that defines his view of a healthy and heroic self: "see what you can do if you're completely psychotic," he tells the cheering throng. The American myth gets a new heroic type.

Yet the central structure of the myth remains in force. Riches, fame, and class mobility remain the universally acknowledged goals; class-rising is reconfirmed as both desirable and easily achieved. More importantly, the film produces a closure that validates the media as the sole maker of significance. Unlike the plays of Bertolt Brecht or the films of Jean-Luc Godard, *Zelig* never reflects on its own production, nor on its relation to the system of material production of which it is a part. Having reconstructed the sign system of the American myth, it falls silent. In this it is representative of that tendency within postmodernist political aesthetics which privileges sign production over material production and hence isolates itself from the latter realm.

Calvino's fables represent another possibility available to postmodernist representational politics, one that recognizes the dangers inherent in the Zeligian direction. First, the stories establish a class subject whose experience and imagination produce meanings at odds with the dominant cultural sign production system. By indirection then, Calvino's fables acknowledge the arena of material production and the class relations they establish as a place in which meanings are contested and created. Though postmodern in their fabulation, these tales move not toward an enclosed formalism, but toward a realist sense of content and theme. In fact, several wryly attack the dominant forms of ideological discourse—the media, the law—because they exclude and render invisible the lives and imaginations of workers. When the TV production, *August Follies* comes to Marcovaldo's city, it not only excludes from view his imaginative vision of an organic city, but reduces him once again to invisible labor. The image of the movie star frolicking in the fountain, a complete invention of the media, supplants both the everyday working world of the city and any counterposed imaginative vision that has its source in the mind of a worker like Marcovaldo.

Calvino demonstrates this exclusion of the working class from cultural sign production in another fable. In order to warm the wintry hearth of his small apartment, Marcovaldo, recalling his peasant past, decides to poach wood from a suburban forest. His thoroughly urbanized children, however, mistake a clump of billboards for the woods and proceed to cut them down. Marcovaldo sees they have a point. On the night he decides to collect more wood, Officer Astolfo, investigating reports that "a bunch of kids was knocking down billboards," has positioned himself to survey the signs. On one he sees an "ad for a processed cheese, with a big child licking his lips"; on another, "a suffering human face painted in the midst of a foot covered with corns: an ad for corn remover." A third ad is comprised of "a gigantic head of a man, his hand over his eyes in pain." Officer Astolfo fails to notice the thieving Marcovaldo, "who had scrambled up to the top with his saw, trying cut off a slice." The officer "examined it very carefully and said: 'Oh, Yes. Stappa Tablets. Very effective ad! That little man up there with the saw represents the migraine that is cutting the head in two. I got it right away'" (39). The representative of the law misreads the sign, failing to comprehend the needs and discontent of the working class Marcovaldo.

This criticism of the media and the law opens Calvino's fables out to social reality. In an essay, "Readers, Writers, and Literary Machines," he acknowledges the awesome power of sign production machinery in the media, in literature and in culture generally, but he refuses to allow it to be the sole arbiter of meaning. Refusing the glib, Zeligian closure Calvino argues that meaning is "found not alone on the linguistic plane . . . but is slipped in from another level activating something that is of great concern to the author and his society." By playing all "the permutations possible on a given material . . . the poetic result will be the effect of one of these permutations on a man endowed with consciousness and an unconscious, that is empirical and historical man. It will be the shock that occurs only if the writing machine is surrounded by hidden ghosts of an individual and his society" (31).

The "Author's Note" to *Marcovaldo* gives a glimpse of those social ghosts: "These stories take place in an industrial city of northern Italy. The first in the series were written in the early 1950s and thus are set in a very poor Italy, the Italy of neo-realist movies. The last stories date from the mid-60s, when the illusions of an economic boom flourished" (n.p.). The "ghosts," then, are a period of scarcity, a period of an "illusion of prosperity" and the representational forms of "neo-realist" movies.

From those movies, Calvino calls up the ghost of realism's code for the representation of working class characters. In that code, workers generally constitute a sign of need, of deprivation. That presentation most typically comes through the "report" of a narrative voice to a middle-class audience assumed to be both rational and charitable—and to possess enough economic and political power to ameliorate the conditions of the oppressed and powerless working class which can neither articulate its own needs nor organize to achieve them. These narratives positively present the working class as suffering, honest, befuddled, and vulnerable victims like Dickens' Stephen Blackpool in *Hard Times* or like the figure of the female orphan in more sentimental works. When these works represent workers capable of speaking, organizing and acting in their own economic and political interests, they are presented as morally dishonest agitators foreign to the otherwise virtuous class. Often enough these types are determined to take over an innocent and virgin nation by force; Disraeli's Bishop of Wodgate in *Sybil* is a characteristic example. Those modes of representation are the consequence of a middle class perception which argues for some charitable relief for the working class before it reverts to mob or criminal action.

Calvino's fables locates themselves ironically in relation to realism's positive code. Unorganized and politically inarticulate, Marcovaldo survives in his bumblingly comic way both the poverty of the fifties and the consumerism of the sixties. But rather than focusing on the worker defined by his need, by an absence, Calvino reveals him as a source of an inexhaustible and imaginative desire for a social plenitude. In these fables Marcovaldo comes to represent his class' infinite production of signs that express a desire for a new and fulfilling society. In short the working class is the source of the sign production of social desire which the media and the law exclude, misread, ignore.

In one story, he discovers some mushrooms growing "in an encrusted strip of earth beneath the avenue's line of trees" (1, 2). While the mushrooms ripen, he watches carefully and he hopes secretly so that he need not share his good fortune with others. Unfortunately on the day they are ripe, he notices a whole crowd inspecting the plants and with the impulsive generosity that is so much a part of the code of working class representations, he tells them that the mushrooms are edible and invites them to share them with him. The next scene is the hospital where Marcovaldo is cursed and beaten by fellow diners poisoned by the mushrooms. In another, he finds a gloriously blue patch of river filled with leaping fish. Returning home with a goodly catch, he is stopped by a policeman who not only tells him he must pay a fine for fishing in a prohibited spot, but is informed that the blue of the river is the result of a chemical spill and the fish poisoned. In another, he takes his sons out to the edges of the city to show them what fields and forests are like, only to learn that the place is now a mental institution and open only to patients. In other stories, Marcovaldo's desire for space, better working and living conditions, fresh air and water, and for a nourishing city is similarly defined and then frustrated.

Another set of stories pits Marcovaldo's imagination of a just city against the corrupt consumerism of the 1960s. In one, he and his family fill their pushcarts with groceries they cannot afford simply to see what it would feel like to buy what one wanted. However, the game becomes serious when they traverse the aisles and floors hoping to find a way out of the maze that doesn't lead to the check-out counter. Surprisingly, they succeed; discovering an area of new construction, they sneak out of the building on a projecting beam only to find themselves scooped up in the giant maw of a crane.

In the final story, Marcovaldo is assigned the task of delivering gifts to important customers and corporations, dressed, of course, as Santa Clause. His own children, imbued in school with a notion of giving to poor children and blinded by ideology to the fact that they themselves are poor, go with him one day when he delivers a gift to a rich child who already has received over three-hundred gifts. The spoiled child complains nastily and Marcovaldo's children decide he must be poor. For gifts, they give him matches, a hammer, and a slingshot with which the child destroys all his other gifts. The child's father turns out to be the head of the Society for the Implementation of Christmas Consumption and immediately sees the virtue of the gifts and so ushers in the era of the destructive gift, thus guaranteeing further consumption. The bitterly ironic story not only shows Marcovaldo's exclusion from the bloated consumerism of his society, but reveals its economic roots in a policy of deliberate destruction. This destructive consumption, the social embodiment of the capitalist imagination, is pitted against Marcovaldo's imagination of a just society with cities that provide their inhabitants with fresh air, decent space in which to live, walk or play, labor that is less harsh and more meaningful, and entertainment that in some way relates to the lives of ordinary citizens. The longing of Marcovaldo for these emerges as decent, sane and above all fully human.

Marcovaldo, then, is not only a sign producer, but a sign of the fully human desire for a more just, a nourishing society. Calvino has created a type rarely found outside Marxist writing: the worker neither as needy, suffering victim, nor as violent social rapist, but the sign of potentiality, of human social fulfillment. His imagination—not the law, not the media, not the conventions of realism—contains the human future.

Yet, as sign, he is encapsulated in realism's earlier code. As Zelig takes his place as a new type within the myth of success, Marcovaldo is encased in a code which gives the worker no mode of political or social organization with which he can embody imaginative vision. Calvino's fables render only desire and its prohibition, never a hint of the vehicles of its embodiment in social reality. Calvino concludes the final Christmas story with a fable that links these tales with the conventional rhetoric of nineteenth century middle-class reform. A hungry wolf tracks a rabbit through the dark and snowy woods: "At the point where the prints ended there should be a hare and the wolf came out of the black, opened wide his red maw and sharp teeth, and bit the wind" (120). The fleeing hare can only ponder the location of the wolf, the location and time of the next strike. It is a fable remarkably similar to one Dickens uses in *Hard Times*. Dickens warns his middle-class audience that they had better attend to the needs of the working class lest "they and a bare existence come face to face," in which case "Reality" might take a "wolfish turn and make an end of you" (125). Like the Dickens novel, Calvino's fables stand not as a call for a working class uprising, but rather as a warning to an indifferent middle class to heed the discourse of need and desire put forward by the working class.

These two works, each in a different fashion, demonstrate serious limitations in postmodern politics. First, while each succeeds in creating a new representative character—*Zelig* a new heroic type, *Marcovaldo* a new significance for the working class—each reproduces an older code. Zelig is encased in the old myth of success, Marcovaldo in a sign system that cannot represent workers as politically effective. More importantly, each reveals the boundary of postmodernist politics which takes the cultural production of sign systems as the central if not the exclusive arena of struggle. In its formalism, *Zelig* encloses itself in its own world of sign production; all significance, all meaning and therefore all change is produced in that realm. While *Marcovaldo* creates an opening to the arena of material production and the relationships inherent within it by pitting its character's bumbling imaginative vision against the media, the law, and a consumer society, the fables provide no clue to the means by which that vision can be embodied. The stories acknowledge a source of sign and meaning production outside the dominant discourses of capitalist society, but cannot envision a vehicle by which that meaning can be translated into action. Postmodernism's privileging of sign production over material production limits its representational modes to either the narrow formalism manifested in *Zelig* or the disembodied social ghosts that hound Calvino's tales. These limits, these boundaries, bring postmodernism to the problem of content, in particular, of class content. The relation of the text and the artist to political struggle based in the arena of material production and the relationships it produces turn out to be important. Viewed from that perspective, *Zelig* looks isotropic with the claims of a new class fraction composed of information and communications specialists for a slice of the American Pie; *Marcovaldo* looks coincidental with middle-class reformist rhetoric. Postmodernism's representational politics undercuts its theoretical premises and reveals itself a class based and contained movement.

Notes:

1. See Hal Foster's "For a Concept of the Political in Contemporary Art," 139-155, for a similar summary of postmodernism's cultural politics.

References:

Bürger, Peter. *Theory of the Avant-Garde.* Trans. Michael Shaw. Minneapolis: University of Minnesota Press, 1984.
Calvino, Italo. *Marcovaldo or the Seasons in the City.* Trans. William Weaver. New York: Harcourt Brace Jovanovich, 1983.

_____. "Readers, Writers and Literary Machines." *The New York Times Book Review,* 7 September 1986: 1, 30-31.

Dickens, Charles. *Hard Times.* Ed. George Ford and Sylvere Monod. New York: W. W. Norton, 1966.

Foster, Hal. "For a Concept of the Political in Contemporary Art." *Recordings: Art, Spectacle, Cultural Politics.* Port Townsend, WA: Bay Press, 1985. 139-156.

Scholes, Robert. *Fabulation and Metafiction.* Urbana, IL: University of Illinois Press, 1979.

Ulmer, Gregory L. "The Object of Post-Criticism." *The Anti-Aesthetic.* Ed. Hal Foster. Port Washington, WA: Bay Press, 1983. 83-110.

Inversion and the (Dis)place of the Other in the Poetics of Paul Celan

Véronique M. Fóti
Pennsylvania State University

Language as such, according to Heidegger, is "poesy" in the essential sense because it lets beings become manifest as such. This bringing to manifestation derives from no arbitrary human doing, but rather from the fact or the given that language forms the hermeneutic bond of reciprocity between human existence and the epochal granting/withdrawal of Being (*Unterwegs* 95-99; trans. 1-54). The unbroken bond of language allows epochal destinations to occur; and even in the unsettled intervals between destinings, language alone is not radically disfigured or undone. It remains therefore possible, even in a "destitute time," for thinkers to entrust themselves to the re-orienting guidance of poets. Heidegger himself turned, not to strictly contemporary poets like Paul Celan, but to poets for whom likewise the bonds of language had not ruptured, since they did not have to ask themselves whether, "not only after Auschwitz, but even about Auschwitz, lyric poetry is still possible,"[1] and possible, moreover, in the German language. For Celan, Auschwitz and the German language define the mandate and destined condition of his poetry.

Heidegger indicates that his own disquiet about his

involvement in National Socialism, his searching efforts to come to grips with the power of totalitarian rhetoric (linked, for him, or displaced upon the totalizing stance of technicity), provoked his deep engagement with certain poets, notably with Hölderlin (*Spiegel* 53). Whereas Heidegger traces even in Rilke's late poetry the metaphysical movement of inversion and internalization, the closure of *Erinnerung* (which seeks to complement calculative rationality with a logic of the heart), he finds Hölderlin to be a poet who reaches into the abyss, who traces the trace of the lost trace, which is the holy, the element of divinity, the salutary and healing ("Wozu Dichter?" 249f; trans. 92f). In exposing himself to the danger of the abyss, such a poet is nevertheless still sustained by the bond of language; and Heidegger places him, moreover, into the tradition which links Heraclitus, Eckhart, and Nietzsche ("Germanien" 127, 134). Though the "place" of this tradition is one of extremity and need (*Not*), those who follow the poet are not deprived of speech, of world, or of community, but can hope to renew "the still reserved earliness" of another beginning ("Die Sprache im Gedicht" 67ff; trans. 175ff). Heidegger thus seals off his meditation on poetry and language from a postmodern sensibility which has suffered displacement and has gone through a devastation of meaning cutting any nurturing bond. Celan, reflecting on the first of his two meetings with Heidegger (July, 1967; Heidegger being then seventy-eight, Celan forty-seven years old), indicates in his poem "Todtnauberg" that Heidegger has failed to hear the call of the destituted other and withheld the hoped-for "word" of atonement and halting consolation:

> Arnika, Augentrost, der
> Trunk aus dem Brunnen mit dem
> Sternwürfel drauf,
> in der
> Hütte,
> die in das Buch
> —wessen Namen nahms auf
> vor dem meinen?—
> die in dies Buch
> geschriebene Zeile von
> einer Hoffnung, heute,

auf eines Denkenden
kommendes Wort
im Herzen,
Waldwasen, uneingeebnet,
Orchis und Orchis, einzeln,
Krudes, später, im Fahren,
deutlich,
der uns fährt, der Mensch,
der's mit anhört,
die halb-
beschrittenen Knüppel-
pfade im Hochmoor,
Feuchtes,
viel.*

In re-enacting this meeting's halting and apprehensive intensity of approach, its hope, and the unfulfilled parting, Celan's poem engages several prominent Heideggerian themes, notably those of the thinker's dialogue with the poet, of the lacking name for Being, and of the questioning "woodpaths" of thinking. The Heideggerian dialogue remains unresponsive to the poet's hope and central concern, leaving poet and thinker separate like "orchid and orchid"; and it is in no way enabled by the listener. The singularized name of the survivor which, unlike the lacking name for Being, is bereft of tradition and is a placeholder for untold effaced names, is not inscribed in the book of life but among the names of strangers, some of whom may have been in complicity with the murderers. Heidegger's woodpaths of questioning do not address the senseless brutality lurking, for Celan, even within the tranquil

---

*Arnica, eyebright, the / draft from the well with the / star-die upon it, / in the / hut, / into the book, / —whose name did it receive / before mine?— / into this book / written, the line about / a hope, today, / for a thinking one's / coming / word / in the heart, / woodland swards, unlevelled, / orchid and orchid, singly, / things left rough, later, in driving / distinct, / he who drives us, the human being / who listens in, / the half-trodden rod- / paths in the high moor, / of the moist, / much.[2]

rural scene: they ignore the insistent memory of the levelled mass graves[3] or the terrorizing use of the rod (*Knüppel*); they become too "moist" and break off halfway.

Celan's poetry as a whole casts its sombering "counter-light" on Heidegger's envisagement of a pure and originary *phainesthai*, a shining forth, even in poetic concealment and denial, of Being's granting/withdrawal. Such *phainesthai*, indeed, remains for Heidegger intimately connected with *logos* in its poetic aspect.[4]

Given not only the aborted dialogue between Heidegger and Celan, but also the lasting importance of Heidegger for the poet's intellectual orientation and, on the other hand, Heidegger's rather lukewarm appreciation of Celan (he read "The Meridian" and some of Celan's poetry to discuss it with Pöggeler[5]), it falls to the reader to seek the import of this difficult and largely unexplored interrelation.

I

At the outset of Celan's "The Meridian," art is ironically unveiled, as if on a puppet stage, in three traditional guises thematized in the works of Georg Büchner: as form, as reproductive *mimesis*, and as artifice or mechanical trick. These guises are enduringly familiar because they can adapt themselves to any *status quo*, even one of destitution. Heidegger, of course, found it necessary to envision art differently: as an instigation of strife, as conflictual opening, as a push or *Anstoss* which shatters the ordinary and accepted interpretations of reality, as an upsurge of strangeness which transposes the familiar into the uncanny ("Der Ursprung des Kunstwerkes"). There remains no room here for either representation or pure form. The unsettling power of art springs from the very matrix of language, the poetic word. The bond which ties the different arts and their historical forms to originary poetic language is as infrangible as the hermeneutic bond which is language itself.

In lifting the curtain upon the scene of art, Celan prepares for a double yet doubly incomplete break, a break with the puppets of the tradition, as well as with Heidegger's closing of that stage.

The break, furthermore, marks a double interval between art and poetry, so as to enable poetry to transgress and exceed art.

In Büchner, Celan identifies two figures of this double interval: Lucile (in *Dantons Tod*) and Lenz (in *Lenz*). When Lucile, at the site of execution (the guillotine) shouts her incongruous "long live the king!" she snaps the wires of the puppet stage by a counter-word, by a poetic word, a word which carries "the majesty of the absurd." Lucile is "artblind" not only because of her shattering loss, but also because she comes up against the materiality of language, against its resistance to transparency and univocity of meaning, while yet, unlike the formalist, she discerns in speaking "breath, which means orientation and destiny" ("The Meridian" 188). The counterword of absurdity opens up breathing space; it affirms dignity; it releases the poetic word from the stage of art. The issues of opening and freeing, of orientation and destiny (though not the metaphorics of vital and smoke-like breath) belong to Heidegger's problematic of un-concealment. Since Heidegger interlinks poetry seamlessly with his thinking on art, language, and Being, he must, however, trivialize absurdity and deny it any particular attention.

Absurdity, nevertheless, does not suffice to define a postmodern poetics, nor does the counterword of any sort; for countering remains dependent upon and thereby preserves that which it counters. Poetry then has to go a step further than Lucile, to take the step which doubles the interval. This further step, Celan finds, is the step of Büchner's Lenz who "on the twentieth of January went through the mountains." And as he walked along, he found only one thing "disagreeable"—that he could not walk on his head. Celan's comment, though deservedly much quoted, bears repeating: "He who walks on his head, ladies and gentlemen,—who walks on his head has heaven beneath him as an abyss" (195). The abyss for which he relinquishes the once assured conviction of a ground is not some counter-pole nameable by a counterword; it cuts one's breath and deprives one of speech. However, this abyss is not only the Heideggerian abyss of the withdrawal of Being or of the fail of the holy; it is first of all the abyss which the atrocities of this century have opened up beneath us, depriving us of the assurances of meaning. Celan stays closer to Heidegger in treating the figure of inversion as no longer speculative and restitutive, but abyssal.[5]

If restitutive rather than elliptical inversion is indeed "the canonical form of the lyric," due to its privileging of subjectivity and of the constitution or restitution of meaning (Hamacher, "The Second of Inversion" 279), and if its abyssal undoing threatens with aphasia, how then can poetry expose itself to the abyss and still speak? How can it speak from out of the moment or *Augenblick* of glimpsing the abyss, given that this *Augenblick*, as the ellipsis of presence and self-presence, is a "blinking of the eye" which disrupts speculative vision and effects a momentary blinding?

Surprisingly, perhaps, the poetry of the turned breath does not, as poetic thinking does for Heidegger, try to speak of the self-withdrawing and nameless which cannot be shown forth in language. It speaks cryptically but not, Celan insists, hermetically (Hamburger, "Introduction" to *Poems* 21), since it always speaks for its time and date. Even the Augenblick has its date. What is novel about poems written today, Celan remarks ("The Meridian" 196) is precisely that they remain faithful to their dates, dates such as Büchner's "20 Jänner." (This date, written in dialect form, is not only the date of Lenz's departure from Strassburg, which led him into madness and death, but also of the Wannsee Conference of 1942 concerning the "final solution" to the "Jewish question.")

Is Celan, after all, in stressing the actual date, counselling a return to representation, the very anathema of a postmodern and post-metaphysical orientation? He will not permit the poet to treat *mimesis*, thus understood, as surpassed; but neither will he let the poet return to it. To leave such *mimesis* completely behind would be to ignore the place and the call or silence of the other, thus cutting the tie of art to human existence and to the socio-political dimension in favor either of a self-contained formalism, or of a philosophical meditation which remains aloof from ontic concerns, noble and solitary like the wild orchid of Celan's poem.

There is, nevertheless, no possible return to representation, since one who has glimpsed the abyss knows the relentless disfiguration of self-identity and of meaning as projected and temporalized in the space of language. Celan notes in his Bremen speech that he writes poems "so as to orient myself, so as to find out where I was and where I might be going, so as to project reality for myself" (*Werke* 3: 186). Can one then perhaps say that the abyssal and the mimetic lie in the same direction; and if so, how is one to mark, within a changed understanding of *mimesis*,[6] the interval between "the alien and the alien," the unnameable abyss and the place or claim of the other?

The poet, one who is "most uncannily in the open," can approach this question only by addressing him- or herself to language. Celan writes of going to language with one's very being, "wounded by reality and seeking reality" (*Werke* 3: 186). How then can language, self-alienated and dispersed in the "second" of the cutting of the breath, reconfigure itself to articulate the turning of the breath?

II

Not language as such, Celan insists, is at work in the poem (as against Heidegger's "die Sprache spricht") but rather an "I" who speaks from under "the specific angle of inclination of its existence," and who seeks "a you capable of being spoken to, a reality capable of being spoken to" (*Werke* 3: 186). One cannot then for long talk about poetry as such or about the figure of the poet, erasing, as Heidegger tends to do, the differences among the historical contexts and forms of poetry, among its languages, among those who write significant poetry, and among their individual poems. Celan notes that to speak, in any sense, of *the* poem, the absolute poem, is to speak of what does not exist ("Der Meridian" 199). The paths of contemporary French and German poetry, for instance, must diverge; and German poetry can no longer rejoin its tradition and speak with an accustomed voice.

The fact that Celan, a resident of Paris for most of his life, a translator of Russian poetry into both Rumanian and German, as well as a translator of French, Italian, Portuguese, English, and Hebrew poetry, chose nevertheless to write strictly in German should not go unremarked. German, his "destined" language (*Werke* 3: 189), the literary language treasured by his mother, but also the language of the murderers of his mother, family, and race, is for him the one thing which has remained "near and reachable" amidst devastation. It is the one possible source of meaning, of a possible responsive relationship; it is the "word" which stoops low for the "crumb of light," and whose failure to seize that crumb would bring utter darkness ("Der Reisekamerad," *Werke* 1: 66).

The German language, Celan remarks, "passed through and gave no word for what happened; but it passed through this happening. Passed through and could again emerge. . . ." It did not, however, he concludes, pass unchanged through "this terrible falling silent, through the thousand darknesses of death-dealing speech" (*Werke* 3: 186). In the passage, it was stripped of its ability to mediate, to nurture, and to respond. A possible healing of such a language could perhaps come about, but come about in only one way: if its very violations, its ruptures, its silences, could allow, could be made to allow—in this language and no other—for the marginal and oblique inscription of the obliterated, for their indelible remembrance. It is poetry which (once again, just possibly) has the power of such inscription. One might be tempted to look also to philosophy, but it has remained far too reticent; and, of course, Heidegger, who perceived the need critically to rethink the Platonic philosophico-political censure of poetry, refused the word of atonement and sorrow. Although Celan's poem "Tübingen, Jänner" (*Werke* 1: 226) addresses Hölderlin's madness and takes up his metaphor of the poet as swimmer, a critique of Heidegger appears to be implied:[7]

> Zur Blindheit über-
> redete Augen.
> Ihre—"ein
> Rätsel ist rein
> entsprungenes",—ihre
> Erinnerung an
> schwimmende Hölderlintürmer, möwen—
> umschwirrt.
>
> Besuche ertrunkener Schreiner bei
> diesen
> tauchenden Worten:
>
> Käme,
> käme ein Mensch,
> käme ein Mensch zur Welt, heute, mit
> dem Lichtbart der Patriarchen: er dürfte,
> spräche er von dieser

Zeit, er
dürfte nur lallen und lallen,
immer-, immer-
zuzu.

("Pallaksch. Pallaksch.")*

Not only does the eyes' assent to blindness invert the
Heideggerian notion of un-concealment, but the blinding is effected
by the persuasion of *über / reden;* and both parts of this compound
verb are significant. Whereas the poet as swimmer and diver carries
out a meaningful if perilous transition and retrieval, (such that
Untergang or sinking/drowning becomes *Übergang*), this mission
fails if the poet (like the mythical swimmer Leandros) is plunged
into darkness. Blindness ensues when speech or the word, rather
than remaining a "crumb of light" (a crumb like the ones which,
in fairytales, guide those who are lost), becomes excessive and
over-whelming (senses of *über*) and thereby approach the *Gerede*
or idle talk which Heidegger speaks of in *Being and Time.* Celan's
allusion is probably in part to the complex issue of Heidegger's
enlistment (the military metaphor is not foreign to him[8]) of the
vocabulary of contemporary political rhetoric in the interest of a
retrieval, in the manner of *Erinnerung* (interiorizing remembrance),
of the enigma of origins. Heidegger, of course, comments
extensively on Hölderlin's cited lines concerning the
mysteriousness of the purely originated in his lecture course of
1934/35, the second part of which addresses Hölderlin's Rhine
hymn ("Der Rhein," *GA* 39: 155-276).

---

*Eyes talked into / blindness. / Their—"an enigma is the purely /
originated,"—their / remembrance of / floating Hölderlin-towers, gulls /
whirring about them. / Visits of drowned joiners to / these / diving words:
/ If there came, / came a man / came a man into the world, today, with
/ the light-beard of / patriarchs: he could, / were he to speak of this / time,
he / could only babble and babble, / ever, ever, / onon. / (Pallaksch.
Pallaksch.)

The swimmer's or diver's passage through the perilous element is a mediation between what is one's own and what is other. The philosophical or poetic mediation must fail, however, if "this / time" which it must start from and return to (rather than, as in the case of Leandros, the destination) cannot be illumined—not even by one with "the light-beard of patriarchs." The speech of such a one can now only return, as it were, to the origins of a child's meaningless babbling (lallen). "Pallaksch," a word of Hölderlin's madness (which also suggests the sound of lapping waves over the "diving words") leaves the whole issue of the continued possibility of philosophical and poetic mediation undecidable, since Hölderlin used this invented word for both assent and dissent.

How then can Celan who is no patriarch and who refuses to "reach over time" find the words to speak of and to mediate this time? How can he inscribe the unnameable into a language which has become unresponsive?

III

The inscription must reject the euphonic, sonorous, or mellifluous, the captivating metaphor or pattern of rhymes, all of which showed themselves able to "sound alongside or in league with the most fearful, remaining more or less unaffected" (Werke 3: 167). Celan insists on severity and precision of language, a precision, however, which is not the absence but the compounding of complexity, so that the saying becomes a "crystal of breath." In "Der Meridian," Celan describes the poem's images as what is apprehended, and to be apprehended, "once, and always again once, and only now and here" (199). This "attentiveness" and "concentration" lavished upon the now and here as "figure of the other," but also of the other's disfiguring takes the place, for Celan, of Heideggerian commemorative thinking or Andacht with its detachment from the other.

Hamacher has delineated, in Celan's early and middle lyrics, a prominent and radicalized figure of inversion. The radicalization seeks to undo the speculative closure of classical inversion by frustrating its restitutive power. Language assimilates itself to the very movement of temporality as relentless alteration.[9] Although such proliferation of alterity is abyssal, the poet, in espousing it, does not ultimately renounce restitution. Since, as de Man has shown, temporality allows one to recapture a point of origin only in its displacements; language, assimilated to the movement of temporality, becomes a negative energy of unification ("The Rhetoric of Temporality" 222; also Hamacher 286). Renunciation converts itself into restitution, so that, through the saying, negativity can be given form and be received—not, indeed, as positivity or presence, but perhaps in the manner of Celan's virtual or semblance-nothing, the *Abernichts*. Poems, Celan points out in a letter, are also gifts for the heedful (*Werke* 3: 178).

It is essential to this transformation by inversion or to what Hamacher calls the poetization of lack (284) that the gift be in fact received, or at least receivable, as destined by the sender. The importance of this closure of the sending can be seen clearly in one of Celan's early poems, "In Ägypten" (*Werke* 1: 46), a poem which shows a prominent inversion structure:

Du sollst zum Aug der Fremden sagen: Sei das Wasser!
Du sollst, die du im Wasser weisst, im Aug der Fremden suchen.
Du sollst sie rufen aus dem Wasser: Ruth! Noëmi! Mirjam!
Du sollst sie schmücken, wenn du bei der Fremden liegst.
Du sollst sie schmücken mit dem Wolkenhaar der Fremden.
Du sollst zu Ruth und Noëmi and Mirjam sagen:
Seht, ich schlaf bei ihr!
Du sollst die Fremde neben dir am schönsten schmücken.
Du sollst sie schmücken mit dem Schmerz um Ruth, um
    Mirjam und Noëmi.
Du sollst zur Fremden sagen:
Sieh, ich schlief bei diesen!*

---

*Thou shalt say to the eye of the strange woman: be the water! / Thou shalt seek those whom you know to be in the water in the stranger's eye. / Thou shalt call them out of the water: Ruth! Noëmi! Mirjam! / Thou shalt adorn them as you lie with the stranger. / Thou shalt adorn them with the stranger's cloud-hair. / Thou shalt say to Ruth and Noëmi and Mirjam: / Behold, I sleep with her! / Thou shalt adorn the stranger next to you most beautifully. / Thou shalt adorn her with the sorrow for Ruth, for Mirjam, and Noëmi. / Thou shalt say to the stranger: / Behold, I slept with these!

The repetitive diction of the Biblical commandments, the language of the law of freedom, is spoken "in Egypt," in a condition of bondage which cannot be transgressed. He who is commanded can love the dead only by seeking them in and assenting to the abyssal element which he encounters in the stranger's eye. Given the abyssal structure of inversion, union is achieved neither with the inaccessible dead nor with the stranger; the mirror or water of the eye subverts each in its identity by a reflection of the other; and in their anticipation of union, the lovers are called upon to witness the reflections. There is a restitution, nevertheless, in virtuality and displacement; and its possibility depends upon the address. The stranger's eye and the gaze of the dead must heed the imperatives addressed to them and respond to the call to bear witness, so that the poetic saying, as a "loving unification of time and language" (Hamacher 286), can convert the obliterating waters into the water of life, and sorrow into a stranger's "cloud-hair" (suggesting her compassionate tears) which is offered to the dead.

In diving into the abyss, the poet continues, like Hölderlin's poet as swimmer, to mediate because what he retrieves can be handed over and received at least in virtuality. Yet the very image of swimming (frequent also in Celan) already appears as errant drift and blind venture ("in the black-light of the wild-steering strokes") in poems from the collection Die Niemandsrose (1963) such as "Die Silbe Schmerz" ("The Syllable Pain," Werke 1: 280f), which I cite here in part:

> Vergessenes griff
> nach zu-Vergessendem, Erdteile, Herzteile
> schwammen,
> sanken und schwammen. Kolumbus,
> die Zeit-
> lose im Aug, die Mutter-
> Blume,
> mordete Masten und Segel . . .*

*Things forgotten reached for / the to-be-forgotten, continents, heart-parts / swam, / sank and swam. Columbus, / the time- / less one in his eye, the mother- / flower, / murdered masts and sails. . . [10]

The eye of the voyager (an ad-venturer rather than one who mediates and remembers) is set upon transient *colchis*-flower, the virginal matrix of time which, in league with language, works the aberrance of the sendings:

> . . .ein blindes
> **Es sei**
> knüpfte sich in
> die schlangenköpfigen Frei-
> Taue—: ein
> Knoten
> (und Wider- und Gegen- und Aber und Zwillings- und Tau-
> sendknoten), an dem
> die fastnachtsäugige Brut
> der Mardersterne im Abgrund
> buch-, buch-, buch-
> stabierte, stabierte.*

Sender and recipient are constituted in the entanglements of discourse where "one/ knot" immediately replicates, complicates, and counters itself, exposing itself, in its murdered literality, to grotesque dismemberments. The disseevered literality is the "staff of the book" (the etymological meaning of *Buchstabe*, the letter) which mediates the sending. As Hamacher points out, the ineluctable aberration of the sending "opens in the poetic speaking a hole which the logic of inversion is powerless to close" (284), so that restitution must yield to ellipsis.

One should, I think, mark here a second break or lacuna; this time in what is sent. Restitutive inversion, even in its abyssal reiteration, depends on the semantic assurances of language. The negativity which, for Celan, erodes these assurances is no longer

---

*. . .a blind / **may it be** / knotted itself into / the snake-headed free / cables—: one / knot / (and anti- and counter- and virtual- and twin-and thou- / s(e)nd-knots which / the carnival-eyed brood / of the marten-stars in the abyss / letter-, letter-, letter- / ized, literalized.[11]

of a piece with negativity for Hegel or even for Rilke. It is not only the negativity of lack, death, or the failure of meaning, but a shattering of the very possibility of meaning, an irremediable disfiguration. Quite apart from the displacement of sender and recipient which makes for an aberrance of the sending, the gift cannot be sent or handed over since it will not cohere. Inversion is powerless to restitute coherence in place of disintegration.

It is as much for this reason as on account of the errance of the sending that language, in Celan's later poetry, becomes what Hamacher calls "a figure of the plunge" (288). I would trace a more pronounced demarcation than does Hamacher between abyssal inversion and the figure of the plunge or, similarly, between this plunge and the Hölderlinian figure of the poet as swimmer and diver.

IV

If language shows itself not only as the scene but as the enactment of violation, as a fissioning im/partment or, in Hamacher's words, as "a self-disruptive, self-dispersive, and disseminating speaking" (292), this is not, I think, what fascinates Celan in its own right. It concerns him, rather, as the possibility and the uncircumventable condition of enacting (in the most literal sense of the speech act) and inscribing the unspeakable im/partment, not of time as such, but of *this* time.

There are two things to be considered here. Firstly, if the mutilation and disruption of language (particularly of its semantic assurances) allows the poet to articulate the violation and destitution which, in the intact language, could not be spoken of, then the poet himself must violate, must implicate himself in what he is bringing to word, letting the word come fourth as *eine Leiche*, i.e., both as what has not been said and what has been murdered.[12] Secondly, the instability of language which makes this violative bringing to word possible may also be, in the end, what renders it impossible. If language shows itself ultimately to be self-referential, if it brings nothing really to word, if no truth can step "into the midst of the flurrying metaphors" ("Ein Dröhnen," *Werke* 2: 89), then the anguished self-implication has failed in its aim.

One of Celan's chief means of semantic destabilization is paronomasia. Hamacher distinguishes, in the poems, between an explicit paronomasia (e.g., *eingeschreint* (enclosed with boards) *dein Schrei* (your cry)), and an implicit paronomasia which exposes every word in the text to the possibility of being an alteration of a lost paradigm resolutely drawing back from rational or divinatory reconstruction (289). The withheld word is not merely the forgotten word (such as Heidegger's absent name); it may also be the dreaded word or name which lurks unrecognized in seemingly innocuous speech and which opens up a vista upon another scene of language. An example of this may be found, for instance, in the implication (discussed by Pöggler) of the *Reichskristallnacht* of 1938 in some of Celan's references to *Kristall* (crystal). In a more playful vein which, however, is telling in this context, Celan remarks in "Der Meridian" that quotation marks (which, in German, may be referred to as *Gänsefüsschen*, "little goose feet") should perhaps be thought of as *Hasenöhrchen*, "little rabbit ears," listening constantly "beyond themselves and beyond the words," but not without fear.

Paronomasia erodes not merely the monosemy of the word or name, but also metaphor and other linguistic tropes which depend upon a reasonable stability of linguistic entities. The poem, Celan remarks, "is the place where all tropes and metaphors want to be carried *ad absurdum*" ("Der Meridian" 199), which is to say, where the swimming (itself a metaphor of *metapherein*) becomes errant and comes close to the perilous plunge. What, for Celan, is in the end still carried over by *metapherein* is *Wundgelesenes*: it has been wounded, injured, worn raw in the linguistic labor of gathering/reading; it is gathered by one who is wounded; it wounds in the reading (cf. Gadamer's discussion of Celan's "Dein vom Wachen" in *Wer bin ich. . . ?* 76-79).

Such a wound-gathering/reading accomplishes what Celan calls a "straitening" or "leading into the narrows"[13] where, with language destabilized and eroded, the poem, brought to the verge of silence by attrition and encrypting, plunges as *dieses / Hinab* (this/ Downward) into the gaping fruiting-ground (*Fruchtboden*), the cleft stigma of dehiscent and disseminating language. A demarcation between abyssal inversion and the poem as uprooted, unfathered, dematricized downward plunge can be traced, for instance, by a comparative reading of "Radix, Matrix" (*Die Niemandsrose, Werke* 1: 259f) and the earlier poem "Vor einer Kerze" ("Before a Candle," *Von Schwelle zu Schwelle* (1955), *Werke* 1: 110f), both of which are poems exploring their own possibility. "Vor einer Kerze" opens with these two stanzas:

> Aus getriebenem Golde, so
> wie du's mir anbefahlst, Mutter,
> formt ich den Leuchter, daraus
> sie empor mir dunkelt inmitten
> splitternder Stunden:
> deines
> Totseins Tochter.

> Schlank von Gestalt,
> ein schmaler, mandeläugiger Schatten,
> Mund und Geschlecht
> umtanzt von Schlummergetier,
> entschwebt sie dem klaffenden Golde,
> steigt sie hinan
> zum Scheitel des Jetzt.

What gapes open here is not language, but the wrought gold of the candelabra or menorah, the finely crafted form of the poem which costs anguished hours of labor. This labor carries out the mandate of the mother who commended to the poet the language and its literary heritage. A candelabra (*Leuchter*) is something which gives light; and as light is most precious, the candelabra itself is made of the most radiant and precious of metals, gold. Since this alchemical gold, however, is wrought in such a way as to gape open, to bring about undecidability and abyssal inversion, its illumining

---

Out of wrought gold, as / you commended it to me, mother, / I formed the candelabra out of which / she darkens forth for me amidst / splintering hours: / your / being-dead's daughter. / Slender of form, / a narrow, almond-eyed shade, / around mouth and sex / dancing slumber-creatures, / she floats out from the gaping gold, / she mounts / to the hair-part of the now.

does not clarify and delimit, but "darkens forth" as an attenuated shade, a sister-figure which redoubles and alienates the self-identity of the poet.[14] She is brought to this shadow-birth since, by her insistent yet lifeless presence, by remaining inexorably "a dead woman's child, / consecrated to the No of my longing, / betrothed to a fissure of time," she is able to bear witness. The poem as a bringing to birth from the dead, as an engendering in renunciation, still accomplishes restitution.

In "Radix, Matrix," however, the poem bears no witness but speaks as if "to the stone," the emblem of inertness and refusal. The hands of mother/sister, of a semblance-you (*Aber-Du*), which grasp "with my hands" for the murdered *Geschlecht* (race, family, sex) grasp into nothingness; radix and matrix jut black into the sky, grotesque in their lifeless separation. The poem cannot speak for its obliterated *Geschlecht* by any alchemy of inversion; it can only plunge upended into the fruiting-ground of language (which first of all spawned the murdered race in its linguistically constituted identity):

Ja,
wie man zum Stein spricht, wie
du
mit meinen Händen dorthin
und ins Nichts greifst, so
ist was hier ist:

Auch dieser
Fruchtboden klafft,
dieses
Hinab
ist die eine der wild-
blühenden Kronen. *

In its downward plunge, the poem, "what is here," expends itself without restitution, crowning the lightless depths with its wild-flowering.

---

* Yes, / as one speaks to the stone, as / you, / with my hands, reach there / and into nothingness, so / is what is here: / This fruiting-ground / likewise gapes, / this / downward / is the one of the wild- / flowering crowns.

V

To speak of one of the crowns is to indicate the place of the unnamed other. The parting of the crowns frustrates the dialectical mediation which seeks to render self and other "phallically / united in the one" (Celan, "Aus Engelsmaterie," *Werke* 2: 196). Hamacher perceives in this partition of crowns (the "hair-part" of every now, of the "crown of roots") a self-cancelling of the figure of inversion, a self-vitiating by the differing which it presupposes, which is to say, a "thoroughgoing break in all compositional positions" (302). The import of this break remains, for Hamacher, a matter of the self-referentiality of language; it is the self-exposure of language as a movement of alteration, and thus the undoing of the singular (said or unsaid) poem with its matrix of inversion, of the reflux of its discourse to the originating and gathering source (Heidegger, "Die Sprache im Gedicht," *GA* 12: 54).

"La poésie," Celan has indeed noted in his one (and precisely dated rather than timelessly presented) French saying, "ne s'impose plus, elle s'expose" ("Poetry no longer imposes itself; it exposes itself," *Werke* 3: 181). This self-exposure, however, ruptures the self-referentiality of language (which is perhaps still another guise of its negativized energy of unification). The rupture points into a profoundly ethical dimension. An adequate discussion of the inter-involvement of an ethics of alterity with the im/parting of language would require a philosophical labor engaging the thought not only of Heidegger and Derrida, but above all of Levinas, a labor which cannot be undertaken here. The partial discourse of the present essay concludes, therefore, by indicating some way-markers, so as to stake out an entirely preliminary orientation in the *topos* of this inter-involvement.

A circle returns to itself while ceaselessly displacing the point of return; it is therefore "a detour of self-encounter," of returning to the *topos* of one's provenance, which one can reach only in displacement, but from which one can also not dissever oneself. Since the self, on this circle-path, can encounter itself only in a fissioning partition, the circle becomes a figure of encountering the other—the self as other, and the other as self. As Derrida has pointed out, the singular, placed date (such as the "20 Jänner") is as such unreadable because unrepeatable; it must repeat itself in the cipher of the other to become decipherable (*Shibboleth* 32). Precisely by remaining faithful to and by mimetically repeating its own dates, by frequenting the "ownmost narrows," the poem extends itself to the other.

Since the encounter of self-as-other and other-as-self, the reciprocal encroachment of their *topoi* comes to pass within the space of discourse, it must inscribe itself into the "open and empty," the dehiscence or dissemination of language. This dehiscence is both atelic and anarchic. As concerns the figure of the circle, which is Celan's figure of the meridian, Pöggler points out (with reference to a letter from Celan) that Kepler compared God to the sphere formed by the totality of meridians, man to the single meridian (*Spur* 62). Kepler's sphere, like the Parmenidean sphere or the Leibnizian *géometral*, is the reconciliation of alterity, the *arche-topos* which interrelates all *topoi* and which functions as the one legitimate place of encounter. Celan's single meridian, by contrast, is already the *topos* of a perpetually displaced encounter. It crosses out both totality and utter discreteness, crossing "gaily" even the turning-points of inversion, the tropics or tropes (*Tropen*).

This anarchically displaced situation in "u-topia" enables poetry to inscribe, obliquely, the ruptures and gaps, the blanks of the unwritten, and to leave itself open to the unforeseeable alterations of reading. The poem, as Celan indicates by his metaphor (if one can still use this term) of *Flaschenpost* (a message cast adrift in a bottle, *Werke* 3: 186), is no longer a swimmer's trajectory but has given itself over to the instability of the elements in its quest for encounter.

Is this "mystery of encounter," then, the other of the wild-blooming crowns, sisterly and yet parted from the poem? We must, I think, be careful here. The circle-shape of the meridian, notwithstanding the ceaseless displacement of the point of return, is self-complete, a figure of perfection rather than of parting, a Hegelian figure which converts "the place of a nothing that does not coincide with itself" (Hamacher 305) into a *topos* of (self)encounter. The circle recalls the sphere.

The circle is perilously ruptured, however, if, in the displacements of self-encounter, one cannot approach the extremity of the other, the effaced place of the other's dying. The "ownmost narrows" are, for Celan, precisely these dis-owning and impassable straits which the poem, even by the ruse of casting meaning adrift, struggles to cross. One must enter these narrows with language—Celan must go there with his art—yet the poem, even in its transgression of art, cannot rejoin the other's utter abjection and dying. It cannot respond to the unvoiced call of "eyes, world-blind, / eyes in the dying-clefts" except in its own undoing, in a self-relinquishing plunge and fall through the "snowbed" of language, after which, at least, self and other become "one flesh with the night. / In the tunnels, the tunnels" ("Schneebett," *Werke* 1: 168).

Alan Udoff has perceptively pointed out that Celan's *Sprachnot* and laconic encrypting attest to a shame without classical parallel, a "shame of being" and a "muteness of defilement" characteristic of those who, in a position of passivity, have witnessed the holocaust (Udoff, "On Poetic Dwelling. . ." 329ff). Whereas shame, classically understood, leaves the self essentially intact, the shame of being erodes it, undercutting narrativity and mediation. Poetry, given this erosion, can no longer assure itself of its ability to mediate understanding or to take the measure of human existence, of history. This failure marks the crossroads at which Celan and Heidegger must part; and for Celan, the plunge which—beyond the possibilities of the poem—rejoins the other's dying may have remained, at last, the only possible mode of responsive affirmation. Celan speaks in a late poem, a poem of his journey to Jerusalem (1969), of this relinquishing of the figure of the meridian: "the poles / are in us, / not to be crossed / waking, / we sleep across, up to the Gate / of Mercy" ('Die Pole," *Werke* 3: 105).

Notes:

1. Harald Weinreich, "Kontraktionen," in D. Meinecke, ed., *Über Paul Celan* 216. The question is first raised by Theodore Adorno in *Negative Dialectics*. Pöggeler prefers to speak of Auschwitz and Hiroshima; but an adequate conjunciton of place names to stand witness for the atrocities of this century would be unwieldy. I therefore let the name Auschwitz stand both for the holocaust and for other contemporary forms of what Edith Wyschogrod has called the "death event."

2. Celan's prose as well as poetry is quoted from B. Allemann and S. Reichert, eds., *Gesammelte Werke*. All translations from the German are mine. In translating Celan's poetry, I have consulted Michael Hamburger's translations in his *Paul Celan: Poems* and in "Poems by Paul Celan." I have followed them on some points but departed from them on others.

No English translation can convey the literal meaning of *Augentrost* ("eyebright"), which is "consolation of the eyes." Arnica is used in herbal medicine to heal wounds.

3. Normally, of course, one does not expect woodland swards to be levelled. This normal condition contrasts, however, with the fact that around Auschwitz the naturally rolling ground was levelled with the ashes of the dead (Pöggeler, *Spur* 266).

4. Relevant texts here include section seven of *Being and Time* (which disregards poetry), Heidegger's lectures and essays on Heraclitus, his correspondence with Emil Staiger concerning Mörike's poem "Auf eine Lampe," and the essays and lectures on Hölderlin.

5. Pöggeler, *Spur* 12f. Celan presented the speech "The Meridian" in Darmstadt in 1960, on the occasion of accepting the Georg Büchner prize in Literature. By that time, he had published three collections of poems (not counting the withdrawn and reworked *Der Sand aus den Urnen*): *Mohn und Gedächtnis* (1952), *Von Schwelle zu Schwelle* (1955), and *Sprachgitter* (1959). By the time of Heidegger's first meeting with Celan (the second took place in March, 1970, shortly before Celan's death by drowning), *Die Niemandsrose* was in print (1963) and *Atemwende* had already appeared (1967). While one must make some allowance for Heidegger's age, his neglect of Celan's poetry is nevertheless striking, given the prominence, at the time, of Celan on the German literary scene.

6. On this issue, see Lacoue-Labarthe's analysis in *L'imitation des modernes*. Concerning the non-imitative aspects of the Greek concept of *mimesis*, see Eva C. Keuls, *Plato and Greek Painting*.

7. "Ein Räthsel ist Reinentsprungenes," cited in "Tübingen. Jänner," is a verse in Hölderlin's hymn "Der Rhein" and is extensively discussed in Heidegger's lectures on that poem (*Hölderlins Hymnen*), in the context of the origin and destiny of an historical people.

Concerning Hölderlin's metaphor of the poet as swimmer, I am indebted to notes for a lecture on "Hölderlin and the Poetry of History" by Glenn W. Most. This material which, to my knowledge, is still unpublished, was brought to my attention by Professor Kathleen Wright of Haverford College.

8. See, for instance, Heidegger's talk about "Einrücken in den Machtbereich der Dichtung" (a (military) march into poetry's domain of influence or power) in "Germanien," *Hölderlins Hymnen*, ch. 1, section

5. For a somewhat conciliatory discussion of Heidegger's ambiguously political vocabulary, see Graeme Nicholson, "The Politics of Heidegger's Rectoral Address."

9. Concerning the relation of the inversion structure in Celan to inversion and the partitioning middle in Hölderlin's "Hälfte des Lebems," compare Bernhard Böschenstein, "Celan als Leser Hölderlins und Jean Pauls," *Argumentum e Silentio* 183-198. This problematic could be expanded to include the figure of the mirror in Georg Trakl's poetry, given Celan's self-assimilation to Georg Trakl.

10. The translation cannot do justice to the parallel between *Erdteile* ("continents") and *Herzteile* ("heart-parts," one of Celan's neologisms formed by composition). I have translated "die Zeit / lose" literally as "the time-/less one," although *die Herbstzeitlose* is the autumn crocus or *colchis*, an important figure in Celan's poetry.

11. An English translation also cannot do justice to the transformation of *Tausendknoten* (thousand-knots) into *Tau-* the unknotted cable, and *sendknoten* (send-knots), effected by the line break. Likewise, it cannot capture the connotation of murder (Mödrer is "murderer") in *Mardersterne* (marten-stars). Finally, *buchstabieren* is to spell and *Buchstabe* the letter; but the break-up frees the semantic energy of the etymological components ("book" and "staff").

12. *Eine Leiche* is a dead body; but in printer's jargon it is an omission or elision in the text. See Celan's poem "Nächtlich Geschürzt," *Werke* 1: 125f.

13. The reference is to "Engführung" (*Werke* 1: 147-204). See here Peter Szondi, "Durch die Enge geführt," as well as the discussion between Derrida, Böschenstein, Bollack, *et al.*, following the translation of this study in "The Criticism of Peter Szondi."

14. The allusion is both to the sister figure in Georg Trakl's poetry and to the figure of the burnt sister in Celan's own work.

References:

Adorno, Theodor. *Negative Dialectics*. Trans. E. B. Ashton. New York: Seabury Press, 1973.

Büchner, Georg. *Gesammelte Schriften*. Ed. Paul Lander. Berlin, 1909.

Celan, Paul. *Gesammelte Werke*. Ed. Beda Allemann and Stefan Reichert. 5 vols. Frankfurt am Main: Suhrkamp, 1983.

Colin, Amy D., ed. *Argumentum e silentio: International Paul Celan Symposium*. Berlin / New York: de Gruyter, 1987.

de Man, Paul. *Blindness and Insight: Essays in the Rhetoric of*

Contemporary Criticism. Theory and History of Literature, vol. 7. Minneapolis: University of Minnesota Press, 1971, 1983.

Derrida, Jacques. *Shibboleth: Pour Paul Celan.* Paris: Éditions Galilée, 1986.

Gadamer, Hans-Georg. *Wer bin ich und wer bist du? Kommentar zu Celan's "Atemkristall."* Frankfurt am Main: Suhrkamp, 1973.

Hamacher, Werner. "The Second of Inversion: Movements of a Figure through Celan's Poetry." Trans. William D. Jewett. *Lesson of Paul de Man. Yale French Studies* 67 (1985): 276-311.

Hamburger, Michael. *Paul Celan: Poems.* Manchester: Carcanet New Press, Ltd., 1980.

_____. "Poems by Paul Celan." *Temenos* 6 (1985):

Heidegger, Martin, "Die Sprache im Gedicht." *Unterwegs zur Sprache.* Vol 12 of *Gesamtausgabe (GA).* Frankfurt am Main: Klostermann, 1985. 53-78. (Trans. Peter D. Hertz and Joan Stambaugh. "Language in the Poem." *On the Way to Language.* New York: Harper and Row, 1971. 1-54.)

_____. *Erläuterungen zu Hölderlins Dichtung.* Vol 4 of *GA,* 1982.

_____. *Hölderlins Hymnen "Germanien" und "Der Rhein."* Vol 39 of *GA,* 1980.

_____. "Only a God Can Save Us: The *Spiegel* Interview." *Heidegger, the Man and the Thinker.* Ed. Thomas Sheehan. Chicago: Precedent Publishing, Inc. 1981. 45-66.

_____. *Sein und Zeit.* Vol 2 of *GA,* 1977.

_____. "Der Ursprung des Kunstwerkes." *Holzwege.* Vol 5 of *GA,* 7-66. (Trans. Albert Hofstadter, "The Origin of the Work of Art." *Martin Heidegger: Poetry, Language, Thought.* New York: Harper and Row, 1971. 17-87.)

_____. "Wozu Dichter?" *Holzwege,* 248-295. (Trans. "What are Poets for?" Hofstadter, 91-142.)

_____. "Zu einem Vers von Mörike." Correspondence with Emil Staiger. Vol 13 of *GA,* 1983. 95-109.

Keuls, Eva. *Plato and Greek Painting.* Columbia Studies in the Classical Tradition. Leiden: Brill, 1978.

Lacoue-Labarthe, Philippe. *L'imitation des modernes; typographies II.* Paris: Éditions Galilée, 1986.

Meincke, Dietlind, ed. *Über Paul Celan.* Frankfurt am Main: Suhrkamp, 1970.

Nicholson, Graeme, "The Politics of Heidegger's Rectoral Address." *Man and World* 9.2 (1987): 171-187.

Pöggeler, Otto. *Spur des Worts: zur Lyrik Paul Celans.* Freiburg/Munich: Karl Albers, 1986.

Szondi, Peter. "Durch die Enge geführt." *Celan-Studien.* Frankfurt am

118 • Fóti

Main: Suhrkamp, 1972. 47-111. (Trans. D. Caldwell and S. Esh. "Reading 'Engführung': an Essay on the Poetry of Paul Celan." *Boundary 2* 11.3 (1983) 231-264.)

Udoff, Alan, "On Poetic Dwelling: Situating Celan and the Holocaust." *Argumentum e silentio.* Ed. Amy D. Colin. 320-339.

Wyschogrod, Edith. *Spirit in Ashes: Hegel, Heidegger, and Man-Made Mass Death.* New Haven: Yale University Press, 1985.

Heidegger, Rorty, and the Possibility of Being

(for Robert Scharlemann)

"Alles is Spiel, aber Spiele . . ."
—Rilke

Lyell Asher,
University of Virginia

In a paper he delivered at Berkeley a few years ago, Richard Rorty divided Heidegger's commentators into three groups when he suggested that "if one is going to write about Heidegger at all one has to either use terms which he himself has said were irrelevant, or use his jargon, or create a new jargon" (1983: 18). Given the difficulty of adopting the last alternative and the apparent presumption of adopting the first, most writers sympathetic to Heidegger's thinking have, to greater and lesser degrees, chosen the second. It is probably not surprising then that Rorty's inclination to use the forbidden terms of the tradition anyway has left these more orthodox Heideggerians at odds with themselves. They like the idea of Heidegger being taken seriously by Anglo-American philosophy but worry that this new accessibility has been purchased at the price of substantial misinterpretation.

The most sustained articulation of this concern is John Caputo's "The Thought of Being and the Conversation of Mankind: The Case of Heidegger and Rorty" (1983), an essay sympathetic with Rorty's ecumenical intentions but critical of his practice. In general Caputo argues that Rorty, like Derrida, has emphasized the deconstructive moment of critique at the expense of the constructive moment of recollection. As Caputo puts it at one point, "I do not hear in either the voice which calls us back to ourselves, which bids us to say what we already know" (685). Though Caputo has recently been cited by Charles Guignon (401) for having pointed out the fundamental differences between Heidegger and Rorty, as will become apparent in the first section of this paper I think Caputo's essay actually clarifies less than it might have about the differences between them, though, as I argue in sections two and three, the differences are real enough, and important.

I. Rorty's Heidegger: More or Less?

We can think of Heidegger as having taken Husserl's insight that every thinking is a thinking of something, and expanded it to include the thinking of a world, a network of relations of which this something is an integral part and from which it gets its relational meaning. According to Rorty this step just disabuses us of the notion that talk is anything more than human behavior, that our language could ever hope to put the world in something like its own terms. He distinguishes the early Heidegger from the late by interpreting the more radical and mystifying versions of the *Seinsfrage* as pedagogical devices designed to give us *Being and Time*'s sense of finitude and contingency through rhetorical rather than philosophical means. On this view, all of Heidegger's god-terms—being, language, the clearing, enownment, that-which-regions—refer to what Wittgenstein called, less dramatically, a form of life. To ask *the* question of one's form of life is not merely to ask about "beings," i.e., particular features of this form, such as one's political affiliation, marital status, or dietary habits, but to ask about the very vocabulary in which questions are asked and answered. This is pedagogically useful because it reminds us, as Rorty puts it, "of what it was like to have a sense that we were talking about *something*, without any sense that we had a criterion for telling whether we were talking about it correctly" (1981). Being authentic, then, means giving up the search for eternally compelling evidence because one has recognized that the language one uses and the form of life that accompanies it are ultimately no more justifiable than any others, since the evidence one might bring to bear on the subject is itself necessarily articulated in a particular vocabulary and authorized by a particular set of cultural practices. To help us remember this sense of contingency, to help keep alive the distinction between correctness and truth, Heidegger asks those large, stultifying questions which frustrate our search for evidence precisely by calling into question the very world in which such evidence counts.

For Caputo, Heidegger's critique of metaphysics asks us not only to remember our finitude, but to retrieve the still unthought origin of metaphysics, to attend to the "matter for thought," to transform mere philosophizing into thinking. To sever Heidegger's retrieval from the critique, says Caputo, "is no overcoming of metaphysics . . . but its simple negation which in fact contents itself with the charred ruins of metaphysics" (669). In reiterating the line taken against Sartre in the "Letter on Humanism," Caputo has readily divined Rorty's habit of filtering out Heideggerian hope by first reading him through the more stringent Sartre. Yet despite his protestations to the contrary, at crucial moments in his argument Caputo himself ends up taking what he accurately and disparagingly describes as "the first and last refuge of the Heideggerian epigones who think that to understand Heidegger is to talk as Heidegger talks, to write as Heidegger writes and to read Heidegger on one's knees—*die knieende Philosophie*" (662). In the following passage, for example, it is clear that Caputo wants to disagree with Rorty, but his Heideggerian vocabulary makes it difficult to see what it is he is disagreeing about.

> Heidegger rejects objectifying thought not because every attempt to build a bridge [between a worldless subject and an object] is a failure—although he agrees that it is—but because man *already belongs* to Being (the world) in a more primordial way, long before propositional discourse arrives on the scene. (668)

Worth noting is a certain reluctance throughout the essay to use either "Being" or "world" alone, despite the fact that we are assured parenthetically of their synonymity. My suspicion is that "world"—as Dasein's totality of involvements— lends itself too easily to an anthropological interpretation, whereas "Being" lends itself to almost no interpretation at all. In tandem, though, each covers the other's weak spot: "Being," with all of its "mystifying effects," (683) gets you out of anthropology, and the homier "world," described as "the place of birth and death, growth and decline, joy and pain" (683), gets you out of negative theology.

This turns out to have more importance than we might first imagine, since the intelligibility of the "Being" half of the conjunction—and what it means to say we are "claimed by Being"—is precisely what it is at issue here. Or, to put it more simply, the question is whether Being could possibly mean anything more than the matrix of possible moves constitutive of any given language game, anything more than the network of relations that make up a world. Caputo certainly makes it sound as if it offers us something more, but he does this only by suggesting that Rorty's "philosophy of words" (671) offers us something less. For instance, we are told that for Rorty we are under "linguistic house arrest," "restricted to the words we use" (668; note 13), and that his remedy for ocularism is to sever the bonds between being and thinking "in favor of purely linguistics relations" (670). But the trouble with tags like "purely linguistic," "restricted," and "sever" is that they make it sound as if Rorty, like Kant, thinks that although there is some kind of noumenal reality, since we are trapped inside our own language game (just as for Kant we are stuck with our transcendental faculties) we had better simply content ourselves with talk that is *just* talk. But what I hear him saying is that the metaphysical problem of trying to describe reality in something like its own terms is one that is written into the system; to overcome metaphysics is not just to abandon the problem as insoluble, but to abandon the problem as a real problem, i.e., one that metaphysics created rather than found. From this point of view, saying that we are restricted to the words we use and saying that it is in language that our world is disclosed are just two ways of making the same point at different stages in a conversation, or in response to two differently posed questions. The first point, for example, is best offered to someone making a play for non-linguistic experience. But once a concensus is reached— and Caputo claims to agree with Rorty, Sellars, and everyone else who has criticized such a notion—"restricted" becomes obsolete since it is not at all clear what our words could restrict us from, except, of course, another "set of words", equally restrictive. The second follows up the first by pointing out that since we have nothing to validate our representations of the world which is not itself just another representation, we should just give up the notion of representation altogether. To disclose is not what one vocabulary does better or more accurately than another; it is simply what having a vocabulary allows you to do and what not having a vocabulary keeps you from doing.

This mention of vocabularies brings me to my next point, and that has to do with Caputo's offering Heidegger's notorious dictum *die Sprache spricht* as a rejoinder to Rorty's understanding of language as, to quote Caputo, "entirely a human doing, a product of human freedom and subjectivity" (674). On first glance the two statements do seem to make contradictory claims, but attention to the context of these remarks will show that they are actually just emphasizing two aspects of the same point. On my interpretation, "language speaks" means among other things that we can only say what our vocabulary makes available for us to hear. Of course this is not to deny that each of us is more or less free to choose what we want to say, any more than Rorty's remark denies that the matrix of possibilities is set out for us by tradition. In the essay "Language," Heidegger himself says:

> Are we, in addition to everything else, also going to deny now that man is the being who speaks? Not at all. We deny this no more than we deny the possibility of classifying linguistic phenomena under the heading of 'expression.' (1971: 198)

And I see nothing in Rorty's discussion of Heidegger that is at odds with any of this. To say that language is "entirely a human doing" is not to deny that "language speaks"; on the contrary, it is to buttress this claim by pointing out that there is nothing in either an entity itself or in the structure of the mind which demands that an entity be spoken of in one way or another. Nor is the characterization of language as "a product of human freedom and subjectivity" meant as a counter to the observation that one's language is something that he or she is born into. Indeed, it attempts to emphasize the role of tradition by denying us the luxury of assuming that our language was originally and is now dictated by the things themselves rather than by human arbitration. Caputo's reference to "the things themselves" always has a Husserlian sense about it though, and I suspect that this disagreement with Rorty stems from his refusal to disavow Heidegger's early phenomenological attempt at a fundamental ontology. For example, though he agrees with Rorty that "Heidegger does indeed disavow making ontological claims," Caputo then goes on to qualify that agreement in the following:

> . . . but only inasmuch as we are always and already *(immer schon)* claimed by Being and hence the posture of making propositional claims upon Being is the *hauteur* of metaphysics. Thinking does not make claims upon Being but is claimed by it *(ins Anspruch nehmen)*. We do not enunciate 'proposition' which have ontological 'commitments' to reality because we are always and from the start 'pre-committed' to Being and world. Hence the critique of metaphysical correspondence has the effect of imbedding thought more deeply into Being than is dreamt of in metaphysics, of acknowledging the 'identity' *(Zusammen-gehören)* of Being and thinking. (669)

This suggests that the problem with attempts to validate the correspondence theory of truth is not that they are ill-conceived and self-defeating, but that they are, in some sense, redundant. This redundancy has at least two senses, the first of which echoes Husserl's anti-Cartesian point that there is no such thing as a worldless subject, a thinking that is not, to use Caputo's word, "precommitted" to the something of which it thinks. That is to say, we need not try to prove the being of the things themselves since thinking and reality are always already in a kind of super-correspondence, an "identity." But this brings us dangerously close to just presupposing the reality of the external world, a position criticized in *Being and Time* as another version of the real *Skandal der Philosophie* (1962: 249-250).

If this first sense of redundancy emphasizes *that* thinking is already "claimed," the second sense emphasizes the *way* in which it is claimed by drawing a distinction between a poetic thinking which serves to thicken and preserve the primordial world of lived experience, and the derivative metaphysical thinking which serves only to thin out that experience and, in the last stage, make all our relations to and in the world technical ones. Though throughout his career Heidegger himself made motions in this direction, I think Rorty is right in saying that if he is to be consistent he cannot claim that poetic descriptions are any truer than scientific ones, only more recognizable. On this view, we should read Heidegger's meditations on the "thingly"character of things as attempts to put the poetic account of beings on the same ontological footing as scientific accounts—footing that is equally provisional and contingent.

It may be objected that this suggested reading does some violence to what Heidegger genuinely believed, but at least in the middle period, roughly the period after *Being and Time* and before the so-called "turn" in his thinking, Heidegger's own texts support Rorty's interpretation of him as the poet of contingency. Whether it is true that, as Hannah Arendt has surmised, the turn toward *Gelassenheit* would be effected in part by his growing disaffection for National Socialism, it seems clear that during the interval marked on the one end by *Vom Wesen der Warheit* (1930) and on the other by, say, "Hölderlin und das Wesen der Dichtung" (1936) or the first group of Nietzsche lectures, "Der Wille zur Macht als Kunst" (1936-37), the historicist side of Heidegger, the side sympathetic to Nietzsche's *Wille* and, by extension, to American pragmatism, was dominant.[1] Though it can be misleading to take bits of his essays out of context, toward the end of the Hölderlin essay Heidegger provides an unusually straightforward summary of what he has been saying thus far in the essay and, I want to suggest, thus far in his career:

> . . . poetry is the inaugural naming of being and of the essence of all things—not just any speech, but that particular kind which for the first time brings into the open all that which we then discuss and deal with in everyday language. Hence poetry never takes language as a raw material ready-to-hand, rather it is poetry which first makes language possible. Poetry is the primitive language of a historical people. (1967: 283-284)

The force of that last line might be clearer if we altered it to read: the primitive language of a historical people is poetry. That is to say, the original, violent act of naming things by bringing them into a particular context is the free, criterion-less creation of a

world. Thinking becomes sophistic—prosaic rather than poetic—
to the extent that it understands this world not as a vocabulary's
attempt to establish being, but, so to speak, as being's attempt to
establish a vocabulary. As Heidegger writes in "On the Essence
of Truth": "Sophistry appeals to the unquestionable character of
the beings that are opened up and interprets all thoughtful
questioning as an attack on, an unfortunate irritation of, common
sense" (1977: 138).

If this can be taken as a reliable account of Heidegger's general
mood in the 1930s, then it becomes clearer why Rorty should be
most sympathetic with the texts of this period. But even in these
essays Heidegger begins to suggest that he does not believe, as
Rorty says he does, that being is just what man says it is, that it
is simply the "referent" of the going final vocabulary. Even in this
early essay on Hölderlin, Heidegger maintains that poetry is not
simply a product of human subjectivity, but that it is subject to
what he calls a "two-fold control":

> The establishment of being is bound to the signs of the gods.
> And at the same time the poetic word is only the interpretation
> of the 'voice of the people' . . . the essence of poetry is joined
> on to the laws which tend towards and away from each other.
> The poet himself stands between the former—the gods, and
> the latter—the people. He is one who has been cast out—out
> into that *Between*, between gods and men. But only and for
> the first time in this Between is it decided, who man is and
> where he is settling his existence (1967: 287-289).

One hesitates to make anything like an argument out of this, but
I take Heidegger's "Between" as a name for the place where
continuity and discontinuity meet and define one another. The
voice of the people, the language game being played at any given
time, would become static and increasingly self-evident ("correct")
were it not for the poet who has the power to alter the game in
ways that his more prosaic peers would never have dreamed of.
The poet stands in "the between" because he understands the
vocabulary of his fellows but knows that this vocabulary is just
one among many, that it does not say all that can be said. In
opening himself to what stands outside the voice of the people,
outside the not-so-final final vocabulary, the poet re-makes the

poem of his people and the world in which they dwell.

I should make it clear though that I do not find here confirmed Caputo's "Heideggerian" critique of Rorty's supposed belief in language as self-enclosed system; here "the signs of the gods" means something not yet heard or thought, something novel, poetic. The only bone of contention between Rorty and Heidegger might be whether a vocabulary of reception is better than a vocabulary of invention for describing what it is that the poet does or, as the case may be, undergoes. Well, which is better? On this point Rorty's and Caputo's interpretations of Heidegger coincide, though as the following passage indicates, Rorty abjures what Caputo seems to have been celebrating:

> The trouble with the word 'disclosure' (and with all the other terms which he uses to translate *alethia*, to express the sense of 'truth' which is more than mere 'correctness') is that it connotes discovery rather than invention. It relies on metaphors of depth and of illumination. In short, as Derrida has pointed out in detail, it embodies precisely the imagery of the metaphysical tradition which it is supposed to overcome (1985: 22).

But alternatively one could understand Heidegger's revelatory terminology as an attempt to capture phenomenologically the experience of poetic invention, an experience made uncanny by what Paul Ricoeur, in a different context, says is enigmatic about metaphorical discourse in general: "that it 'invents' in both senses of the word: what it creates, it discovers; and what it finds, it invents" (1977: 239). The many versions of *alethia* may just testify to the inappropriateness of a vocabulary of the will to describe the sudden, overwhelming, and insistent presence of certain radical re-visions of our world—redescriptions which will only be thought of as such when the immense reality of their disclosure suffers eclipse. As a conscientious pragmatist one may, when pressed, readily admit that a particular trope or a particular account of our world is just the product of intellectual history and personal temperament, serving what William James called the "marriage-function" of old truth to novel experience; but to be struck by the unexpected pertinence of a metaphor, or persuaded by the self-evident truth of a paradigm—this is also, I think, to be stubbornly, if unjustifiably, ethnocentric in one's sense that something has been revealed rather than contrived.

II. Undermining The Pragmatists

Rorty characterizes the various versions of the *Seinsfrage* as a pedagogical devices designed to bring us face to face with our contingency by posing questions which we have no criteria for answering. All such questions teach their lessons by confronting us with the fact that no matter how thoroughly we explicate the implications of the language game we happen to be playing, the game itself remains inexplicable. This, at least, is how the device functions in an argument against the verificationists, where it can be said that Heidegger is indeed arguing for a sense of contingency, finitude, and historicity—a sense of the infinite number of possible language games we could be playing, of worlds in which we could be dwelling.

And if this were all Heidegger were arguing for, Rorty would be perfectly right in saying that the Nietzscheans, Sartreans, Deweyans, Goodmanians, and pragmatists are being slighted since they too have stressed the absence of any real constraints which could determine for us one right way of thinking about the world. Indeed, it does seem that, if anything, the moderns are *less* likely than the Greeks to put much stock in a single version of the world since we have so much more evidence to suggest that history will continue to embarrass those who do.

In the end, though, I just don't think that their supposed forgetfulness about the many alternate vocabularies we might inhabit is what the later Heidegger holds against the pragmatists. Of course that would be the argument if we took the early works like "On the Essence of Truth" as his final word. But Heidegger's later view that the thinking in these early works "remains on the path of metaphysics" (1977: 140) indicates a desire to convey something more than a sense of contingency, finitude, and historicity. Indeed, I shall suggest in this section that, *pace* Rorty, Heidegger may have wanted to forget about such a sense altogether.

In *An Introduction to Metaphysics* Heidegger claimed that the Greeks could have retained the original truth of Parmenides' maxim only by "raising (it) to a still more original unfolding" (1959: 145). But only later, in *What Is Called Thinking?*, does he suggest what this more original unfolding—his own "retrieval"—might look like. Speaking about Parmenides' "*khre to legein te noein t'eon emmenai*," Heidegger says:

> *Eon emmenai* directs that which constitutes the fundamental character of thinking—the *legein* and *noein*—into its own nature. What so directs is what calls on us to think. . . . To the extent to which we make the effort to take it so to heart, we are asking the question 'What is called thinking?' in the decisive fourth sense:
>   What is That which calls on us to think, by so disposing the conjunction of *legein* and *noein* that it relates to It. (1968: 231)

The early Greeks understood *legein* and *noein* in their to-getherness, and it is to this relation that, according to Heidegger, Parmenides here responds. But the "origin" of this saying is not the understanding itself, but what allows for this under-standing—the imperceptible background, the forgotten question that Heidegger wants to remember by asking what "It" is that brings *legein* and *noein* together in the first place. As Heidegger explains early in the essay: "The thinkers of the fateful beginning of Western thought did not, of course, raise the question of the calling, as we are trying to do now. What distinguishes the beginning is rather that those thinkers experienced the claim of the calling by responding to it in thought" (1968: 167).

Whether one accepts the claim that this question is somehow hidden in Greek thinking, a likely result of asking such a question as "What calls for thinking?" is that and single answer will seem woefully inadequate and outclassed. Again, Heidegger himself confirms Rorty's claim that such questions serve to open us to infinite possibilities, to our freedom, when he says that above all it is not an object, but we ourselves who are "put in question," that what is most important is "to make the question problematical" (1968: 116; 159). But "possibility" for the later Heidegger has a far different sense than it does for Rorty, who, like Sartre and the Heidegger of the early thirties, thinks of it in its negative sense, as the absence of constraint, as the not-yet-actual.

And it is just this conception of possibility and freedom that Heidegger begins to disavow in his "Letter On Humanism" when he writes:

> Of course, our words *möglich* and *Möglichkeit*, under the dominance of 'logic' and 'metaphysics,' are thought solely in contrast to 'actuality'; that is, they are thought on the basis of a definite—the metaphysical—interpretation of Being as *actus* and *potentia*, a distinction identified with the one between *existentia* and *essentia*. (1977: 196)

To get some insight into what Heidegger means by *Möglichkeit*, consider his designation of man as a "thrown projection." As interpreted by existentialism, the expression means that man is, in Sartre's words, "condemned to freedom." That is to say, although man is not responsible for the initial fact of his existence, for being "thrown," "abandoned" in the world as a human being, once there he is nothing but this responsibility inasmuch as he alone, as a free subject, has to project himself onto the concrete possibilities that will constitute his own way of being. But since Heidegger's point of departure is decidedly not the Cartesian *cogito*, what he has in mind can have nothing to do with man conceived of as a free subject. The word "projection" suggests (and perhaps more pointedly than *Entwurf*) that what it signifies is neither subjective nor objective, and still less some combination of the two. Projection does not simply mean for Heidegger as it does for Sartre that man always has a virginal future before him which, in contrast to the necessity of this past, remains open to what the *pour-soi* has yet to be—by which Sartre means, what it has yet to actualize. Rather, "projection" is to be thought, as Heidegger writes, "in the only way the 'understanding of being' in the context of the 'existential analysis' of 'being-in-the-world' can be thought—namely as the ecstatic relation to the lighting of Being" (1977: 207). In other words, "projection" does not refer to the subjective act of choosing goals and trying to actualize them, but to what makes this possible: to man's way of being in the future, present, and past already, before particular plans and "projections" (as Sartre understands the word) can take shape. Man does not project, but insofar as he is at all, he is "projectingly."

Rorty may well object to his being allied with Sartre on this point, though, since the latter often neglects the extent to which one's freedom is, at some level, always constrained by the language in which one's possibilities are laid out. In fact, we can still square Rorty's interpretation of being as what vocabularies-as-wholes are about with Heidegger's understanding of *möglichkeit* by thinking of both as disagreeing with Sartre's account of throwness as something that ends, as it were, with one's being thrown into the world at a particular time and place.[2] For Heidegger, man is always thrown, sustained in the world—in the *"da"* of *Dasein*, in the *"ek"* of *eksistence*—by the grant of being itself, by the *es gibt* that first enable man to be in a situation or to have a world at all. Or in Rorty's terms, man is always sustained by a final vocabulary, a language game by virtue of which it first becomes possible to have a place to be—a world to be in. Sartre's mistake was perhaps just a failure of imagination, a failure to emphasize that every expression of freedom, every projection, takes place within a relatively narrow field of possibilities determined in advance by the language we happen to be speaking, and the ways we happen to be acting.

But if we jump ahead to the later essays the differences between Heidegger and Rorty's account of him are less easily reconciled. In the "Letter On Humanism" there are already implicit rejections of the notion that being could be equated with vocabularies-as-wholes, that, in Rorty's words, "Being is no more and no less than what Dasein says it is" (1984: 20), though I think that at this point Heidegger was not quite sure how to suggest the difference. The claim that "being lights all beings" and that "language is the house of being" does seem to support Rorty's interpretation, and yet Heidegger insists that the line from *Being and Time*, "Only so long as Dasein is, is there Being," "does not say that Being is the product of man" (1977: 216). I take the new terms Heidegger uses in the forties and fifties—the fourfold, the appropriation, the clearing, etc.—to represent a surrender of the term "being" to just this sort (Rorty's) of interpretation, as well as an attempt to dig beneath the *Seinsfrage* so construed, by asking what it leaves unthought."[3] The result of this philosophical burrowing finds its clearest formulation in "The End of Philosophy and the Task of Thinking," where possibility is no longer just what one becomes aware of when he or she comes to understand the arbitrariness of a final vocabulary, but what one becomes aware of when the fact that one can have a vocabulary at all is given explicit attention. A sense of this possibility is a sense of what Heidegger once called "the region of all region" or in "The End of Philosophy," the "opening":

> Light can stream into clearing, into its openness, and let brightness play with darkness in it. But light never first creates openness. Rather, light presupposes openness. . . . We must think *alethia*, unconcealment, as the opening which first grants Being and thinking and their presencing to and for each other. The quiet heart of the opening is the place of stillness from which alone the possibility of the belonging together of being and thinking, that is, presence and apprehending, can arise at all. (1977: 384; 387)

In these passages Heidegger has raised everything up a notch: while it is still true that "Being lights being," this light presupposes a clearing by virtue of which Being and thinking are made appropriate to one another; as he writes in *Identity and Difference,* "the appropriation appropriates man and Being to their essential togetherness" (1969: 38). Or, to put the matter in Rorty's terms, while it is true to say that the arbitrary configuration of one's final vocabulary determines what will count as correct and incorrect, what will count as possible and impossible, we should not also think it arbitrary, a matter of choice, that we should *have* a final vocabulary. Or to mix the two: a final vocabulary grids an open space in a particular way, but does not create the open space that it grids.

  Now this shift does not so much alter the set of descriptions that can be correctly applied to our thinking as it does one's conception of which descriptions are really important, "essential" we might say. It may be "correct" that thinking is finally ungrounded, that it represents the poetic, historically contingent creations of finite beings; and to be sure, there is no higher court of appeal from which to judge one's final vocabulary. But I think the later Heidegger came to see such descriptions as unwittingly metaphysical, as strategic ways to characterize human being in an argument with the Platonists, but no truer for that. Indeed, Heidegger's desire to "leave metaphysics to itself" stems from the recognition that the winning move against Plato harbors within it dangers that only a new way of thinking can avoid.

The danger is not, I believe, *pace* Rorty, just that the Nietzscheans, Sartreans, and Goodmanians will develop a vocabulary that closes in on itself, that keeps them provincially unaware of the other worlds that their own form of life excludes. The real danger may be that a vocabulary which is itself finalized, so to speak, by the abjuration of final vocabularies will forget that its conception of man as maker of worlds rather than a knower of essences, as one whose task consists in proliferating and disseminating versions of being rather than homing-in on the Absolute—will forget that this conception requires its dialectical antithesis in order to retain its veracity. To forget this, to forget the history of being in which nihilism has its place, is to over-emphasize the correct belief that human beings are finite and historical because one has forgotten the contingency of the very context—metaphysics—in which such an emphasis is appropriate. *Merely* temporal, *merely* historical, *merely* finite will come to be thought of as what human being *is*—as if such designations were true independently of the conversation with those who thought of our essential natures as something beyond the temporal, historical, and finite.[4] In order to save human being from this inauthentic nihilism, from what he describes in "The Question Concerning Technology" as the illusion "that everything man encounters exists only insofar as it is his construct" (1977: 308), Heidegger recalls the contingency of this conversation that started with the Greeks, and hopes that by doing so he might be able to forget *both* Plato's sense of the eternal and Nietzsche's sense of the contingent. To go beyond this conversation, then, is to agree with Nietzsche that thinking does not measure up to the standard Plato imposed on it, but to qualify this agreement rather severely by interpreting this conclusion as being just the inevitable result of Plato's first having judged thinking, as Heidegger puts it, "by a standard that does not measure up to it" (1977: 195).

III. Finding Ourselves Making

What standard does measure up? To quote from one of Heidegger's favorite Hölderlin poems,

> Is there a measure on earth? There is
> None.

In that last line we hear: There is no unique name, no poem that could tell us once and for all what it means to dwell in the world as a mortal. Heidegger himself remarks that this must be the poet's reply, "because what we signify when we say 'on the earth' exists only insofar as man dwells on the earth and in his dwelling lets the earth be as earth" (1971: 227).

Yet in order to clarify how Heidegger would take us beyond the network of binaries that has made this reply sound as though it were only the confession of a lack, I suggest that we think of this line as the naming, rather than the simple negation, of a measure. None, or the nothing, *is* the measure. But how on earth does the Nothing measure? How does Nothing designate something other than Rortian finitude, something other than the lack of a link to the eternal in the absence of which we must see ourselves as *mere* mortals?

Understood superficially, the Nothing measures the self by standing on either side of the self's sequence of "nows"; mortality, then, is the condition of having to have this sequence discontinued at some point by one's physical degeneration. But fundamental to Heidegger's explication of "being-towards-death" in *Being and Time* is his critique of the onto-theological treatment of finitude as something imposed from the outside, "tacked-on" to man. Not only the Christian, but the everyday understanding treats mortality as a deprivation of immortality, as something which happens, as it were, *to* life, stopping its otherwise uninterrupted persistence. To the Christian notion that God sends death at a particular time corresponds the average understanding of death as a possibility that has not yet been actualized; and both, according to Heidegger, suggest that Dasein's usual way of dealing with death—even, or perhaps especially, when one is most attentive to it—is to cover it up. For typically such attention is given in the language of *das*

Man: death is always there; this or that person's demise is a case of death; I too will die some day, but not yet—all of these "recognitions" of our finitude assure us that death is something that happens to everyone, and therefore, says Heidegger, to no one. To wrench oneself from the they-self is to anticipate death not as some abstract possibility that will affect me, as it affects everyone, sometime in the future, but as the definite possibility which involves me now by being most my own. In the section on "Authentic Being-towards-death" in *Being and Time*, Heidegger writes:

> In anticipating the indefinite certainty of death, Dasein opens itself to a constant threat arising out of its own 'there.' In this very threat Being-towards-the-end must maintain itself. (1962: 310)

On this interpretation, the very act of existence is a thinking of death, though not, to be sure, a dwelling on death that sponsors moods of listless despair or careless frenzy, both of which entail an inauthentic view of what life ought to have been, of what it would have to be like in order to be meaningful, and consequently construe death as a kind of imperfection. For what Heidegger wanted was to see the self not against the background of eternity and the absolute, where it always appears diminished—finite, historical, contingent—but rather to see it against the background of the Nothing, of one's own death, where the sense of Dasein's finitude is itself surpassed by the wonder at the self and this world happening at all.

At this point the contrast I drew earlier between Heidegger's sense of *möglichkeit* and Rorty's can be made more concrete. In his recently published essay "The Contingency of Selfhood" Rorty comments on a poem of Philip Larkin's in which the poet contemplates his own death and confesses how unsatisfying it seems now, at the end of his life, to have traced "the blind impress / All our behavings bear . . . Since it applied only to one man once, / And that one dying." Rorty writes:

> There is no such thing as fear of inexistence as such, but only fear of some concrete loss. It is not enough to say that poets, like everybody else, fear death, or that they fear nothingness.

> 'Death' and 'nothingness' are equally resounding, equally
> empty terms. To say one fears either is as unhelpful as
> Epicurus' attempt to say why one should not fear them.
> Epicurus said, 'When I am, death is not, and when death is,
> I am not,' thus exchanging one vacuity for another. For the
> word 'I' is quite as hollow as the word 'death.' To unpack such
> words one has to fill in the details about the 'I' in question,
> specify precisely what it is that will not be. (1986: 11)

Specifying his own odd selfhood was what Larkin had made his
life's work, and so Rorty thinks his dissatisfaction affected,
"because I doubt that any poet could seriously think trivial his own
success in tracing home the blind impress borne by all his
behavings—all his previous poems" (1986: 11). For Rorty,
trivializing such an enterprise is not the work of poetry but
philosophy, which finds value only in those things which apply
indiscriminately to all men for all times.

But I wonder if there isn't a more urgent contrast to be found
here that has less to do with differences between poetry and
philosophy than with the more pedestrian one between living and
dying. In his memorial poem to Larkin, "This Is Your Subject
Speaking," Andrew Motion records another confession of Larkin's
which reads: "You see, there's nothing to write / which is better
than life itself, no matter / how life might let you down, or pass
you by" (139). "Life" can doubtless seem as hollow a term as any
of its peers—"death" and "nothingness," for example—but Larkin's
dissatisfaction with filling in the details of his life may have
stemmed from his discovery that such details—whether poetic and
contingent, or philosophic and eternal—seem trivial in comparison
to the very process of their accumulation, to the very possibility
of identifying the blind impress, regardless of his success or failure.
To see the self in this way is, roughly, to think of Plato's respect
for the eternal and Nietzsche's for the idiosyncratic as being
confined to a dialectic that remains oblivious to the simplest and
most startling fact of all: "that a thinking is," as Heidegger once
put it, "ever and suddenly" (1971: 11).

And this is, indirectly, the great value of Caputo's contention
that "language originates not in the inventiveness of subjectivity
but in the openness of Dasein, not in the subject's ingenuity but
in letting be" (674), for what this sense of the Nothing brings us

up against is the overwhelming strangeness of the self having a world, and—by virtue of having a world—being a self. But Caputo often betrays his own good intentions when instead of emphasizing the phenomena of language *qua* language, world *qua* world, he talks about a particular language ("A man does not create his language but is born into it" (674)), and a particular world ("What I hear is a call back to the human setting of our lives, back to a sense of human finitude and mortality, to the joy and tragedy of the human condition. . . " (684)). Again, shuttling back and forth between language as such and a particular language, between the worldhood of the world and a particular world, Caputo seems reluctant to stay with what is an essential part of Heidegger's fundamental project: the attempt to think of death not just as a deprivation of this joy or that disappointment, of a particular way of being in the world, but as the negation of the clearing, of possibility as such— as the collapse of the region where anything can be said to have been at all. But rather than return to Heidegger at this point, I want instead to quote from Richard Wollheim a passage that captures a sense of things remarkably close to Heidegger's own:

> It is not that death deprives us of some particular pleasure, or even of pleasure. What it deprives us of is something more fundamental than pleasure: it deprives us of that thing which we gain access to when, as persisting creatures, we enter into our present mental states and which, from then onwards, we associate in some special way with our past mental states and our future mental states. It deprives us of phenomenology, and, having once tasted phenomenology, we develop a longing for it which we cannot give up: not even when the desire for the cessation of pain, for extinction, grows stronger. (1984: 269)[5]

Getting a sense of what it means to gain access to this phenomenology depends on our being able to gain an awareness of its negative condition, of what it's like *not* to have access to it, and this, I will admit, defies a certain logic. But I think that some conceptions of death are better than others, if only because the ones they surpass seem to have, so to speak, too much life left in them. And Heidegger thought that this would make a difference because he understood that so much of what we are depends on how we construe what we are not. If the negative function of the *Seinsfrage* is, as Rorty contends, to short-circuit those traditional attempts to measure human being by reference to something either far beyond or deep within us, its positive function, I have been suggesting, is to bring into view the possibility of that very measuring—the simple, constant, and irresistible spanning of our lives.

Notes:

1. For Arendt's analysis, see *The Life of the Mind* II, 172-173. For a critique of Arendt's views see David Krell's "Analysis" at the end of *Nietzsche IV: Nihilism*, esp. pp. 272-276

2. See *Being and Time*, p. 330: "Throwness, however, does not lie behind it as some event which has happened to Dasein, which has factually befallen and fallen loose from Dasein again; on the contrary, as long as Dasein is, *Dasein*, as care, *is* constantly its 'that-it-is.'"

3. Hence Heidegger's remark at the close of "The End of Philosophy and the Task of Thinking": "Does the title for the task of thinking then read instead of *Being and Time*: Opening and Presence?" (1977: 392).

4. See Rorty, *HAP*, p. 20. In his "Analysis" of Heidegger's Nietzsche, Vol. II, Krell points out that Heidegger's neglect of Dionysos may be an attempt to saddle Nietzsche with the bad form of nihilism, a form that Dionysos, according to Krell, surpasses. In this regard it's worth noting the following entry in *The Will To Power*: "The supreme values in whose service man *should* live, especially when they were very hard on him and exacted a high price—these *social values* were erected over man to strengthen their voice, as if they were commands of God, as 'reality,' as the 'true' world, as a hope and *future* world. Now that the shabby origin of these values is becoming clear, the universe seems to have lost value, seems meaningless'—but that is only a *transitional stage*." 5. I take this to be the upshot of the following passage from *Being and Time*: "*The closest closeness which one may have in Being towards death as a possibility, is as far as possible from anything actual.* The more unveiledly this possibility gets understood, the more purely does the understanding penetrate into it *as the possibility of the impossibility of any existence at all.* Death, as possibility, gives Dasein nothing to be 'actualized,' nothing which Dasein, as actual, could itself *be*. It is the possibility of the impossibility of every way of comporting oneself towards anything, of every way of existing" (306-307).

6. My thanks to John Caputo for his generous reception of a shorter version of this paper at the IAPL Conference held in Lawrence, Kansas, April 30-May 2, 1987; and to Richard Rorty for access to his unpublished book on Heidegger.

References:

Arendt, Hannah. *The Life of the Mind.* 2 vols. New York: Harcourt, Brace, Jovanovich, 1977-78.

Caputo, John. "The Thought of Being and the Conversation of Mankind." *Review of Metaphysics* 36 (1983): 661-685.

Guignon, Charles. "On Saving Heidegger From Rorty." *Philosophy and Phenomenological Research* 46.3 (March 1986): 401-417.

Heidegger, Martin. *An Introduction To Metaphysics.* Trans. Ralph Manheim. New Haven: Yale University Press, 1959.

_____. *Being and Time.* Trans. John Macquarrie and Edward Robinson. New York: Harper and Row, 1962.

_____. *Existence and Being.* Ed. with introduction by Werner Broch. Chicago: Henry Regnery-Gateway, 1967. ("Hölderlin and the Essence of Poetry, " trans. David Scott.)

_____. *What Is Called Thinking?* Trans. J. Glenn Gray. New York: Harper and Row, 1968.

_____. *Identity and Difference.* New York: Harper and Row, 1969.

_____. *Poetry, Language, Thought.* New York: Harper and Row, 1971.

_____. *Basic Writings.* Ed. David Krell. New York: Harper and Row, 1977. ("On the Essence of Truth," trans. J. Glenn Gray; "The Question Concerning Technology," trans. William Lovitt; "Letter On Humanism," trans. Frank Capuzzi and J. Glenn Gray; "The End of Philosophy and the Task of Thinking," trans. Joan Stambaugh.)

_____. *Nietzsche IV: Nihilism.* Ed. David Krell. Trans. Frank Capuzzi. New York: Harper and Row, 1978.

_____. *Nietzsche II: The Eternal Recurrence of the Same.* Ed. and trans. David Krell. New York: Harper and Row, 1984.

Motion, Andrew. "This Is Your Subject Speaking." *TLS* 7 February 1986: 139-140.

Nietzsche, Friedrich. *The Will to Power.* Trans. Walter Kaufmann and R. J. Hollingdale. Ed. Walter Kaufmann. New York: Random House, 1967.

Ricoeur, Paul. *The Rule of Metaphor.* Trans. Robert Czerny. Toronto: University of Toronto Press, 1977.

Rorty, Richard. "Heidegger Against The Pragmatists." Presented to the Second Leonard Conference, "Hermeneutics," Reno, Nevada,

October 15, 1981. (An uncorrected version of this paper appears in German under the title, "Heidegger wider die Pragmatisten," *Neue Hefte für Philosophie* 23 (1984): 1-22.)

_____. "Ironists, Metaphysicians, And Heidegger." Presented at the NEH Council for Philosophical Studies Dissemination Workshop on Intentionality in Continental and Analytic Philosophy, March 24, 1983, Berkeley, California.

_____. "Heidegger on Contingency and Belatedness." Unpublished manuscript, 1985.

_____. "The Contingency of Selfhood." *London Review of Books*, 8 May 1986: 11-15.

Wollheim, Richard. *The Thread of Life*. Cambridge: Harvard University Press, 1984.

Simulations:
Politics, TV, and History in the Reagan Era

"Maybe Alzheimer's disease is only the body's adaptation
to a new world in which the sense of history is no longer
necessary or even desirable"
　　　　　　　　　—Pat Wilkinson-Bus

"History is not a text, not a narrative, master or
otherwise, but that, as an absent cause, it is inaccessible
to us except in textual form."
　　　　　—Fredric Jameson, *The Political Unconscious*

Robert Merrill,
Institute for Advanced Cultural Studies

　　　To account for the success of Ronald Reagan's political
project—and I need to insert a word here about the current
Iran/*Contra*gate scandal for I am convinced that at question in the
scandal is not the foundation of the political project itself, of which
the overtures to Iran and the creation/funding of the *contras* are
only the tip of the iceberg, but rather at question is only a failure
of certain individuals to follow prescribed channels for inviting
Congressional participation along with some panic now about a
loss of direction in the Reagan agenda (my own feeling is that when
the operations are advantageously narrativized, the scandal will
become publicly quite acceptable)—at any rate, to account for
Reagan's ability on the world political scene during the last seven
years to set an agenda and manufacture public consensus (a
simulated consensus—I will argue in the following pages) for a
mean-spirited ethnocentrism and economic imperialism, a case is

often made that Ronald Reagan is the first TV president; his second American Revolution appeals to Americans in general in the same way that television does and for the same reasons. But is this not to announce also that Ronald Reagan is the first postmodern president? Postmodern—that is, in the sense of ultra- or hyper-modernism now advocated by French theorizers such as Baudrillard, Dubord, and Lyotard—Reaganism may be seen as the triumph of simulation and narrative over history. All of the apocalyptic themes implicit in this reversal of signs are, moreover, acted out in Reaganism; in spite of all his vaunted conservatism, his record shows him to be destructive of his own traditions in the imploding manner identified by the cultural critics of postmodernism. This may be the final irony of Reaganism: the cultural logic of neo-conservatism projects itself toward what turns out to be a great reversal of inertia, leaving the movement itself in ruins, unable to secure the primacy of ideology and economy it promised.

Typically, two forms of the argument about TV and political power dominate critical discourse: the first cites TV as the cause of an evolution in electoral politics toward a conflict of personalities and consequently the cause of an erosion in congressional government in favor of an imperial presidency. The proof here finally rests on technical and formal limitations—or strengths, depending on how you view them—of TV as a medium: television is more visual than verbal and it does better showing a close-up of a single person than it does of a group, especially a group as large as Congress where image recognition (and thus valorization) for the mass audience is bound to be very low. Televisual narrative, both fiction and news reporting, tends toward the presentation of a single hero or at most a pair, and that presentation is almost invariably anecdotal. The anecdote and ultimately the image take on tremendous symbolic power to represent or symbolize reality, and by logical extension from the image the viewer infers an entire world, including his or her own place in it. This is why we have an imperial presidency—so the logic of the televisual medium implies—and why we cannot have anything else. This logic points toward what Jean Baudrillard pronounces to be the Precession of the Simulacra.

What TV narrative celebrates is a *fin de siècle* cult of

supermen; those whose images rise above the inscrutable bureaucracy, the fragmentation, and frustrations of modern industrial society to get things done. This cult includes men— still almost always men—from business, finance, and government like T. Boone Pickens, Lee Iacocca, Carl Icahn,Oliver North, or H. Ross Perot and their character is pre-defined and valorized by television heroes like Blake Carrington, J. R. Ewing, Sonny Crockett, or *Lifestyles of the Rich And Famous.* The Summer's billing of Oliver North as national hero depends upon the establishment of a simulacrum within popular consciousness of heroes who take the problems of the state into their own hands and operate outside of the law (by lying and consorting with drug-lords, terrorists, and weapons traders) but in the national or public interest, a simulacrum established to a large extent by the character of Harry Callahan and disseminated more widely by Rambo, Mike Hammer, the A-Team, and MacGyver—all hyper-ingenious operatives who get things done no matter what the bureaucratic impediments or what the shortage of resources. North is MacGyver—that and nothing more will turn out to be the burden of the Summer-long Congressional hearings into the Iran/*contra* affair. Though "higher-ups" like Daniel Innouye or any TV police lieutenant are often annoyed and embarrassed by the methods of renegade operatives and may scold them with stern faces, they prove to be, nonetheless, glad to have the work done. And so do most other Americans in this late stage of capitalism when the general panic about an inability to compete in world marketplaces is compounded by military and ideological frustrations presented in the collapse of American hegemony in Iran and Nicaragua.

The other account of this present political scene puts the administration in charge, suggesting that media specialists, of whom Michael Deaver is most renowned, have always known how to market their candidate in a way that generates high ratings. TV is only the latest electronic fad. The essential technique is the "photo opportunity" in which the press and the world are allowed only glimpses of the *Man.* Some reports indicate that Reagan spends as many as two-thirds of his working (waking?) hours on public relations and much of that on photo opportunities which place him in contexts or semiotic matrices that can be readily decoded by a viewing public always already educated by the rest of TV programming to interpret such stimuli in ways that augment the personal popularity of the president and an identity of the viewer's interests with the president's policies. This view is taken in *The Triumph of Politics*, where David Stockman, now a dissenter, essentially blames the excessive fascination with and devotion to telemarketing for the failure of supply-side economics. Stockman writes, "The President's non-revolutionary instincts and sentimentality were vastly compounded by the inveterate tube watching of the 'fellas,' [Deaver, Meese, Baker, Nofziger]. . . . Our revolutionary blueprint required relentless hot pursuit of the politicians, interest groups, and organized constituencies which resolutely defended all of the unaffordable largesse. It required taking huge political risks. . . . But the 'fellas' would have none of that. It would have meant worse than the Atlantic story. It would have meant a bad time at reality time—every night at 7:00 P.M. They never read anything. They lived off the tube" (11-12). Stockman's self-serving self-narrativization is right in saying that supply-side policies failed in attaining historical or material goals (i.e., the trickle down) but wrong in thinking the administration has been unsuccessful in making the basic tenets of finance capitalism part of accepted American reality.

To my mind, these arguments demonstrate pretty well the mutual dependency of media (especially TV) and the world of the state up to Reaganism and may account for the co-optation of network news personnel (how else to explain the teflon phenomenon?), but they do not go far enough in explaining the bizarre reversal in semiotic fields that we are beginning to recognize in Reaganism. The rise of the imperial presidency can be traced back certainly to Theodore Roosevelt (with its roots firmly in James Madison and James Monroe), both in presidential action and in the press (see Schudson, "The Politics of Narrative Forms"), and it is impossible to think of a time when a government, and everyone else with the means to do so, did not manipulate the media. What seems genuinely new is what Arthur Kroker and David Cook aptly call in *The Postmodern Scene* "a panic philosophy," the predominance of an intertext of TV and dominant class imperialism passing as hard reality that the present government and general public simply respond to—the mediascape replaces the landscape and the imaginary becomes the real in a reversal that Jean Baudrillard calls the Precession of the Simulacra:

> It is no longer a question of imitation, nor of reduplication, not even of parody. It is rather a question of substituting signs of the real for the real itself, that is, an operation to deter every real process by its operational double, a metastable, programmatic, perfect descriptive machine which provides all the signs of the real and short-circuits all its vicissitudes (*Simulations* 4).

Another way of looking at this historical moment in which the political machine as simulacrum becomes first reality and history comes after is that of Max Horkheimer and Theodor Adorno who observe that when the "enlightenment returns to mythology"in order to shore up legitimations that can no longer be realized in material production or in social desires it gives up the historicity of its rhetoric about liberation, justice, equality, and human rights to assert only its own totality (*Dialectic of Enlightenment* 27). This is panic politics at the end of an epoch. "Enlightenment is totalitarian"(6), Horkheimer and Adorno also say, and, in this historical moment under Reagan, political choices have always been made in favor of ideological extension, even when that obviously means revoking basic human rights and the material benefits of the Englightenment. The Reagan doctrine(as symbolic counter to the Breshnev doctrine) centers around the creation or maintenance of simulated democracies in the Third World: El Salvador, Brazil, Israel, Argentina, Philippines, Panama, South Africa, Taiwan, Korea, Honduras, and the list could go on. These simulations are testimony to the triumph of "democracy" over communism as a social and economic model. No attention is paid to the historical conditions of the indigenous populations. If we are to speak plainly on this subject of Reaganism as a moment in modernism and the Enlightenment, then we must recognize it as the point in American history at which a long tradition of rhetoric about individual rights and liberation becomes its opposite: a naked fascism and overt determination to dominate the world political scene. This panic politics, however, seems to be emerging just at the point where for the United States such a deep desire is also becoming materially impossible, making its simulation in the production of signs of mastery all the more necessary and satisfying.

Because TV is primarily oriented to the individual and concrete situations, television cultivates an experience of simulated primary exposure and a consciousness, therefore, of a world of unmediated facts (why, for example, TV news frequently will not run stories for which they have no good film footage)—all which derive, however, from the requirements of narrative construction of reality rather than a representation of history or of real events. The penetration and conquest of the consciousness, as Fredric Jameson observes in *The Political Unconscious*, is the last frontier of capitalism, and of course it was George Orwell who in *1984* showed that fascism is really about the process of locating "the real" in the mind rather than outside of the mind in history and material reality: "But I tell you, Winston, that reality is not external. Reality exists in the human mind, and nowhere else. . . . The Party is not interested in the overt act: the thought is all we care about"(205-209). I do not want to suggest the sentimentality of a truly objective or unmediated reality or history—as one finds in the radical right-wing objectivist epistemology of, say, Ayn Rand—rather I concur with Jameson when he writes that history is *real* but that it is always the absent referent, what is unrepresentable absolutely: "our approach to it [history] and to the Real itself necessarily passes through its prior textualizations, its narrativization in the political unconscious" (35). We must be careful here about the differences in the positions taken by TV and Jameson. TV and Ayn Rand, for that matter, act *as if* reality is external, while *in fact* the reality presented is thoroughly simulated in the mind by narratives. TV asserts, therefore, an identity of the mental and the extra-mental. Jameson, on the other hand, knows that such an identity is always impossible. The question put to TV representations by critical theory, then, is *how* and on the authority of *whom* are history and the real narrativized? Who's story is being told? I will return to this in a moment, but first a case in point.

The current hysteria over drug abuse and all of the government's much publicized actions against a "Colombian Mafia" are much more the result of shows like *Miami Vice* or *60 Minutes* and needs of the administration to imitate in real life the simulacrum of a government protecting its citizens than of any real, sudden surge in drug use or any material concern on the part of officials over drug importation or use. The "Dialectic of Enlightenment" is the principle by which "Every spiritual resistance it encounters serves merely to increase its strength" (Horkheimer and Adorno 6); in other words, and in contrast to the Carter approach, Reagan needs enemies or oppositions in order to make his own project grow. Thus we get in the mediascape narrativizations of wildly escalating conflicts between drug-lords and the police, while statistics from the National Institute on Drug Abuse indicate that in 1985 only 17% of highschool students reported trying cocaine at least once and the figure has been at 16% ever since 1979. Marijuana use has actually declined over the last five years, but this is not the way the drug crisis is narrativized on TV.

Drugs always appear as a photo opportunity for the police and other officials to act heroically. Increasingly horrible enemies are required for increasingly total policing—even if that means the police must abet the drug trade. The point is the consciousness of Americans, not whether anyone uses cocaine. The Washington-based Christic Institute has recently filed suit in a Miami Federal District Court charging (among other things) top officials from the Drug Enforcement Agency, the National Security Council, the Central Intelligence Agency, and other "assets" with drug smuggling to support the various "contra" wars around the world; in other words, with increasing clarity, we are learning, as Daniel Sheehan, Director of the Institute, asserts that the administration itself has been largely responsible for the importation of cocaine into the U.S. during the last six years ("Christic Institute Special Report"; see also "CIA, Contras Hooked on Drug Money," *In These Times* 15-21 April 1987). This is of course not the reality that newsmagazines, network news programs, government officials, and the general public has in mind. Alcohol abuse is up, but drugs make better TV and, of course, political leaders need the kind of fight drug enforcement provides to create the desired simulacrum—or, that is more precisely, to imitate the simulacrum that already exists in TV narrative.

What strikes me as so interesting about the fulfillment of the imperial presidency under Reagan is the certainty of its implosion, and with it this time the collapse of Western culture as world hegemony. In a chapter titled "The Divine Irreference of Images," Jean Baudrillard describes the reversal latent in simulations:

> the iconolators were the most modern and adventurous minds, since underneath the idea of the apparition of God in the mirror of images, they already enacted his death and his disappearance in the epiphany of his representations [photo opportunities] (which they perhaps knew no longer represented anything, and that they were purely a game, but that this was precisely the greatest game—knowing also that it is dangerous to unmask images, since they dissimulate the fact that there is nothing behind them. (*Simulations* 9)

Reagan could not have had Baudrillard's analysis of the death of God in mind when he released an autobiography called *Where's the Rest of Me*, and one can only speculate about what the producers of *Max Headroom* had in mind when they conceived of a person's image taking on an independent life in television circuitry, but the technique of simulation serves both in the same way. The faithful—i.e., those possessed of what Nietzsche calls the will to truth (*The Gay Science* 282)—cannot help inferring that some "rest" does exist and contains all of the qualities they desire but which are only modestly hinted at and implied by the real Reagan which we see almost every day on TV. That is, the material Reagan only points to the simulated president and world leader with all of the competence and knowledge that are clearly not present in the Reagan of sense experience but must be present in the more real Reagan which arises from the formal requirements of the office itself—that is, from the qualities of narrative itself. Jean-François Lyotard in *The Postmodern Condition* shows that reality is always whatever satisfies public desires, but, of course, desire too is simulated in the mediascape. One only needs to read a few issues of the myriad of magazines for the upwardly mobile like *Town & Country* to see that the theme of the 80s is, as one advertisement boldly proclaims, "An Illusion That Surpasses Reality" (March 1987). Reagan's persistent references to the misery and pessimism of the 70s and the Carter years, stimulate public desire for greater satisfactions than the political experimentalism and marginality the little man from Plains could offer. Lyotard explains, "When power assumes the name of a party, realism and its neoclassical complement triumph over the experimental avant-garde by slandering and banning it—that is, provided the 'correct' images, the 'correct' narratives, the 'correct' forms which the party requests, selects, and propagates can find a public to desire them as the appropriate remedy for the anxiety and depression that public experiences" (*The Postmodern Condition* 75). Above all, the simulated Reagan—though he is certainly a fascist—is publically satisfying.

This is not an isolated condition of political life. The same processes toward the the production of signs of mastery and away from the production of goods characterizes the corporation in the United States as well as the work life of the most privileged class in the 80s, the Yuppie. Instead of building fuel-efficient cars (at least ones that meet federal guidelines), General Motors and Chrysler advertised new, lean corporations and worked secretly to have the regulations changed. T. Boone Pickens and Carl Icahn claim a moral imperative to take over corporations that have become fat and inefficient. As a whole, businesses in the United States will spend over 1.3 billion dollars in 1987 paying professional athletes to represent them. In fact, Barry Bluestone and Bennet Harrison in their *Deindustrialization of America* envision a time when the American corporation will be nothing more than a huge and opulent façade behind which nothing is produced but vast sums of money are moved in and out as the corporate executives trade commercial paper to inflate the wealth of stockholders. Whatever wealth is generated will go into trading paper even more intensely. Such a flurry of economic activity will accordingly show tremendous economic growth and national well-being in the "leading economic indicators"—the simulacrum of commodity production. David Roderick, CEO of the former US Steel, openly admits that he is no longer interested in making steel but now only in making wealth, and so changed the name of the corporation to USX—where X is the sign of whatever produces wealth— that is now, the sign of wealth itself (*Time*, 21 July 1986: 54). Americans, if the reactions of the press, especially the *New York Times* and the *Wall Street Journal*, can be taken as representative, now seem much more satisfied with USX than in those troubled days when it bothered to make steel and compete with the Koreans and

Japanese. It is, of course, in these postmodern times more important to look marvelous than it is to be marvelous, as *Saturday Night Live* has taught millions of Americans to say.

Reaganism is, then, only the vanguard of a global movement in which violently reactionary politics and rhetoric are producing ever greater signs of mastery while at the same time losing control. "We are living through a great story," Arthur Kroker writes, "an historical moment of implosion, cancellation and reversal; that moment where the will to will of the technoscape ... traces a great arc of reversal, connecting again to an almost mythic sense of primitivism as the primal of technological society" (*The Postmodern Scene* 15). Reaganism is the postmodern scene—a global Laffer curve in which simultaneous tax cuts for the wealthy and massive increases in government spending move with absolute precision toward a balanced national budget and economic equity. This principle of reversal, so well exemplified by the Laffer curve (i.e. lower taxes to increase governmental revenue), underlies also the desire to "impose" democracy and peace on a nation such as Nicaragua by destroying the productive capacity of the nation and killing or maiming upwards of 40,000 people (one could mention here too Namibia, Mozambique, Angola, Kampuchia, black South Africa, Afghanistan and more). The narrative structure of these explanations is struggle, conflict, and tension. As a subscriber to "Current Policy" publications of the White House and Department of State, I have been amazed over the years at the high proportion of topics of public policy that are cast in the form of a struggle or fight against some external opponent. Perhaps the memoirs of the Reagan administration will be titled "mein kampf"—who can tell.

This reversal is important to an understanding of the postmodern condition, if we first understand two things that postmodernism is not: it is not a fascination with theory or an intellectual fad that will soon go away, as Stephen Knapp and Walter Benn Michaels among others seem to think ("Against Theory"); nor is postmodernism a desire or nostalgia for cultural transcendence, as one in moments of sentiment and anger might wish it to be. It is, rather, the conditions of life as we find them around us every day and the enforced interpretation and narrativization of these conditions within the cultural logic of modernism (both Marxism and capitalism) which have arrived at a point of deep crisis, a crisis in which political and social theory become less able every day to point out useful solutions to the problems we face. The struggle now is one of re-legitimization for both Marxism and capitalism, if they are not to pass simply into the realm of the quaint practices of dead civilizations. Both Marxism and capitalism now face the problem of boosting their appeal to a much higher level and this means dropping back to the level of narrative to see which dominant can be most persuasively narrativized.

This is why postmodern discourse—which is concerned with theorizing the historical moment, as is all philosophy (Paul Bové, "The critical mind must address the politics of the moment" 22)—must be concerned not only with texts but also go beyond them to the partisans of texts and the exercise of power in the struggle to re-ground and re-legitimate cultural dominants. We can never endorse the nostalgia of the critic "waiting in the wings ever since the late sixties for such boring annoyances as critical theory, feminism, affirmative action programs, and so forth to disappear [so that] we can go back to doing business as usual, waging our polite and sensible battles over the sources and significance of some line in Pound's *Pisan Cantos* or Joyce's manuscript drafts of *Finnegans Wake*" (O'Hara 37). The struggle is really, as Fredric Jameson sees it, a conquest or re-conquest of forms of representation ("Interview" 87): who's story will get to be the one repeated in the sitcoms, the crime dramas, the soaps, and the nightly news programs in America. Will it be as Jameson so cogently argues the

> Marxism [that] offers a philosophically coherent and ideologically compelling resolution of the dilemma of historicism. . . . Only Marxism can give us an adequate account of the essential *mystery* of the cultural past, which, like Tiresias drinking the blood, is momentarily returned to life and warmth and allowed once more to speak, and to deliver its long forgotten message in surroundings utterly alien to it. This mystery can be reenacted only if the human adventure is one; only thus . . . can we glimpse the vital claims upon us of such long-dead issues as the seasonal alternation of the economy of a primitive tribe, the passionate disputes about the nature of the Trinity, the conflicting models of the *polis*

or the universal Empire, of apparently closer to us in time, the dusty parliamentary and journalistic polemics of the nineteenth-century states. These matters [i.e. human life itself] can recover their original urgency for us only if they are retold within the unity of a single great collective story; only if, in however disguised and symbolic a form, they are seen as sharing a single fundamental theme—for Marxism, the collective struggle to wrest a realm of Freedom from a realm of Necessity. (*Political Unconscious* 19)

Or will it be the vision of American world hegemony Ronald Reagan delivered to the graduates of Glassboro high school in the Summer of 1986:

Certainly the American story represents one of the great epics of human history. Yet ours is a story of goodness as well as greatness. After World War II, our goodness received a dramatic manifestation in the Marshall Plan—the vast program of assistance to help war-ravaged nations recover from World War II. And we can be proud that we helped restore not only our allies but those who had been our enemies as well. Pope Pius XII said of us at that time, 'The American people have a genius for splendid and unselfish action and into the hands of America, God has placed the destinies of an afflicted humanity.' And in our own times, the United States continues to bear the burdens of defending freedom around the world. Listen to the world of former Prime Minister of Australia John Gorton: 'I wonder if anybody has thought what the situation of comparatively small nations would be if there were not in existence the United States, if there were not this great, giant country prepared to make those sacrifices. . .'

If ever in the coming years you grow disillusioned with your nation—if ever you doubt that America holds a special place in all the long history of humankind—remember this moment. . . . Call it mysticism if you will; I have always believed there was some divine plan that placed this great land between the two oceans to be found by people from every corner of the earth—those people who had in common that extra love for freedom and that extra ounce of courage that would enable them to pack up, leave their friends and relatives and homeland to seek their future in this blessed place.

In 1984 Walter Fisher called for a "'narrative paradigm' of reasoning so that we can reconceive the role of the expert: 'Experts are storytellers and the audience is not a group of observers, but are active participants in the meaning-formation of the stories.' On this view, counselors of state, professional administrators, and nuclear physicists should be brought down from high platforms of public authority to storytellers amidst the people, where their business is disseminating knowledge as social lore or public wisdom" (McGee and Nelson 143; Fisher, "The Narrative Paradigm").

The creation of this social lore or political reality is, of course, precisely what Reaganism has been so successful at doing. Current policy is rationalized not so much as implementation of constitutional ideals, the improvement of social conditions, or the enactment of some political science but as action within a structure defined by determinants modeled on narrative presentation, a response to conditions confronting the state in the same way that a character in a narrative becomes involved in the opening conflict of a TV drama. What is often called Reagan's pragmatism is only his responsiveness to situations that are constructed as narratives. To blame Reagan for always being one step behind in world politics and therefore always playing "catch-up" as we so frequently hear from the Peter Jennings-type is to miss the point entirely. Reaganism is not aimed at solving human problems at all. It is aimed at dramatizing them—and quite naturally the situations in South Africa, the Middle East, and Central America have continued to grow worse. The object of political action under Reagan is human consciousness and its goals are revolutionizing the way people conceive of situations in order to re-legitimize the project of modernism in the popular consciousness. To do this, the world has to be represented entirely on a basis of conflict and opposition. That is what people are supposed to see so that they can become accustomed again to picking out the good side from the bad.

The logic used year after year by Caspar Weinberger to justify the Defense Department budgets works this way: Pentagon expenditures cannot be related to domestic economic conditions and an assessment of military strength or adequacy but must respond to any Soviet actions, in a move- / counter-move fashion.

It is the manner of existence of this "Soviet threat" that arises as an intertext of TV and political aims. In modernist (and by logical extension, capitalist) narrative, the character of the protagonist arises as a function of his interaction with the antagonist. In narrative, one is allowed to create whatever sort of antagonist he chooses, and in TV the antagonists are created as ways of valorizing or demonstrating the prowess of the protagonist. What could be said of Beowulf had there been no Grendel capable of eating thirty men, precisely reputed strength of Beowulf's handgrip? The same is true for Sonny Crockett, Hunter, and the *Equalizer*—whose very name suggests that he will respond to any criminal with a level of violence equal to that which confronts him. TV narrative elevates this necessity of suitable enemies to the level of a concrete universal, and so much of Reagan's popularity must be attributed to his creation of suitable enemies for him to battle with, beginning with the Air Traffic Controllers and continuing on through Daniel Ortega, head of what Reagan now tells us is a 600,000 man army determined to over-run Harlengin, Texas.

Another, perhaps clearer example is the remarks of Attorney General Edwin Meese to the California Peace Officers Association about the destruction of the MOVE family and an entire Philadelphia neighborhood. Meese makes it clear that the decisions of government officials were only a natural response to a crisis and a real threat of terrorism created by someone else—that is, MOVE. He said, "The public has got to know from the top public officials available that the situation that gave rise to the tragedy was caused by the criminals not the police." In Meese's view the role of the expert becomes that of fabricating or fictionalizing enemies or situations in which the authorities can act in a way that demonstrates their mastery and power—in a way that shows they are the authorities.

Certainly the true event involved no criminal acts on the part of MOVE; it was a police riot or a military-type invasion with the sole intent of murdering a group of people whom the police had long hated and who had been marked for extermination (along with other Black Panthers) ever since the days of the FBI COINTELPRO, but that is not the way it was reported and narrativized. According to Meese, we need to understand exactly what the police and the mayor were responding to in such an exemplary manner. It is crucial that the response is exemplary: "I think that Mayor Goode in Philadelphia, for example, in the very rational and reasonable way he's handling a very difficult situation there is a good example for us all to take note of" (*New York Times*, May 18, 1985: A26).

Meese in the genre of George Orwell's newspeak suggests that the use of water canons, 10,000 machine-gun bullets, and bombs in a residential neighborhood is reasonable in response to—we must ask—what. What is Meese seeing, and indeed what are the vast majority of Americans asked to see, that calls out such as response. It is certainly not the true event; there was nothing to call out such a response. But something is implied or posited by the narrative frame or a situational thinking derived from the narrative determinants of TV; in other words, the reported event had to imitate not the real event but the simulacrum of all such events: TV crime drama. Images of the MOVE family presented on TV and the irresponsible use of the term "radical" by reporters and top public official enables anyone educated by television to script a drama in which terrorists irrationally and violently threaten the safety of hundreds, even thousands, of people. The enemies of the police are always scripted in terms worthy of whatever weapons the police choose to employ. This is what we have seen in hundreds of news reports and crime dramas with increasing frequency during the last ten years. TV needs opportunities to display the workings of sophisticated weapons, and so the script writers create enemies who can only be stopped by the use of these tremendous weapons. But abundant evidence now exists (presented by PBS "Frontline") to show that the police in concert with the FBI planned to use high-explosives four months before the actual confrontation, when no threat existed at all.

In crime drama, negotiating with the enemies of the police would destroy the tensely charged plot. Heroes simply must have enemies as implacable and as violent as themselves. I am not aware that anyone has counted the number of dead left by the heroes of *Miami Vice, Hunter, The Equalizer, Spenser, Stingray, MacGyver,* and many more, but what is important is that the plots are increasingly confrontational and the motivation of the heroes is increasingly personal hatred for their enemies. In an episode of *Crime Story,* Lieutenant Mike Torello on a courtroom witness stand was asked if he had any personal feelings about the accused mobster, Ray Luca. He answered in a remarkable tirade that he hated the man, regarded him as an animal, and held a vow to see Luca dead no matter what the cost. In fact, the real appeal of *Crime Story* is the personal hatred between these two. The personalization of conflict is, of course, just as prominent in night time soap operas; what really makes J. R. Ewing and Cliff Barnes such successful businessmen is their deep and abiding hatred for each other. The same hatred and jealousy fuels Alexis Colby-Carrington.

The construction of political reality during Reagan government involves much of the same kind of emphasizing animosity between rivals and the personalization of global conflict. The prominence of conflict as a way of narrativizing historical events in the 1980s is revealed very sharply by comparison with the rather conciliatory policies of Jimmy Carter. Carter's administration can probably be characterized by his pardoning of Vietnam War draft evaders, his turning over of the Canal Zone to Panama, his refusal to supply Anastasio Somoza or the Shah of Iran with weapons during revolutions in their countries, his de-funding the CIA, and the Camp David accords. "Detente" is the word generally applied to international relations in the late sixties and seventies. In the eighties, Carter is regarded as simply a wimp and a weak and boring president. What is sometimes called the "Reagan Doctrine" is a dialectical intensification or a reopening the cold war by scaling up the level of conflict in every sector of the world society where at all possible, what Jonathan Kwitney in his recent analysis of US foreign policy calls the creation of "Endless Enemies." The great problem facing Reagan and the reopening of the cold war of US world dominance is that of general popular acceptance. What is needed is a general consciousness of a reality filled with hostility and violence; filled, that is, with suitable enemies for an increasingly aggressive United States. For general public acceptance of American global domination, the Reagan government had to bring its own conception of political reality in line with terms set by the structure, internal logic, and self-referentiality of TV narrative.

TV narrative is the simulacrum which politics under Reagan imitates. The enemies of TV heroes are constructed in order to highlight some quality of the hero. And so early in the administration, the Soviet Union became the "evil empire," inherently evil and the source of all evil on earth. As a mirror opposite, journalists, especially the cynical George Will and the vindictive Charles Krauthammer, began painting the United States as inherently good and, therefore, entitled to employ whatever means were necessary to spread its good to all people of the earth. The French rightist, Jean-François Revel, warned that unless western democracies (read, "the inherently good guys") began bullying and terrorizing the smaller nations they would lose the global competition to the totalitarian nations (*How Democracies Perish*). The big spenders in Congress, symbolized by the overweight Tip O'Neill, similarly were drawn into a melodramatic plot. Tip O'Neill in a PBS interview credits Reagan with creating him as the most important Speaker of the House in history, a consummate villain whom Reagan could confront and defeat. In the heat of the tax battle, Reagan borrowed a line from Harry Callahan, threatening the big spenders in Congress to "go ahead, make my day." The Muammar al-Qaddafi of public consciousness is almost entirely a symbolic counter for Reagan's increasing militarization of the oceans. A recent article in the *Philadelphia Inquirer* reported on fifty operations in which the United States has since 1980 supplied money, weapons, and mercenaries to insurgency groups around the world, all in the name of counter-terrorism. Nicaragua, Afghanistan, Chad, Kampuchea, Angola, South Africa, Mozambique, Lebanon, Guatemala, and El Salvador are merely the names people recognize. These are real wars, the secret wars alluded to in the Iran/*contra* hearings, but they arise and are legitimated from a simulacrum of conflict and counter-terrorism that exists only on television and, perhaps, in the minds of the Wills, Krauthammers, George Shultzes, Elliot Abrams and other script-writers of "America," the protagonist of a global crime drama.

Narrative offers powerful means for legitimating any social position because the grounds for legitimation lie within the structure of the plot itself and are thereby protected from testing against hard and empirical data. The low intensity wars just mentioned are episodes in a continuing drama in which a reified and anthropomorphized America battles the forces of evil on all fronts. "America is back" is both the advertising banner of the new Chrysler corporation and of the Reagan government—no one ever questions whether or not it was ever absent, or by what means it intends to come back, or just where it intends to go back to. Just as Lee Iacocca permits us to think that he is battling the Japanese auto imports, Reagan lets us think he is battling another foreign invasion. The truth is that 80% of the components of Chrysler cars are manufactured in Japan or outside of the U.S., and the enemies Reagan is conscious of are his own creations (see Philip Agee's *The White Paper Whitewash* for a clear example of how these enemies are created by so-called CIA intelligence) but—significantly—they take him back to fighting the cold war. He is expressly clear about his goal to return to a condition of pre-Vietnam cold war, as he told a group his friends last September at the White House:

> Restoring America's strength has been one of our Administration's highest goals. When we took office, we found that we had ships that couldn't leave port [and] planes that couldn't fly. . . . In the last five and half years, we've begun to turn that desperate situation around. We've restored the morale, the training, and the equipment of our armed forces. And let me just say that around the world and here at home, I've met many of our young men and women in uniform over the last several years. It does something to you when you're standing up there on the demilitarized zone in Korea and a young fellow standing there in uniform says, 'Sir, we're on the frontier of freedom.' (Dept. of State, Current Policy, No. 869).

The intertext is, of course, that the frontier of freedom brings us face to face with the new enemy, exactly what innumerable crime fighters and corporate magnates do on television every night.

Mass culture and the economy in the 1980s are uncannily enchanted with power and specifically with a power to destroy, as we see in any crime drama where cars are crashed and bombed, people killed by the score; or in any night time soap opera like *Dallas*, the *Colbys, Falcon Crest,* or *Dynasty* where destroying one's enemies is practically the nature of business. This huge simulacrum is parodied in more representations for public consumption such as TV championship wrestling, monster "bigfoot" trucks crushing rows of cars and school buses, and professional sports. The 80s have been years of hostile takeovers, leverage in the market, corporate aggressiveness, union smashing, and deindustrialization. While T. Boone Pickens, Carl Ichan, Ivan Boesky, and Donald Trump may behave rather civilly in public, what they do with their power in the marketplace can only be imaged forth by stars of *Dallas* and *Dynasty*. Kroker and Cook call this spirit of the age "a pleasurable voyage under the sign of 'viciousness for fun'" (27). And it is the necessary connection between viciousness and fun (or satisfaction) we are meant to understand as the nature of life in the present world, a resurgeance of social Darwinism in which the biggest and fiercist survive by natural right.

This discussion does not argue for a flow of causation in either direction, from TV or from government, for it seems rather more important to recognize the narrativizing of political reality or the politicizing of TV narrative in relation to the historical moment of legitimation crisis or the death of the "grand récits" of modernism. The point of convergence between government and TV, as pointed out above, is the strategy for re-legitimating dominance by a dialectical intensification. Let me assert again that modernism in the American experience is about mastery under the signs, however, of liberation, wealth, and equality; the moment of postmodernism is about the fear of the loss of mastery as "the old legitimation, 'everyone will prosper,' has lost its credibility" (Lyotard, "Rules and Paradoxes" 210). The culture of the 80s is saturated with the signs of mastery and representations of those who have prospered, but these are panic significations by those whose historical mastery is now threatened by rise of marginal groups (i.e., women, blacks, third world nations) and from the increasing failure of traditional methods for achieving mastery to provide it. Narrative solves the problem of legitimation in the way the protagonist arises from the conflict or plot and in his counter-position to the antagonist. It, moreover, socializes an interpretive community to structures of human relations built on dominance which are then taken to refer to historical social structures. If the Reagan government wishes to return to the basic policies of the pre-Vietnam *pax Americana* without accepting the old forms of legitimation which led those policies to the crisis of Vietnam, then it becomes clear that the Reagan era will have to end with a re-narrativizing or a re-writing of the history of the Vietnam war.

Representations of that war during the 60s and 70s, under the sign of pluralism and free expression, problematized all of the assumptions of American governance about the conflation of popular sentiment and national unity of interests. The war gave some truth to the cliché about the enemy being us and the insight that injustice occurs on both sides. The War against Vietnam touched-off, consequently, a legitimation crisis that has been true focus of government policy ever since. The war, along with other simultaneous social movements, especially the civil rights of Black Americans and feminism smashed the notion that all Americans hold the same interests. If one listens carefully enough to the criticism of Reed Irvine about the PBS series entitled "Vietnam: A Television History," it is quite clear that PBS told the story of Vietnam in a way that prevented viewers from drawing a stable conclusion or meaning. That narrative was postmodern to the extent that the depicted war became more and more indefinable and ungraspable as the series went on. No single theory accounts for the war. Motivations were not sufficient or plausible, characterizations were inconsistent, and no polarization of good and evil forces developed steadily throughout the series; instead, multiple viewpoints emerged and developed, and much of the action appeared simply as senseless and aimless. In this way, the PBS series very accurately summarized the problem of the TV representation of the war during the 60s and 70s.

The increasing anger of Accuracy in the Media and conservative columnists during the airing of the series made a nice register for what was unacceptable to the conservative consciousness of the 1980s. The series lacked closure; there were rather a plurality of closures, each refuting and undercutting the other. Reed Irvine's rebuttal called "Television's Vietnam: The Real Story" played exactly like a freshman thesis and support essay; the selectivity of supporting detail was transparent and naturally any attempt to rehabilitate the Vietnam war on logical grounds is doomed to fail. The problem with the war itself is that it was a postmodern war; Irvine wanted to see a clear dynamics of good and evil, and that is the way his closure interpreted the PBS series. My own view is that Francis Ford Coppola's depiction in *Apocalypse Now* as an incoherent, murderous, and nihilistic frenzy arising from, as Conrad's original story makes clear, the recognition of a terrible emptiness within the heart of Western European master narratives is about right. The war had very little to do with enemies but everything to do with American hegemony; the paradox of Colonel Kurtz is the paradox of Enlightenment. The delivery of peace and democracy to any people by means of seven million tons of explosives cannot be rationalized. No one can produce factual evidence for the validity of that hypothesis.

Television coverage of the war contributed significantly to problematizing rational explanations of it. Television was perhaps infatuated with its own power to present images, and so presented simply too much information (not enough, really—just more than most people could handle), and because the war was actually being fought on many fronts—the battlefields as well as university campuses, within families whose son refused to obey the call of the government, on television, and in government itself—the process of generalization made possible by traditional narrative distancing announced by some form of "in those days" or "in a far off country" could never be carried out with any degree of unanimity or certainty. So much information, moreover, prevented polarities required for motivating the narrative conflict from standing up to the laws consistency of characterization required for a modern plot. Vietnam profoundly confused just who was good and who was evil. Following the war against Vietnam was and remains to this day like reading a postmodern novel, say, Marquez's *One Hundred Years of Solitude* or Pynchon's *V*; just when you think you have discovered a pattern or theme upon which to base an interpretation, the pattern permutates into something that deconstructs those first glimmerings of interpretation. In any subsequent wars, there won't be so much information; new laws restricting press access to war events have been tested in Grenada and are rehearsed in the yearly troop maneuvers in Honduras, Panama, the Gulf of Sidra, and many other places.

The project of Reaganism, then, is to re-establish a narrative framework for televising history in precisely the way that the war against Vietnam could not be. Validity in narrative depends not upon correspondence to anything outside of the narrative but rather on the coherence of the narrative itself; if something can be shown to fit coherently into the internal logic of the narrative then it is judged valid. Thus, any action in a narrative is real if it is plausible;

that is, if it is sufficiently motivated by other actions in the narrative. Narrative is self-referential. If the conflict of the plot is resolved, then the particular ordering of experience or the conceptions of the agent of that resolution, the hero, are categorically legitimated. What the hero did works at resolving his problems—nothing else really matters. This point about modern narrative looks back, of course, to the deism of the eighteenth century, when the world was conceived of as a closed system or a vast machine, operating upon universal laws so that "Whatever is, is right" (Pope, "Essay on Man"). And so it is with the project of Reaganism; imitating a simulated machine means whatever he does is right, provided that the machine preceeds the act itself. Lyotard best phrases the human implications: "the system seems to be a vanguard machine dragging humanity after it, dehumanizing it in order to rehumanize it at a different level of normative capacity" (*Postmodern Condition* 63).

The unique power of TV and the project of Reaganism to confer this new kind of postmodern "reality" on an event is well understood by George Bush who after his vice-presidential TV debate with Geraldine Ferraro told a reporter inquiring about certain mistakes in his presentation, "You can say anything you want in a debate and 80 million people will hear it. If reporters then document that a candidate spoke untruthfully, so what? Maybe 200 people will read it, or 2,000, or 20,000. So what?" What Bush understands is that TV has attained the status of public ritual in the United States, largely because of its pervasiveness, but more importantly because of its style of realism. Television, according to John O'Neill in "Televideo Ergo Sum," universalizes personal experience and creates "a phenomenology of everyday life that is largely a spectacle of things" (226). Anyone who reads in a newspaper about the untruths Bush mentions cannot help associating the revelation with some particular editorial writer, a Jack Anderson or James Reston who along with Bush is referred to by the words themselves printed on the page. Reality thus mediated is suspect and secondary. TV images on the other hand are *hyperreal*, leaving an impression that belongs uniquely to the viewer, as if she were viewing events in and of themselves by direct sensory grasp without mediation or the filter of a reporter. Through TV, the individual experiences the mystery of the real—like the

Challenger making its great "**Y**" of white smoke against the blue deep sky, the mystery of the thing itself—"*why.*" We are all witnesses and the scene will be imprinted forever on the imaginations of nearly every American.

So accustomed are we to the hyperreal that it seems perfectly natural to interpret—that is to see first—the merely real Tom Selleck as the hyperreal Magnum, P.I. Actors and actresses frequently complain that they cannot rid themselves of the image they acquired in their first starring TV role. The Andy Griffith of public consciousness will always be the sheriff of Mayberry, in spite of whatever else he does. No one's sense of reality is offended by Marcus Welby (can I even say Robert Young) giving advice on caffeine consumption. That television is now the primary arbiter of what is taken as real in America can be judged by the fact that no social movement can be taken seriously or hope to succeed until it has been on television, until it has had a media-event.

I disagree sharply with popular critics of TV who argue that television watching induces passivity. In fact, the opposite is true. Television succeeds because it empowers viewers; as Kroker concludes, TV is finally Nietzsche's *Will to Power*. Because the viewer is the only omniscient intellect in the ritual, television provides viewers with a simulacrum of mastery—the final desire of the Western mind. Television privileges the viewer's perspective and therefore simulates mastery in three essential ways—which may account for why television watching can be so satisfying and even addictive. Typical television editing structures the narrative in a series of anecdotes or vignettes, all of which are known only to the viewer and thereby give him a knowledge of the workings of the plot that no one in the program itself even has. Today, the "deus ex machina" is the viewer himself.

In addition, it is quite common for fictional characters to step out of the context of their particular series to speak directly to the viewer about an upcoming special or as in the case of *Moon Lighting* make critical comments on the show itself and how the actors played their parts. We often see TV heroes entering our own lives by telling us not to use cocaine, drink and drive, or to buy a certain brand of soft drink, wine cooler, and vote because its our right to do so. The televisual world is further realized when characters from real life move into the sphere of fiction, as when

Lee Iacocca, Mayor Koch, or G. Gordon Liddy take roles in *Miami Vice* or when fictional characters discuss contemporary events and even comment on or watch other TV programs. The viewer's sense of omniscience is further enhanced because he knows a great deal more about the characters than even their on-screen counterparts do. We see characters like Hunter, Tubbs, Torello, Addison, and so on when they are alone and we know what the insides of their apartments look like, what food or drink they prefer, and how they relieve stresses and frustrations when no one else on the show is looking.

The eye of the TV viewer penetrates into the private tragedies of real people on the local news or in a Barbara Walter's interview with the same relentless privilege that exposes the normally hidden workings of corporate headquarters, police departments, criminal investigations, hospitals, courtrooms; the decision making processes of presidents, dictators, terrorists, murderers, and criminals of all sorts; the social relations between employer and employees, between the sexes, the races, lovers, and competitors.

The extension of the fictional world into the everyday world and the opposite extension does not demarcate the boundaries of the two but rather erases such boundaries, and further privileges viewers who now know Magnum, P.I. or Sonny Crockett in an even deeper and broader way than before. This ability to extend itself into the everyday world gives television a myth making power that goes far beyond anything possible for other media, even film, because TV's mythological status is constantly erased in the viewer's mind. Dominant social values or myths, which television dramatizes almost without exception, become real when they appear inevitable and natural, that is, when the fictionality becomes invisible and whatever is social, cultural, or ideological becomes historical, natural, and true (see O'Neill). Although many commentators joke about the Reagan presidency's adoption of the televisual style, it seems that the strategy is precisely to allow individuals to view Reagan as if he were a TV show and thus participate in all of the privileged mastery that TV simulates. The real Reagan is the simulated Reagan—that is what we are privileged to know.

Now few, if any, viewers are ever unaware that TV is fiction, although the just cited example of Marcus Welby would advise caution. The importation of particular characters into one's everyday life may only represent the fantasy of knowing intimately someone important and powerful, and as McIlwraith and Schallow have shown people's fantasies gradually do come to be built up of material taken from TV ("Adult Fantasy Life" 80-82). But even this fantasizing is the *will to power.* The social function of myth or public ritual is always to privilege participants; those who participate possess insights, understandings, or tokens of value simply not available to non-participants. This insight is a knowledge of the fundamental ways in which this society works and the fundamental norms, values, and principles which order the lives of people and the relations of states. And this is finally, as Michel Foucault shows in *Discipline and Punish* the power to discipline. Panopticism turns the prison outward and generalizes or totalizes the disciplinary society: "On the whole, therefore, one can speak of the formation of a disciplinary society in this movement that stretches from the enclosed disciplines, a sort of social 'quarantine,' to an indefinitely generalizable mechanism of 'panopticism'" (216). TV places every viewer in the Panopticon: "a machine for dissociating the see/being seen dyad: in the peripheric ring, one is totally seen, without ever seeing; in the central tower [the panopticon itself], one sees everything without ever being seen" (202).

The principles of TV narrative construction taken together with the disciplinary function of panopticism reconstruct history; this time placing it in what Foucault describes as a prison:

> This enclosed, segmented space, observed at every point, in which the individuals are inserted in a fixed place, in which the slighest movements are supervised, in which all events are recorded, in which an uninterrupted work of writing links to the centre and periphery, in which power is exercised without division, according to a continuous hierarchical figure, in which each individual is constantly located, examined and distributed among the living beings, the sick and the dead— all this constitutes a compact model of the disciplinary mechanism. (197)

Such confinement involves unspeakable levels of generalized violence against others, as we see in the highly charged and tense plots of TV crime drama and soap operas. The insertion and distribution of individuals in their assigned places is symbolized every night when Magnum, Sonny Crockett, Hunter, Mike Torello, and others finally after nearly an hour of suspense apprehend or kill the criminals they sought. This killing of the criminal resolves the plot and relieves the viewer of the terrible tension of the middle of the drama. The relieving of that tension and the return of sadistic pleasure in violence against others legitimizes the act that produces it, the almost always violent killing of the antagonist. While the viewer feels pleasure in the relief of his tension, he also participates in the violence and learns something else about the workings of society. As George Gerbner and Larry Gross write,

> We do not believe that the only critical correlate of television violence is to be found in the stimulation of occasional individual aggression. . . . Preparation for large scale organized violence [by government, corporations, and class factions] requires the cultivation of fear and acquiescence to power. TV violence is a dramatic demonstration of power which communicates much about social norms and relationships, about goals and means, about winners and losers, about risks of life and the price for transgressions of society's rules. Violence laden drama shows who gets away with what, when, why, how and against whom. Real world violents may have to learn their roles. Fear—that historic instrument of social control—may be an even more critical residue of a show of violence than aggression (178).

The intertext of television and the political agenda under Reagan is a consciousness of a world that must be increasingly policed and of a world in which conflict and dominance are the origin of human relations and the pre-conditions of order. This is a world that the neo-conservatives of the 1980s would like to govern and will be permitted to govern once the general population has been terrorized and re-humanized into a different world constructed after the determinants of TV narrative. Reaganism does not propose to change people in the way liberal democrats have always sought to, but, rather, it leaves them their own power, privileging their perspective on a different simulated world, thus making everyone the police and knowing that through such implication in violence they will change themselves to fit that world. Foucault writes, "It had to be like a faceless gaze that transformed the whole social body into a field of perception: thousands of eyes posted everywhere, mobile attentions ever on the alert" (214), and, we might add, ever ready to punish the enemies of the police—that is, the enemies of themselves and soon even themselves as victims of universal policing.

The real hero, therefore, of an episode of *Heart of the City* in which a drug dealer is surrounded by two dozen policemen armed with handguns, shotguns, and M-16s and is told very clearly that "You have the right to remain silent, you have the right to an attorney—and you could try to make a break for it" is viewer himself standing in the place of Attorney General Edwin Meese who told interviewers from *U.S. News and World Report* that the 1966 Supreme Court decision in Miranda *vs* Arizona is wrong and infamous: "Suspects who are innocent of crime should [be given Miranda warnings]. But the thing is, you don't have many suspects who are innocent of a crime. That's contradictory. If a person is innocent of a crime, then he's not a suspect"(8 October 1985). Similarly, the real hero of *Miami Vice* is the DEA, the Drug Enforcement Agency now aligning itself with the military and national security forces (CIA and NSC) to bring order to drug production in the Third World in the way that Crockett and Tubbs have for the simulated Miami.

References:

Agee, Philip. *White Paper Whitewash: Interviews with Philip Agee on the CIA and El Salvador.* New York: Deep Cover Books, 1981.

Baudrillard, Jean. *Simulations.* Trans. Paul Foss, Paul Patton and Philip Beitchman. New York: Semiotext(e), 1983.

Bluestone, Barry and Bennet Harrison. *The Deindustrialization of America.* New York: Basic Books, 1982.

Bové, Paul. "The Ineluctability of Difference: Scientific Pluralism and the Critical Intelligence." *Postmodernism and Politics.* Ed. Jonathan Arac. Minneapolis: University of Minnesota Press, 1986. 3-25.

A Christic Institute Special Report: The Contra-Drug Connection. Washington, DC: The Christic Institute, November 1987.

Combs, Maxwell and Donald Shaw. "Structuring the Unseen Environment." *Journal of Communication* 26 (Spring 1976): 18-35.

Fisher, Walter R. "The Narrative Paradigm: In the Beginning." *Journal of Communication* 35 (Autumn 1985): 74-89.

Foucault, Michel. *Discipline and Punish: The Birth of the Prison.* Trans. Alan Sheridan. New York: Random House, 1979.

Gerbner, George and Larry Gross. "Living with Television: The Violence Profile." *Journal of Communication* 26 (Spring 1976): 173-199.

Habermas, Jürgen. *Legitimation Crisis.* Trans. Thomas McCarthy. Boston: Beacon Press, 1975.

Horkheimer, Max and Theodor Adorno. *The Dialectic of Modernism.* Trans. John Cumming. London: Allen Lane, 1973.

Jameson, Fredric. "Interview" *Diacritics* 12 (Fall 1982): 72-91.

_____. *The Political Unconscious: Narrative as Socially Symbolic Act.* Ithaca: Cornell University Press, 1981.

Kwitney, Jonathan. *Endless Enemies: The Making of an Unfriendly World.* New York: Cogdon and Weed, 1984.

Lyotard, Jean-François. *The Postmodern Condition: A Report on Knowledge.* Minneapolis: University of Minnesota Press, 1984.

_____. "Rules, Paradoxes, and Svelte Appendix." *Cultural Critique* 5 (Winter 1986-87): 209-219.

Knapp, Stephen and Walter Ben Michaels. "Against Theory" *Against Theory: Literary Studies and the New Pragmatism.* Ed. W. J. T. Mitchell. Chicago: University of Chicago Press, 1985. 11-30.

Kroker, Arthur and David Cook. *The Postmodern Scene.* New York: St. Martin's Press, 1986.

McIlwraith, Robert D. and John R. Schallow. "Adult Fantasy Life and Patterns in Media Use." *Journal of Communication* 33 (Winter 1983): 78-91.

McGee, Michael Calvin and John S. Nelson. "Narrative Reason in Public Argument." *Journal of Communication* 35 (Autumn 1985): 139-155.

O'Hara, Daniel T. "Revisionary Madness: The Prospects of American Literary Theory at the Present Time." *Against Theory.* Ed. W. J. T. Mitchell. Chicago: University of Chicago Press. 31-47.

O'Neill, John. "Televideo Ergo Sum: Some Hypotheses on the Specular Functions of the Media" *Communication* 7 (1983): 221-240.

Revel, Jean-François. *How Democracies Perish.* Trans. William Byron. Garden City, NY: Doubleday, 1984.

Schnudson, M. "The Politics of Narrative Forms: The Emergence of News Conventions in Print and Television." *Daedalus* 3 (1982): 97-110.

Stockman, David. *The Triumph of Politics: How the Reagan Revolution Failed.* New York: Harper and Row, 1986.

Postmodern as Post-Nuclear : Landscape as Nuclear Grid

> "The whole incredible problem begins with the need to reinsert those events of 6 August 1945 back into living consciousness."
> —John Berger, "Hiroshima," *The Sense of Sight*, 287

> "Since Copernicus man has been rolling from the center toward X."
> —Friedrich Nietzsche, *The Will to Power*, 8

Rob Wilson,
University of Hawaii

I. The Sublime Scenario at Alamagordo

When Brigadier General Thomas Farrell groped to describe (in an official government report) the subjective effect of the first atomic explosion at Alamagordo, New Mexico, at 5:29:50 *am* on July 16, 1945, he found himself, like many a would-be writer of the sublime before him, at a loss for adequate terms and tropes— stupefied, dwarfed, reaching for hyperbolic endterms like "doomsday" and "blasphemous" and resorting to spaced-out adjectives such as "tremendous" and "awesome" that nineteenth-century Americans had reserved for more manageable spectacles of God's grandeur such as Niagara Falls or the Grand Canyon. As Farrell registered this history-shattering event, he struggled to produce some rhetoric of ultimacy before nuclear "effects [that] could well be called unprecedented, magnificent, beautiful,

• 169

stupendous and terrifying":

> No man-made phenomenon of such tremendous power had
> ever occurred before. The lighting effects beggared description.
> The whole country was lighted by a searing light with the
> intensity many times that of the midday sun. It was golden,
> purple, violet, gray and blue. It lighted every peak, crevasse,
> and mountain range with a clarity and beauty that cannot be
> described but must be seen to be imagined. It was the beauty
> the great poets dream about but describe most poorly and
> inadequately. Thirty seconds after the explosion came, first
> the air blast pressing hard against people and things, to be
> followed almost immediately by the strong, sustained
> awesome roar which warned of doomsday and made us feel
> that we puny things were blasphemous to dare tamper with
> the forces heretofore reserved to The Almighty. Words are
> inadequate tools for the job of acquainting those not present
> with the physical, mental, and psychological effects. It had to
> be witnessed to be realized. (Barash 64)

Farrell's firsthand experience of figurative inadequacy and
inexpressibility comes about because a terrifying abyss has
suddenly opened between cognition (the language of the self) and
its corresponding object (nature as nuclear force). In aesthetic
terms, this widening gap between man's strongest language and
the death inducing forces of nature was what Longinus and myriad
neo-Romantic critics after him had privileged as the rapture
(*hypsous*) of the sublime. This sublime force of energy released,
in numinous dread, is what Farrell here mislabels the "beauty the
great poets dream about but describe most poorly and
inadequately." Indeed such a scenario of sublime confrontation had
been used by a host of writers (in various genres) to induce—
symbolically, not materially—the death of the ordinary self that,
paradoxically, would awaken a language of passionate elevation
that went on speaking beyond the grave, in literature's *"great time,"*
as exalted textuality (Bakhtin 4). The Grand Chartreuse, as Thomas
Gray's sensitive tourist-self put it in 1739, "would awe an atheist
into belief" and even the most city-weary soul into "religion and
poetry" (Monk 211).

As a classical rhetorician blithely grounding transformations
of language in exalted states of *sublime transport*, Longinus had

located this boundary-shattering, yet art-stimulating experience of the sublime in certain confusing absorptions of the self into the wordless godhead; the self became empowered not so much through dynamical forces of nature (those vast spectacles of energy such as volcanoes, oceans, and hurricanes that Longinus evokes in *On the Sublime*) as through masterworks of figurative transformation (Homer, Moses, Sappho, Plato, Demosthenes and a whole array of textual fragments) that forever alter the imagination and energize the agonistic writer's will-to-create.

Later, building upon the awkward mechanistic psychology of Edmund Burke's *Philosophical Inquiry into the Origin of Our Ideas of the Sublime and Beautiful* (1757), Immanuel Kant's *Critique of Judgment* (1790) more idealistically discriminated the category of *the sublime* from tamer formalities of *the beautiful* by propagating the idea that the sublime vouchsafed a subjective experience of the highest order that, both fearful and awe-inspiring, allowed the rational ego to confront representations of annihilation yet manage to overcome all blockages, obstacles, and form-shattering anxieties of this material otherness through an affirmation of the mind's *a priori* moral grandeur. Nature need not threaten the mind with its spectacles of material violence because the human imagination was always already beyond this force, and need only affirm its own centrifugal, supersensory grandeur.

After Kant's transcendental underwriting of the sublime experience, the *natural sublime*, whether materialized as a volcano, Alpine mountains or Niagara Falls could serve only as some vast staging ground for the soul's emerging recognition of both its moral infinitude and its exalted vocation on earth. Through the sublime landscapes of nature or of art, then, the imagination of the poet came to recognize the cognitive immensity of a transcendental subject forever free and ungrounded in nature, however immense, deadly, or anxiety-inducing. That is to say, the sublime object (whether confronted as nature, as an imagination-affirming text such as Wordsworth's *Prelude*, or later as a work of technology like Whitman's "Locomotive in Winter" or Hart Crane's Brooklyn Bridge) functioned to provide only a finite, secondary landscape out of which the poet could disclose to himself, in a scenario of blockages confronted and terrors overcome, the soul's primary vocation to contemplate its own moral infinitude. The ego remained autonomous, however, in its power to interpret, represent, transcend.

Confronting the sublime landscape of the atomic bomb, then, General Farrell's euphoric emptiness before the first nuclear blast remains—not so easily—grounded in the *telos* of Christian piety, as he fends for American ideology by asserting a moralizing stance to the atomic godhead, which is well in keeping with an all-too-unconscious Kantian scenario of transcendence. Moving perilously beyond the nihilism disclosed by such atomic weapons, Farrell creates his homemade version of the sublime, with what I take to be characteristic *ambivalence*, by reading nuclear power at Alamagordo as at once a Faust-like sign of man's historical depravity and yet of God's form annihilating infinitude unveiling some quasi-apocalyptic purpose in history.

Such "Dynamical Force," to invoke Kant's term for the self-dwarfing and self-transfiguring energies released in the material sublime, can only be sacralized in the spooky deserts of the Manhattan Project through such a self-centered, moralizing interpretation, as Farrell goes on to read the bomb as some kind of (reified) hero about to intervene in the eradication of Nazism and global fascism, starting at Hiroshima. (Needless to say, from a less cheerful Nietzschean perspective on such a will-to-interpret, the bomb could be moralized to fit other purposes, values, powers, and *ends*—bad pun intended.)

General Farrell's description of "the beauty the great poets dream about but describe most poorly and inadequately" that was unleashed in all atomic grandeur by the explosion at Alamagordo will be articulated in this essay as the self-decentering experience of a *nuclear sublime*, impossible to recuperate or evade (see Ferguson, "The Nuclear Sublime"). I will read this by-now-global sublimity as one large-scale consequence of approaching nature through the mandates of technocratic reason and the "value-neutral" imperatives of science, that is, as a sublime generated out of our collective will-to-power over nature and others. Because, whether we will or no, this nuclear effect remains our *postmodern sublime*, an exhilaratingly nihilistic effect of global terror ("deterrence": policies emanating "from terror") daily induced by some eclectric mix of nature and technology that decenters (if not abolishes) the pious subject in his/her power to represent the underlying purpose (*telos*) of such impressive grandeur—the "dynamical force" of Hiroshima.

Though I would like to agree with the popular t-shirt that proclaims **END NUCLEAR TERROR** by anxiously re-situating Edward Munch's tormented screamer of World War I in front of a nuclear cloud, this First World politics of terror will not end until we can (genealogically) imagine the bomb in all its horrific materiality and symbolicity, invoking this specular image of the *nuclear sublime* as a way of keeping more Hiroshimas from happening. As James Hillman (deconstructively) avows in a nuclear symposium, *Facing Apocalypse*: "The translation of bomb into the imagination is a transubstantiation of God to *imago dei*, deliteralizing the ultimate God term from positivism to negative theology, a God that is all images. . . . The task of nuclear psychology is a ritual-like devotion to the bomb as image, never letting it slip from its pillar of cloud in the heaven of imagination to rain ruin on the cities of the plain" (134-135). For if, as social psychologist Robert Jay Lifton has argued about survivors of Hiroshima, the bomb threatens the self with "desymbolization" and a schizoid-like dislocation within history, then we have to represent and re-symbolize the bomb, confront its sublime aura in order to desacralize the force and mystique of technology it entails (*Facing Apocalypse* 42-47).

Whatever General Farrell's firsthand misgivings at Alamagordo, we all now live under the shadow of this nuclear bomb. What he termed the "mental and psychological effects" of this dynamical sublimity—*both positive and negative*—now pervade an American culture that henceforth I will call *postmodern*, meaning here a Cold War framework, *post-nuclear*, *post-Hiroshima*; that is, after the effects of this technological sublime have made their way into the remote recesses of the most transcendental and nature-loving subject.

The mother scowls as she mops up the baby's spilled milk, and turns to the newspaper-reading father: "You may think of this as the nuclear age, but to me it's the paper towel age" ("Family Circus" by Bill Keane, *Honolulu Advertiser*, 23 December 1986). As domestic beings, of course, we all abide within such humble tensions and conflicts, homemade battles that task our motherly love and wit. Yet cartoons of history aside, ours remains the "nuclear age" and there is no repressing this Cold War fact; entailing a technological threat on the horizon, this bigger-than-domestic terror hangs over the daily dramas of the "Family Circus." For the "nuclear family" that Bill Keane depicts so charmingly each day does occur within a "nuclear age," and some of these larger tensions and global uncertainties of deterrence pressure it with cosmic anxieties that I will further map as instances of the *nuclear sublime.*

If we must abide within this repressive nuclear terror in order to live within more manageable confines of domestic routines and organic nature (such comforting sites as the "nuclear family" or the pastoral countryside of long ago—see Terrence Des Pres 9), I would summon up the nuclear sublime from the "political unconscious": a new "landscape" allowing the lofty Kantian—or, as in American terms, Emersonian—subject of moral idealism and sublime grandeur no place to hide, no room in which to transcend the material majesty of technology disclosed at Alamagordo. Even amid the natural loveliness of a place such as Hawaii, we all live as frail spots on this landscape-as-nuclear-grid, all of nature placed "in brackets" by majestic works of technology such as the Soviet Union's TT-09 multiple warhead missiles now and then "'bracketing' the Islands in [a] classic artillery range-firing maneuver" (*Honolulu Advertiser*, 2 October 1987).

II. The Landscape Around Pearl Harbor

> Birch, sumac
>   before
>   the blast

—Lorine Niedecker, "Home/World," *My Life by Water* 102

As I gaze out of my condominium window from the 44th floor of the Island Colony, most days I can take in a vast horizon of the azure Pacific mixing into a cerulean sky, with green hills mauka-side over which mists and rainbows overlap, as in some spectacular play of natural infinitude. Not even the glass-and-concrete highrises of the Hilton Hawaiian, the Ilikai, or the Bishop Tower can disturb this palpable grandeur of water, sky, and valley which constitute the biosphere of Oahu and still give it the dreamy makings of a lush, tropical paradise. The sublime feels palpable here, like some original home, and I find it conducive to metaphors of belonging, even of bodily bliss.

But this perception of immense wonder grounded in nature that I have easily evoked—and which many feel daily in Honolulu as residents or as a flow of awe-struck tourists through the Likelike valleys—this sense of awesome peace and self-loss before the natural grandeur of swaying palms, gigantic waves, and triple rainbows, can come about— in 1988—only by a romantic illusion (self-defensive "hyperbole," Bloom, *Deconstruction* 16) of bliss (*sublime transport*) which perilously depends upon a repression not of Wordsworth but of the Cold War reality of Pearl Harbor. Without such a repression, "Pearl Harbor" becomes a synecdoche, invoking that elaborate stockpiling of nuclear weaponry of air and sea which, since the atom bomb first disclosed America's technological supremacy at Hiroshima, has locked Russia and the USA into an anxious dialogue of atomic terror/wonder that has dwarfed my own personal sense of political and spiritual agency since I entered this Cold War world in 1947.

To be adequate and not aesthetically evasive, our own vocabulary of sublime landscapes would have to include such nature-dwarfing masterworks of American post-war culture as the B52 or the Poseidon's Tomahawk, a warhead with a maximum yield of 250 kilotons (metaphorically, "20 Hiroshimas of nuclear force"). Now multiply this nuclear power by 13, because Pearl Harbor—as far as experts can tell—bases 13 submarines, each equipped with many Tomahawk missiles.) Or take into aesthetic cognizance the P-3 Orion patrol planes based at Barbers Point Naval Air Station that can be equipped with nuclear depth charges of up to 20 kilotons (that is, nearly two Hiroshimas.

Whether the individual ego and nature-beholden birdwatcher chooses to have it so or not, the landscape in Hawaii already exists as a nuclear grid, supporting an invisible vector of military decisions and codes paradoxically aiming to provide domestic security through generating the terror of nuclear deterrence; that is, the production of geopolitical peace through nuclear terror. As the state with the highest percentage of its real estate already devoted to military use, Hawaii (with 29 nuclear-related facilities and 345 nuclear warheads by a conservative estimate) in fact ranks only 14th in terms of nuclear weaponry concentrated within its island boundaries.

My ghoulish portrait of Hawaii as a nuclear landscape, mingling Kant's twin sublimes of dynamical force and mathematical infinitude, remains *merely* specular or "textual" in that this nuclear force cannot be adequately represented or even symbolically confronted. My portrait of Hawaii as a sublime landscape must remain speculative and representational, moreover, a mere *figure of terror*, because in the expert words of the *Honolulu Advertiser's* military reporter, Jim Borg, "Under longstanding policy, the military won't confirm or deny the presence of nuclear weapons anywhere. But it will say which ships, aircraft, and cannons are capable of nuclear firepower, and the list is long" (*Honolulu Advertiser*, 19 March 1985). To complicate this specular decoding, we daily pass more denotative signs that tell us, **RESTRICTED AREA / USE OF DEADLY FORCE AUTHORIZED.** Furthermore, as Peter Hayes has documented in *American Lake: Nuclear Peril in the Pacific* and other public contexts, the Navy has been ordered to treat nuclear accidents at sea as ones involving "conventional weapons," as if this (all-but-Nietzschean) shift in official rhetoric will make any difference to the people and ecology involved!

In order to cultivate my own poetic garden and write about plumerias and Taoist mists over Manoa, it would be better for myself, perhaps, *not* to confront or think through this unrepresentable force, not to think about the threat of such nuclear power to the beauty of the landscape or the grandeur-accumulating project of poetry. Yet from Ewa Beach to Haiku, Maui, wherever I / you look in Hawaii, the landscape can no longer remain innocent in its awe-inducing sublimity; even Haleakala Crater, for example, has been conscripted as a site for Star Wars laser-research and nuclear surveillance. Even the bodysurfing waves of Bellows Beach can function on the nuclear grid as sites of nuclear offense / defense.

More than Niagara Falls, stellar infinitude, Rocky Mountain High, or the engineering wonders of Brooklyn Bridge and the Empire State Building, the nuclear bomb has become the postmodern icon of sublimity, a seemingly final instance of what Kant called the Dynamical Sublime of immense power threatening the self with death. Henceforth, the atomic bomb can help focus for our postmodern era an array of technological achievements that paradoxically entail dwarfing effects of material exhilaration *and* decentering, that is, an experience of self-transcendence that at once incites both awe (the euphoria of power) and terror (the anxiety of evacuated agency).

Dialectically considered, the *positive* effect of the nuclear blast at Hiroshima is that it forever awakened a quasi-religious sense of nature's infinitude, releasing vast latent energies inside the atom waiting to be tapped and channeled: from the time J. Robert Oppenheimer first invoked Hindu scriptures on the bomb as Shiva-the-Destroyer ("I am become death, the shatterer of worlds"), nuclear imagery retains this quasi-religious effect as some kind of technological apocalypse, as some sublime disclosure of nature's awesome power to shatter known boundaries of ego and form.

Yet, more terrifyingly, one large-scale *negative* effect of atomic energy remains that this nuclear sublime dwarfs all sense of human agency and control, hence brings postmodern man up to some shattered limit of moral finitude and political control. The Nuclear Sublime releases an infinite energy that, Shiva-like, threatens fragile biological and human systems—*totally*. We need only picture the body melting bird-like, destroyed from far away, unconsentingly caught up in a (decentered) game of remote delivery systems and Cold War discourse. A science-fiction like anxiety lingers that, as an idealistic yet power-infatuated society, we have somehow transgressed biological/moral limits, and hence are stunned and blocked by our own technological Frankenstein. As Susan Sontag has illuminated, the displaced anxieties of nuclear dread, manifest and latent, in trash Science Fiction movies of the 50s, a "mass trauma" of depersonalization, technologization, and de-individualized death must hover over the postmodern imagination like some primal sign, generating "unassimilable terrors that infect the consciousness" (226-227).

"I've been suffering from my own private case of *acute nuclear anxiety*—not so much for myself but for the whole Hawaiian landscape, the sea and mountains which my ancestors worshipped. So I wrote these poems as a way of expressing my political fears," explained Aaron Whines, a young Hawaiian poet, before reading his poems to the University of Hawaii Peace Institute on "Nuclear

Perspectives" (19 November 1986). I take Aaron's pastoral fear and recoiling attempt to articulate a viable moral stance towards nuclear anxiety to be exemplary, and not at all that singular in postmodern America. Even the paradisiacal scenery of Honolulu cannot repress this fact of nuclear presence, of Hawaii's place in the production of nuclear deterrence: I want to flesh out this landscape-as-nuclear-grid in both *local* (Pearl Harbor) and more *global* senses (as a scenario of the sublime).

Loud, bright, deadly: we live under this nuclear sign in a steady state of Cold War terror, an anxiety barely repressed and easily heated up during political confrontations, or worse yet, accidents (KAL Flight 007 or Chernobyl, for example). Nuclear *deterrence* literally relies upon geopolitical policies of so-called "low-intensity conflict" emanating *of and from terror*, as the Latin etymology suggests (*de-terrere*). This image of global terror is irresistibly fascinating, like something ultimate, overwhelming, dwarfing even a Brigadier General to awe: the ego alone in cosmic space, spinning out its highest rhetoric, propitiating before a scientific godhead disclosed. For the nuclear sublime can be read, to invoke Brian Hallett's paradoxical terms formulated at the University of Hawaii's Peace Institute, as both a constraining image of "nuclear genocide" and of existential freedom. As even President Reagan has come to acknowledge, the post-nuclear question remains, daily, *Where do we go from here?*

III. The Example of William Carlos Williams: "The Bomb Puts an End to All That"

The massive force engendered by the technological apparatus and geopolitical formations of World War II has materialized itself since July 16, 1945 in dynamisms of sublime wonder/terror of which the nuclear explosion at Alamagordo remains a determining instance. As force and sign, the atomic bomb becomes for our postmodern era what Derrida has called a "fabulously textual" and epoch-shattering event. The bomb begets a thermonuclear *heat* that deconstructs instantly our metaphor-making "heliotropes" of poetic *light* that would claim fictive supremacy. If once massive natural formations such as Niagara Falls, mountains, stellar space, and desert landscapes could awe and terrify the ego into self-humility and belief, the site of this sublimity inducing higher credulity has quietly migrated into the mainframes of our best nuclear productions: the bomb exists as force and sign of an ongoing global intimidation.

The American poet, William Carlos Williams, expressed the claustrophobic effect of atomic power upon himself as a flower-troping poet, "The bomb puts an end to all that" (1962: 165). Shaken by the reality of technological terror when an American bomber exploded into the side of the Empire State Building, Williams wrote to James Laughlin on August 7, 1945 that he found the bomb at Hiroshima even more absolutely "mind quelling," meaning, as Paul Mariani puts it, "touching deeper even than the imagination seemed to be able to follow" (506).

Henceforth, as Williams registered in "Asphodel, That Greeny Flower" from *Journey to Love* (1955), a majestic love poem to his elderly wife, Flossie, the atom bomb at Hiroshima had forever altered postmodern consciousness of space and structure, the human conceit of erotic figurations such as "gems" and "flowers" as symbolically efficacious over the "profound depth" disclosed in this abyssmal image of technological deadliness. If the poem "seems to triumph" over the destructive depths of nature (like a dance of light upon the sea),

> The bomb puts an end
> > to all that.
> I am reminded
> > that the bomb
> > > also
> is a flower
> > dedicated
> > > howbeit
> to our destruction.   (165)

"Asphodel" represents in its triadic structure (Three Books and a hyperbolic coda affirming the redemptive power of the poet's metaphor-generating Imagination) a dialectical struggle between heat and light, force and sign—death forces struggling against the light of the poetic imagination. Confronting the "death of love" (162) in his wife as well as recurring heart strokes and the nearness of his own death, Williams raises the figurative ante in Book II of the poem by invoking the absolute image of global death (the nuclear "flower") through the destructive power ("heat") of nuclear energy, partly as a way to figure his own death as well as a way to terrify Flossie back into love's tenuous fold. If the figurative resources of the poet are commonplace (flower, garden, sea, storm, light, queen), the thermonuclear threat is new, a quantum leap into an empty trope-less future.

As a "flower" image dedicated to nothing less than global death, the bomb physically threatens *all* flowers, both natural ones (the asphodel) and rhetorical ones (woman as love's "flowers" or, later, as "flowerlike"). Though the poet speaks—as ever—in figures from the heart's elevation, this figure is no hyperbole in its threat to annihilate the texts of any ground, biological or poetic. Written during the McCarthy era when Williams was subjected to investigation as a Communist, the poem is one of the first in America by a major poet to register complexly the Cold War horizon of nuclear terror.

Taking apart death ("I have to take it apart") in a long poem that is a decreative meditation on atomic energy as much as a love-poem to his wife, "Asphodel" openly represents this struggle of "heat" and "light"—that is, of thermal heat versus figurative light, of material force versus poetic imagination: after evoking the flowers of the ground and of his wife in Book I, the oet dialectically moves from admitting in Book II that heat silences light ("the bomb speaks," 168) to affirming in the Coda that light finally overcomes heat: "the heat will not overtake the light. / That's sure. / That gelds the bomb, / permitting / that the mind contain it" (179). Yet the nagging question remains after the hyperbole of this Coda: Does poetry *geld* the bomb or is it, despite such manly figurative claims, the other way around—a death-force gelding the poet of his loftiest fictions ?

In "Asphodel" we can watch the Petrarchan rhetoric of courtly love, the elevated language of trope and abstract predication, the desperate assertions of manly potency break down, collapse, palpably expire, only to reassert their figurative claims over empty space. Written in syntactic scraps "dancing" over subatomic emptiness, the poem shoots the gap (overcoming blockages and creative anxieties) between silence and speech, death and life, emptiness and power, as the poet struggles to engage nuclear force and poetic figuration by localizing the battle in his own deathbed speech. Despite its compounding of floral hyperboles, the poem's structure is a record of inadequacy, of majestic failure, as poetic language breaks down before the images of terror and death which Williams evokes.

Light does not "geld" force, and this assertion, by an imagination strained to impotent extremity, seems desperate if not silly in the nostalgic imagery of the *Coda*. Confronting the nuclear spectacle, the poet cannot find concepts or terms which are adequate to such extremity, a force such as the one at Hiroshima which can deprive millions of a slow, individualized, domestic death such as the one Williams is affirming.

Williams intuited the psychological effect of the *nuclear sublime* as a force of energy so final in its disclosures of death inducing power that it renders the vaunted "supreme fiction[s]" of the romantic imagination hollow or piously ludicrous. The lyrical subject must confront this nuclear sublime—with mingled awe and terror—as a thermonuclear energy that cannot be bounded nor sublated by the "flowers" of metaphorical language. If "the bomb speaks" with terminal deadliness, effacing the subject and its grand textual traces, poetry must hereafter confront a nothingness that is more than just a post-Nietzschean trope for philosophical nihilism: for writers confronting such nuclear force, as social historian Paul Boyer captures the American literary expression of the bomb from 1945-1950, using the catchphrase of sublime inexpressibility—"words fail" (*By the Bomb's Early Light* 243-256).

"*The bomb speaks*" (Boyer 168), while poetry is quieted, in that atomic power forever empties the time-honored claim of figurative language to transfigure / transcend death through symbolic proliferations of tropes as eternal "flowers," New Jersey asphodels of archetypal loveliness that will bloom even in hell. Williams saw that the atom bomb at Hiroshima had released a force of infinitude forever latent in nature, dwarfing the subject with "its childlike / insistence" of death's presence. Deconstructing molecular "limits that prove to be liminal" (Hartman 150), nuclear fission had unleashed a deadly force that brought the mind up to the *limin* (threshold) of any form as such, devastating the substance of things, rendering earth objects unstable and resonant with subatomic emptiness. The nuclear bomb is no "flower" of loveliness, and Williams's (deconstructive) trope knows it. As George Oppen frontally represents the totality of nuclear threat in "Time of the Missile" from *The Materials* (1962):

> My love, my love,
> We are endangered
> Totally at last. Look
> Anywhere to the sight's limit: space
> Which is viviparous:
>
> Place of the mind
> And eye. Which can destroy us,
> Re-arrange itself, assert
> Its own stone chain reaction.   (49)

Oppen sees that the whole poetic archive is endangered by a force of deadliness so great it signifies this totality of biological / textual closure: or as Williams put it in an earlier draft, "All poems stem from / the Iliad as all life ends / in the Bomb. Repeat it!" (Riddel quoting from the Yale MS of "Asphodel" 184). In the broken winter of 1953, even a little dog injured in the street could evoke for Williams the imminence of his own death and—more shockingly—of the earth, in some irrational association he could not repress: "It is myself, / not the poor beast lying there / yelping with pain / that brings me to myself with a start— / as at the explosion / of a bomb, a bomb that has laid / all the world waste" ("To a Dog injured in the Street" 86).

For the bomb all too literally puts an end to *all that*, those hyperboles of the symbol / image: eternalizing tropes of love as "flower" and "sun" and "gem" and so forth, the enduring Renaissance metaphors based in "light" which oddly proliferate in this late poem, as if a force of fictive language circulating to ward off nuclear "heat" and the death of his wife, if not of the flower-ridden earth. James Breslin describes the poem's peculiarly conventional style: "Formality, ritual, decorum—all these were values that the younger Williams had heaped contempt on. Now, that crude fight is over" (232). In his *Autobiography* (1951), Williams had anachronistically declaimed of Eliot's textual effect in *The Waste Land*: "It wiped out our world as if an atom bomb had been dropped upon it and our brave sallies into the unknown were turned to dust" (174). Now the bomb could physically waste all that, from dogs to majestic epics to the tenderest old lovers. As "Asphodel" shows, the atom bomb had instantly turned *all* modernist figurations of the unknown, whether "rooted in the locality which should give it fruit" (as in *Paterson*) or in some world archive of intertextual sources (as in *The Four Quartets*), into languageless dust: "The bomb puts an end to all that." If the poet speaks in figures to defeat time and death (159), his loftiest words fail to defeat this "flower" of death, this atomic emptiness quietly sublating known tactics of self-preservation.

As Williams sees, the only stance in such collective extremity is to affirm not only domestic particulars, but the whole poetic project as figuring forth imaginative light and a trope of love (the asphodel) that might endure even in hell, even through nuclear fires. Taking apart death in a way the atom was already taken apart, Williams affirms the radium of his own terms by asserting that the light of imagination abides over death: "Only the imagination is real! / I have declared it / time without end." Yet this (highly Kantian) assertion or imaginative autonomy is a desperate one, the metaphors trite and chauvinistic, as if we have to accept the whole program on faith. The voice grows increasingly impotent, as his poetic devices are used up, emptied of their efficacy in some new, unmapped hyperspace of subatomic emptiness which the poem's space-laden form mimes. Veracity is not enough; the flower of the bomb still speaks of a destructiveness which the human imagination has wrought, just as his betrayals of Flossie in the interest of producing more poems (flowers) has brought him to a deadly impasse, where the light of her conjugal love has gone out. Yet the homey parallel breaks down: How can mutual forgiveness be a cure for Cold War superpowers, as they attempt to control the nuclear power they have released?

Ironically asserting the supremacy of poetic fictions in *Paterson* over his beloved locale of time and death, Williams shocked his audience in 1951 when he evoked the nuclear threat to textual grandeur: "The very inner casings of Egyptian sarcophagi, made of paper sheets, are ungummed in the improbable hope that a shred of papyrus found there may contain even a few words from a poem by Sappho. If England is destroyed by Russian bombs it will hardly be a matter of importance to history so long as the works of Shakespeare be not lost" (Mariani 699). Now nuclear fire threatens humanist monuments (Eliot's "ideal order" of literature) with tracelessness, an abolition of the past and future more sweeping even than the natural one Stevens depicted while reading paragraphs on the sublime by the fires of Vesuvius: "The total past felt nothing when destroyed" (*Palm* 252).

Once envisioned as "the metapoem of *Paterson*, Books One-Four" (Riddel 200) but later separated off as an autonomous poem addressed to Flossie, "Asphodel" can indeed be read as a "coda" to William's whole poetic project, as he tries in a final fictive seeing (like Stevens' "The Rock") to ward off the forces of death—personal, mutual, textual, global—with the figurative resources which his new American idiom had made available over the course of some 40 years. If he cannot outtalk nuclear death, he can at least persuade Flossie, through an accrual of poetic figures, to forgive him unto death (which he does: "You have forgiven me / making me new again" 177). A measure invented partly in response to the discovery of radium and the spaces of the atom, the empty-seeming triadic stanza pattern taken over from the "descent beckons" passage in *Paterson* II of 1947 (Breslin 224) is invoked one last time to dance over radical emptiness, to spread flowers ("poems flowers") over the nuclear grave, to speak in loving figures and innovative measures which would overcome death through love, yet acknowledging:

The end

    will come

        in its time. (165)

With his peculiar brand of gallows humor, Bob Hope uncannily joked on a Valentine's Day radio show in 1946 that even the floral poetry of Hallmark greeting cards would never be the same after Hiroshima: "Have you noticed the modern trend in verses this year? No more of this 'Roses are red, violets are blue.' I picked up one and it showed an atom bomb exploding, and under it a verse that read: 'Will you be my little geranium, until we are both blown up by uranium?'" (Boyer 21). "Asphodel" more complexly registers this same nuclear effect on the flower-tropes of the poet and upon the spring flowers of his beloved earth. Nevertheless, fascinated to figurative blockage by this image from *Life* of the atomic bomb as a "mere picture" of death which threatens to annihilate loving subjects such as Doctor Williams and his embittered wife, "we cannot wait / to prostrate ourselves before it" into the technological worship of what Williams depicts as a mechanical death-god, the massively destructive energy which the American World War II project had unleashed, rather than "desert music," at test sites in New Mexico.

As a document kindred to General Farrell's transcendental conjectures, J. Robert Oppenheimer's personal scenario of mingled awe/terror before the explosion of the first atom bomb in New Mexico on July 16, 1945, can also serve as a postmodern text of nuclear sublimity, recording a subjective trace of infrared energy, wherein the ego gets absorbed (raptured) into a nuclear godhead that is domesticated by evoking transcendental scriptures of god-the-destroyer (*Shiva*): "Like the others [on the Manhattan Project], Oppenheimer was stunned by the sheer magnitude of the blast. A passage from the Hindu scripture came to his mind as the mushroom cloud [code-named "Trinity"] rose up toward the heavens: 'I am become death, shatterer of worlds'" (*Ground Zero* 29 ; Giovannitti and Freed 197).

As in the Kantian scenario of ambivalence disclosed by the natural sublime, if such a spectacle of cosmic force *attracts* the dwarfed subject in its magnitude and instant release of the latent infinitude of nature, it also *repulses* as the material agent of pain and death on an unprecedented scale, a new vastness defying the body's measurement, by ton or heat gradient or ethical norm. Not surprisingly, in Ai's recent dramatic monologue in *Sin*, Oppenheimer becomes another in a cast of nature-subduing American visionaries, in love with the spiritual annihilation of his bodily ego, now done on a global scale: "We tear ourselves down atom by atom, / till electron and positron, / we become our own transcendent annihilation" (67).

Byproduct of technological ingenuity and "a kind of / hard-headed pragmatism standing in the empty spaces" (Perelman

"Person" 51), the atomic bomb had originated in American *fear*, of the Germans and Japanese and later of the Russians, as the militant tool if not of death than of an incapacitating truce founded in *deterrence*, lifelong intimidation. As the "new Cold War" discourse of the Reagan administration has made spectacularly clear, as in some specular mirror os Superposer semiotics, the Nuclear arsenal still exists as force—and sign— to induce fear ("intimidation") in the Russians as well as in ourselves, or, as Derrida argues, as massive "missive / missiles" sending global signs that we can eradicate the literary-juridical archive, instantly and forever.

IV. Postmodern as Post-Nuclear

Confronting dialectical images in poems like "Asphodel" and "The Rock"in their hyper-rhetorical confrontations to overcome some disfigured ground of *nothingness* (see J. Hillis Miller for a merely textual reading of this Stevensian abyss), I would read "postmodernism" as a periodizing figure for post-nuclear: the poetry that comes after the fire or that must face the annihilation of the vaunted literary archive, or that must face not only the thermal death of the subject but the death of the earth and its supreme fictions. The bomb puts an end to Stevens' claim to fictive supremacy in a void-dancing poem from 1952: "There it was, word for word / The poem that took the place of a mountain. / He breathed its oxygen, / Even when the book lay turned in the dust of his table" (*Palm* 374). Threatening the earth and its subjects with biological closure and thermonuclear death, the bomb put an end (or at least destabilized) certain ontological claims of High Modernism to presencng in the image, or in its high-minded Stevensian assertion, for one, of poetry as a "supreme fiction" or "idea of order" transfiguring the existential ground of *nothingness* with textual "icons" and "leaves" (as in "The Rock" of 1950) that will last forever—generating that textual infinitude dear to Yale critics of "New senses in the engenderings of sense."

As Fredric Jameson argues in "Periodizing the 60s," while outlining the framework of a Euro-American *postmodernism* whose widely dispersed hallmarks are the death of the subject, the proliferation of an image-culture of the simulacrum ("trompe-l'oeil copies *without originals*") as in the mock-heroic posters of Andy Warhol, an increased play of the signifier and of a foregrounded textuality liberated from any referential pretence to some ontological ground of sacredness as in the Language Poets, pop or mixed genres wherein parodic collage and mixed tones collide as in the "neo-vernacular" style of Venturi's Las Vegasism, a seeming delight in structural overdeterminations such as Foucault's discourse models, the loss of depth-interpretation and essentialism in philosophy if not in psychology, the parasitical attack of the later upon the temporally prior as in Bloom: "postmodernism emerges as a way of making creative space for artists now oppressed by those henceforth hegemonic modernist categories of irony, complexity, ambiguity, dense temporality, and particularly, aesthetic and utopian monumentality" (195).

Hence, "post-modern" needs to be read as a dialectical category, a way for writers to undo, if not to surpass, in diverse cultural genres the canonical traits of High Seriousness and the "Heroic and Original" style of Modernism, within some "Ugly and Ordinary" style of Postmodernism, as in Kenneth Koch's highly irreverent parodies of his American masters, Frost and Williams, or the junk-art flux of Frank O'Hara's *Lunch Poems*. Isn't this a "post-nuclear" effect, furthermore, a semiotic disturbance registered in the semi-autonomous realm of high culture; that is, as Williams depicts in the politically sensitive language of "Asphodel," poetry troping itself wildly, ever more richly and desperately as a way of warding off not so much personal but global death? The ground of nature has been taken away; not even the fences and plastic sheets of Christo, with his parodic megabucks and hightech projects, can surround and capture its desacralized being.

Considering the nuclear horizon of 1945-1985, I would read the pervasive nihilism against which such art desperately tropes, its deliberate undermining of claims to subjective expressivity and eternal high-seriousness, as less a personal choice and more the period effect of nuclear terror, the material effect of infrastructural determinations now registered in multi-megatons and megabucks. Post-modernism does not just come *after* but comes *against* the reified conventions of modernism which defines it as parasite and child, as "Joker and Thief" of its own ensconsed sublimity.

Confronting anti-nihilistic poems like "Asphodel" (1955) and "The Rock" (1950), we need to would interrogate American postmodernism not just formally but socially as a periodizing figure for *post-nuclear*: as the poetry that comes after the terror/wonder of nuclear fire, that must face the annihilation of the vaunted intertextual archive, that must figure in unconsciously not only the thermal death of the subject but the death of nature in what Jameson has termed, somewhat dismissively, our "hysterical sublime" under Capital ("Baudelaire as Modernist and Postmodernist," 1985).

V. For and Against the Nuclear Sublime (For / Against)

My present-day hope is that if we can move towards conceptualizing (representing) the *nuclear sublime* of global technology in language, we can have some dialogical effect—however slight, mediated, rarefied at a symbolic level—upon the collective move towards the nuclear sublime as a death-inducing force. Because if the nuclear sublime happens as history, as some Hiroshima-squared, there will be no need to imagine or conceive: the nuclear sublime *will have been* an accurate hypothesis of sublimity evacuating its own consequences—in a rapture all too material and impure.

Similarly ambivalent, for example, Henry Moore's statue of a skull rising out of Fermi's pile at the University of Chicago creates an atomic icon that aptly mingles positive and negative senses: something rounded, brain-like, polished, scientific; something rough, crude, skull-like, tribal. Moore's image is compellingly *oxymoronic* as a cultural text of the postmodern; his atomic skull contains both positive and negative charges, his own split feelings of horror and awe at this work of contemporary science / art so unlike his typically lounging maternal bodies.

The irony of sublime discourse is that this proud speaking subject of the Humanities (Moore, Williams, myself, you) will not have foreclosed the technological threat of the "new science," or the "new age," through evoking nuclear images of terror and wonder, the progressive move towards semiotic evacuation, the death of symbol-systems however eternal and grand (the epic tradition, for example, or computer libraries, corporate law, etc.). All we can do, will have done, is (like the giddy poet in Robert Pinsky's "Figured Wheel") to imagine nuclear prayer wheels annihilating, in some chain-reaction unleashed to infinitude, the majestic stuff of egos, insects, and languages.

For, as postmodern painters tacitly admit, nuclear power remains unrepresentable except in its grotesque consequences: deformed bodies, parts flying off, funereal blacks and bloods, warped shapes, piles of skulls and carrion birds (even that is too hopeful). John Hersey's *Hiroshima* (1946) remains an analogous narrative instance, as the mysteriously noiseless and sun-like bomb can only be represented in its carnage and gruesome aftermath, in a style of degree-zero neutrality, as six viewpoints struggle to survive as individuals amid mass trauma and mass death.

Postmodernism needs to be mapped, in all its deconstructive glory, as cultural labor forever disturbed by nuclear terror: an evacuation of humanism, an emptiness in response to the nuclear explosion. This effect works its way into culture not so much as theme and content, but as empty form, altering the very modes of perception as a nuclear after-effect. So it is that William Carlos Williams stages the power of the poetic imagination (affirming "the asphodel" that lives beyond the nuclear fire, indeed that blossoms even in hell) over immense emptiness, his syntax having ruptured, broken open into some perdurable scraps of an American measure. Existentialism and confessionalism flourish in the 1950's and beyond as ways of holding on to the unique expressive power of the subject, as unique agents and "voices" with style and flair, Mailer's "white hipsters" defying the bomb? Not so much a glorification of war, of patriotic violence and moral supremacy, as a numbness towards war and its heroic machinery? Even Brigadier General Thomas Farrell intuited that, after the nuclear sublime, there could be no comforting vantage point of subjective transcendence, no safe landscape from which to distance "the strong, sustained awesome roar which warned of doomsday and made us feel that we puny things were blasphemous to dare tamper with the forces" of sublime infinitude (God).

Notes:

I would like to thank the Hawaii Committee for the Humanities, especially Dean Diane DeLuca of Windward Community College and Principal Humanities Scholar, George Simson, of the University of Hawaii, for allowing me to participate in a dialog with international humanists and scientists in the "Perceiving Nature Conference" held in Honolulu, March 21-22, 1987. I would also like to acknowledge feedback from Ron Silliman, Marjorie Perloff, and others at the IAPL conference on "Postmodernism: Texts, Politics, Instruction" held at the University of Kansas, April 30 to May 2, 1987.

References:

Ai. *Sin*. Boston: Houghton Mifflin, 1986.
Albertini, James, Nelson Foster, Wally Inglis and Gil Roeder. *The Dark Side of Paradise: Hawaii in a Nuclear World*. Honolulu: Catholic Action of Hawaii, 1980.
Andrews, Valerie, Robert Bosnak, and Karen Walter Goodwin, eds. *Facing Apocalypse*. Dallas: Spring Publications, 1987.
Bakhtin, M. M. *Speech Genres & Other Late Essays*. Trans. Vern W. McGee. Austin: University of Texas Press, 1986.
Barash, David P. *The Arms Race and Nuclear War*. Belmont, CA: Wadsworth, 1987.
Berger, John. *The Sense of Sight*. New York: Pantheon, 1985.
Bloom, Harold. "The Breaking of Form." *Deconstruction and Criticism*. New York: Continuum, 1979.
_____. *Wallace Stevens: The Poems of Our Climate*. Ithaca: Cornell University Press, 1977.
Boyer, Paul. *By the Bomb's Early Light: American Thought and Culture at the Dawn of the Atomic Age*. New York: Pantheon, 1985.
Breslin, James E. B. *William Carlos Williams: An American Artist*. 1970. Chicago: University of Chicago Press, 1985.
Burke, Edmund. *A Philosophical Inquiry into the Origin of Our Ideas of the Sublime and Beautiful*. Ed. J. T. Boulton. Notre Dame, IN: Notre Dame University Press, 1968.
Derrida, Jacques. "Not Apocalypse, Not Now (full speed ahead, seven missiles, seven missives." *Diacritics* 14 (1984): 20-31.
Des Pres, Terrence. "Self / Landscape / Grid." *Writing in a Nuclear Age*. Ed. Jim Schley. Hanover, NH: University Press of New England, 1983.

Donley, Carol C. "Relativity and Radioactivity in William Carlos Williams' Paterson." *William Carlos Williams Newsletter* V (1979): 6-11.

Ferguson, Frances. "The Nuclear Sublime." *Diacritics* 14 (1984): 4-10.
_____. "The Sublime of Edmund Burke, or the Bathos of Experience." *Glyph* 8 (1981): 62-78.

Giovannitti, Len and Fred Freed. *The Decision to Drop the Bomb*. New York: Coward-McCann, 1965.

Ground Zero [Director, Roger Molander]. *Nuclear War: What's In It for You?* New York: Pocket Books, 1982.

Hartman, Geoffrey H. *Saving the Text: Literature / Derrida / Philosophy*. Baltimore: Johns Hopkins University Press, 1981.

Hayes, Peter, Lyuba Zarsky and Walden Bello. *American Lake: Nuclear Peril in the Pacific*. New York: Penguin, 1986.

Hersey, John. *Hiroshima*. New York: Bantam, 1946.

Hertz, Neil. *The End of the Line: Essays on Psychoanalysis and the Sublime*. New York: Columbia University Press, 1985.

Jameson, Fredric. "Baudelaire as Modernist and Postmodernist: The Dissolution of the Referent and the Artificial Sublime." *Lyric Poetry: Beyond New Criticism*. Eds. Chavia Hosek and Patricia Parker. Ithaca, NY: Cornell University Press, 1985.
_____. "Periodizing the 60's." *Social Text* 3 (1984): 178-209.

Kant, Immanuel. *Critique of Judgment*. Trans. J. H. Bernard. New York: Hafner, 1966.

Kristeva, Julia. "The Pain of Sorrow in the Modern World: The Works of Marguerite Duras." *PMLA* 102 (1987): 138-152.

Kroker, Arthur and David Cook. *The Postmodern Scene: Excremental Culture and Hyperaesthetics*. New York: St. Martin's, 1986.

Laporte, Dominique G. *Christo*. Trans. Abby Pollak. New York: Pantheon, 1986.

Longinus. *On Great Writing (On the Sublime)*. Trans. G. M. A. Grube. Indianapolis: Bobbs-Merrill, 1957.

Lyotard, Jean-Francois and Jean-Loup Thebaud. *Just Gaming*. Trans. Wlad Godzich. Minneapolis: University of Minnesota Press, 1985.
_____. *The Postmodern Condition: A Report on Knowledge*. Trans. Geoff Bennington and Brian Massumi. Minneapolis: University of Minnesota Press, 1984.

Mariani, Paul. *William Carlos Williams: A New World Naked*. New York: McGraw-Hill, 1981.

Miller, J. Hillis. "Stevens' Rock and Criticism as Cure, I and II." *The Georgia Review* 30 (Spring and Summer 1976).

Monk, Samuel H. *The Sublime: A Study of Critical Theories in XVIII-Century England*. Ann Arbor: University of Michigan Press, 1960.

Niedecker, Lorine. *My Life by Water: Collected poems, 1936-1968*. London: Fulcrum, 1970.

Nietzsche, Friedrich. *The Will to Power*. Trans. Walter Kaufmann and R. J. Hollingdale. New York: Vintage. 1968.

Oppen, George. *Collected Poems*. New York: New Directions, 1975.

Perelman, Bob. *The First World*. Great Barrington, MA: The Figures, 1986.

Riddel, Joseph N. *The Inverted Bell: Modernism and the Counter-poetics of William Carlos Williams*. Baton Rouge: Louisiana State University Press, 1974.

Sontag Susan. *Against Interpretation*. New York: Dell, 1966.

Stevens, Wallace. *The Palm at the End of the Mind: Selected Poems and a Play*. Ed. Holly Stevens. New York: Vintage, 1972.

Schwenger, Peter. "Writing the Unthinkable." *Critical Inquiry* 13 (1986): 33-48.

Venturi, Robert, Denise Scott Brown and Steven Izenour. *Learning From Las Vegas: The Forgotten Symbolism of Architectural Form*. Cambridge, MA: MIT Press, 1977.

Williams, William Carlos. *Pictures from Brueghel and other poems*. New York: New Directions, 1962.

——————. *Paterson*. New York: New Directions, 1963.

——————. *The Autobiography*. New York: Random House, 1951.

Wilson, Rob. "Wallace Stevens: Decreating the American Sublime." *American Poetry* 3 (1986): 13-33.

Notes on Contributors

Lyell Asher is a doctoral candidate at the University of Virginia and is completing a dissertation on *The Arts of Confession: Self-Revelation as Creation and Discovery in the Renaissance Lyric*. His publications include an essay on "Hamlet's Moral Wonder."

Anthony J. Cascardi is Associate Professor of Comparative Literature at the University of California, Berkeley. He is the author of *The Bounds of Reason: Cervantes, Dostoyevsky, Flaubert*, and editor of *Literature and the Questions of Philosophy*, among other works. A companion piece to the present essay appears in *Philosophy and Literature* (Fall, 1987).

Véronique M. Fóti teaches Philosophy at the Pennsylvania State University. She has taught at the New School for Social Research and is the author of some twenty articles on Continental philosophy and the history of philosophy. A book to be titled *Poiesis / Sophia / Politeia: Chiasms of Philosophical Discourse* is now in progress. She spent Fall 1987 as Fulbright Lecturer at Banaras Hindu University, India.

Geoffrey Galt Harpham is Associate Professor of English at Tulane University. He has taught at Brandeis, MIT, and the University of Pennsylvania. He is the author of *On the Grotesque: Strategies of Contradiction in Art and Literature* and *The Ascetic Imperative in Culture and Criticism*. Presently, he is at work on a book to be titled *Getting It Right: Language, Literature, and Ethics*.

D. Emily Hicks is Assistant Professor in the Department of English and Comparative Literature at San Diego State University. She publishes regularly on Mexican writers and artists and is a member of the editorial board of the **Border//Culture** Research Project of the Institute for Advanced Cultural Studies.

Eugene W. Holland is Assistant Professor of French and Humanities at the Ohio State University. He received a Ph.D. from the University of California, San Diego, and has taught at Rice, UC San Diego, and the University of Iowa. He has published essays on 19th and 20th century French literature and contemporary critical theory in journals such as *Salmagundi, Boundary 2,* and the *New Orleans Review,* including "The Supression of Politics in the Institution of Psychoanalysis" and "Narcissism from Baudelaire to Sartre." He is presently completing a book on Baudelaire.

Linda Hutcheon is Professor of English and Comparative Literature at the University of Toronto. She has also taught at McMaster University and served as Associate Editor of *Recherches Semiotique / Semiotic Inquiry.* She is the author of *Narcissistic Narrative: The Metafictional Paradox; Formalism and the Freudian Aesthetic; A Theory of Parody: The Teachings of Twentieth-Century Art Forms; A Poetics of Postmodernism: History, Theory, Fiction;* and *The Canadian Postmodern.*

Robert Merrill is Director of the Institute for Advanced Cultural Studies and currently teaches at Catholic University of America and the Maryland Institute, College of Art. He has taught at the Pennsylvania State University and the University of South Carolina. He is the author of *Sir Thomas Malory and the Cultural Crisis of the Late Middle Ages.* Two books are currently in progress: *Morse Peckham, Postmodern Theory, and the Legacy of American Pragmatism* and *The Cain Complex: Further Developments in the Freudian Cultural Analysis.*

Neal Oxenhandler is Edward Tuck Professor of French and Comparative Literature at Dartmouth College. He chairs the Department of French and Italian. He has taught previously at Yale, UCLA, and Santa Cruz, where he was Chair of the Graduate Program in Literature. Among his awards are Fulbright, Guggenheim, ACLS, and Cross-Disciplinary Fellowships. He has served on the editorial boards of *PMLA, Film Quarterly, French Review,* and the University of California and New England University Presses.

Oxenhandler's books include *Scandal and Parade—The Theater of Jean Cocteau; Max Jacob and Les Feux de Paris; French Literary Criticism: The Basis of Judgment;* and a novel *A Change of Gods.* He has published numerous articles on film, theater, psychoanalysis, postmodernism, and literary theory. Two books are currently in progress: *Modern to Postmodern: Aesthetics and Ideology* and *Literary Emotion: History, Theory, Application.*

Richard Wasson teaches English at Rutgers University and chairs the Grievance Committee of the local faculty union. He has published numerous articles and reviews on modern and postmodern literature and criticism. In progress is a book titled *Class, Gender and the Shapes of Desire,* which defines codes for the representation of class struggles from the 1830s to the present in novels, plays, and films.

Rob Wilson is Assistant Professor of English at the University of Hawaii at Manoa. He has published many essays on American poetry and a volume of poems titled *Waking in Seoul.* A book on American poetry, *American Sublime: The Ideology of a Poetic Form,* has recently been published by University of Wisconsin Press.